A SOFTWARE
TOOLS SAMPLER

PRENTICE-HALL SOFTWARE SERIES
Brian W. Kernighan, Advisor

A SOFTWARE
TOOLS SAMPLER

WEBB MILLER

Department of Computer Science
The Pennsylvania State University
University Park, Pennsylvania

Prentice-Hall, Inc., Englewood Cliffs, New Jersey 07632

Library of Congress Cataloging-in-Publication Data

MILLER, WEBB
   A software tools sampler.

   Bibliography: p. 340
   Includes index.
     1. Computer software. 2. C (Computer program
language) 3. UNIX (Computer operating system)
I. Title.
QA76.754.M55 1987   005.36′9   86-30234
ISBN 0-13-822305-X

Editorial/production supervision
and interior design: *Theresa A. Soler*
Cover design: *Lundgren Graphics, Ltd.*
Manufacturing buyer: *Ed O'Dougherty*

© 1987 by Prentice-Hall, Inc.
A Division of Simon & Schuster
Englewood Cliffs, New Jersey 07632

Printed in the United States of America
10 9 8 7 6 5 4 3 2 1

ISBN 0-13-822305-X 025

Prentice-Hall International (UK) Limited, *London*
Prentice-Hall of Australia Pty. Limited, *Sydney*
Prentice-Hall Canada Inc., *Toronto*
Prentice-Hall Hispanoamericana, S.A., *Mexico*
Prentice-Hall of India Private Limited, *New Delhi*
Prentice-Hall of Japan, Inc., *Tokyo*
Prentice-Hall of Southeast Asia Pte. Ltd., *Singapore*
Editora Prentice-Hall do Brasil, Ltda., *Rio de Janeiro*

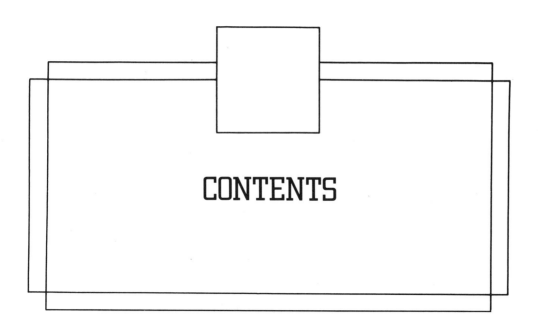

CONTENTS

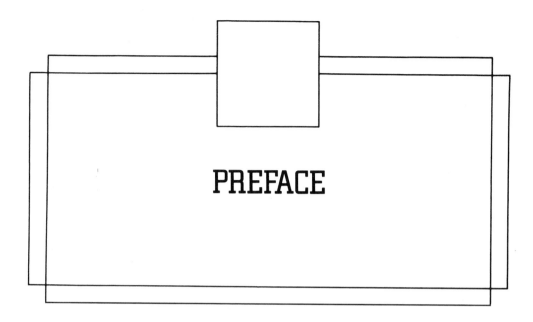

PREFACE

This book contains a small ensemble of useful and interesting *software tools*—programs that help you prepare documents and programs on a computer. Each tool's capability and construction are discussed in detail and enhancements are outlined. After reading Chapter 1 (at most an hour or two if you already know the C programming language) you can go directly to any chapter of interest.

You should get copies of the programs, experiment with them, and change them to suit your needs. All programs listed in this book are available for a nominal charge. For information write:

James F. Fegen, Jr.
Executive Editor
Technical+Reference Division
Prentice-Hall, Inc.
Englewood Cliffs, N.J. 07632

The book's prerequisites are

- Programming experience and a familiarity with systematic methods for program development, such as *top-down design*.
- Experience with data structures equivalent to an undergraduate course on the subject. The terms *pointer, hashing, binary search*, and *dynamic storage allocation* should be completely familiar to you.
- Knowledge of, or willingness to learn the C programming language.

While the tools provide capabilities available from the UNIX[†] operating system, the code is new and UNIX is mentioned only superficially.

The book is a text on software tools. Initial versions were written at the University of Arizona, where the tools course is the first of three upper-division undergraduate classes covering computer system software. The other two classes treat programming systems (compilers, linkers, and debuggers) and operating systems. One of the purposes of this book is to teach about a major category of system software.

The tools course has an additional distinctive goal. It provides many students with their main exposure to complete and realistic software. Earlier courses exhibit only programs that can be built in a day (or an hour) and later ones often construct only toys for programming projects.

Besides use for a software tools class, this book might serve as a building block for a software engineering course. A text such as *Principles of Software Engineering and Design* by Marvin Zelkowitz, Alan Shaw, and John Gannon (Prentice-Hall, 1979) could introduce general software engineering principles, with examples and programming projects drawn from this book.

A third use is for self-study by a well-prepared and dedicated reader. Such a reader might want to turn a non-UNIX system into a more pleasant and productive place to work or might just be curious to see how these software tools can be built.

I have followed in the footsteps of the book *Software Tools* by Brian Kernighan and P. J. Plauger (Addison-Wesley, 1976), which was used for years in the tools class at the University of Arizona. Progress in computer science and improved preparation of the entering students led me to cover substantially more complex tools and to use a different programming language. The resulting class notes became this book.

My sincerest thanks go to Dave Hanson, Gene Myers, and Titus Purdin for reading drafts of this book and offering countless suggestions.

Webb Miller

[†]UNIX is a trademark of Bell Laboratories.

1

INTRODUCTION

Some basic material should be mastered before studying programs in later chapters. Accomplished C programmers can extract the necessary information from this chapter in one or two hours. Others should allot substantially more time and be prepared to consult other sources.

Reading the later programs requires a knowledge of C. This book does not provide a complete language description; for that, you need a book on C. *The C Programming Language* by Brian W. Kernighan and Dennis M. Ritchie (Prentice-Hall, 1978) is an authoritative introduction, and *A C Reference Manual* by Samuel P. Harbison and Guy L. Steele, Jr. (Prentice-Hall, 1984) is an excellent resource for experienced C programmers.

Section 1.1 is essentially an "entrance examination" on C: when you understand the programs given there, read the rest of the book. Of course, newcomers to C will become fluent in the language only after completing several programming assignments from Chapters 2 to 5. Even C experts should look at Section 1.1, since it outlines the book's basic assumptions about the C programming environment.

The remainder of this chapter covers two C programs that lie midway, in terms of size and complexity, between the trivial programs of Section 1.1 and the programs in Chapters 2 to 5. The main goal is insight into the large-scale structure of the later programs. Readers unfamiliar with C may benefit from studying the code in detail.

The programs of Sections 1.2 and 1.3 illustrate the importance of the "decision hiding principle": *a program's structure should confine the effects of each implementation decision to a small, easily identified section of code.* Software

1

conforming to this principle is easy to comprehend (and, hence, comparatively
easy to get working) because relatively few implementation decisions must be
grasped to understand a given module. Moreover, such software is easy to modify,
since revising an implementation decision invalidates a minimal amount of code.
Indeed, the implementation decisions that seem most likely to be changed later
should be hidden with particular care.

Section 1.2 introduces *abstract data types*, an especially useful application
of the decision hiding principle. The general idea is to keep the bulk of the program
from directly manipulating an important data structure; instead, data access is restricted to a few tightly-specified "access functions". Details of the specific data
structures implementing the access functions are hidden from the rest of the program, and the data structures are easily changed.

Abstract data types are the key to understanding much of the large-scale
structure of later programs. Programs are often divided into manageable pieces by
encapsulating each main data structure in a distinct module, then treating those
modules as abstract data types. Typically, the remainder of the code can be mod-
ularized according to relationship to the data modules. For example, the code that
moves data from an input file to data module A becomes module X, the procedures
that access data module A and build data module B constitute module Y, and so
on.

Section 1.3 discusses decision hiding for system dependencies in programs.
Not all programs in this book are portable; some must be changed before they will
run under another operating system or on a different machine. To minimize the
work required to move a program, the nonportable code has been isolated.

1.1 GETTING STARTED

The short programs of this section provide a natural introduction to software tools.
The first group of procedures is used throughout the book. The remaining programs
are complete and useful software tools.

1.1.1 Basic UNIX Command Syntax

In this section, and at isolated points in the remainder of the book, use of a
software tool is illustrated with the UNIX command syntax. Other command languages would have worked as well; the only purpose is to give a concrete idea of
what it feels like to use the tools. The few properties of UNIX needed for these
examples are summarized below. The paper "The UNIX programming environment" by Brian Kernighan and John Mashey (*IEEE Computer* magazine, April
1981, pp. 12–24) is a good source for learning more.

Under UNIX, the user can organize files into arbitrary groupings called *directories*. For example, the source files, object files, and executable file for a
program are often grouped into their own directory.

UNIX programs are run by typing a line that contains the program name, perhaps followed by a list of arguments that are separated by blanks. Arguments often consist of file names or ''flags'' that select options. By convention, a leading minus ($-$) character distinguishes a flag from a file name. For example, the command

```
cc -O thud.c
```

applies the C compiler *cc* to the C source file *thud.c*, with the $-O$ flag requesting optimized object code. Another UNIX convention is that files containing C source code have names ending with the two characters ''.c''.

The UNIX command interpreter, called the *shell*, provides a shorthand notation for specifying lists of file names. Specifically, in a command like

```
cc *.c
```

the string ''*.c'' is replaced by the list of file names in the current directory that end in ''.c'', i.e., all C source files. Thus, if the current directory consists of the files *foo.c*, *thud.c*, and *prog.docum*, the command is equivalent to

```
cc foo.c thud.c
```

A second useful service of the UNIX shell is connecting the output of one command to the input of another. For example, *ls* is the command that lists the names of files in the current directory, and *lc* (pp. 12–14) counts its input lines. The UNIX command

```
ls | lc
```

connects the output of *ls* to the input of *lc*, creating a command that counts the number of files in the current directory (assuming that *ls* lists files one per line). Two commands can be connected this way if the first writes standard output and the second reads standard input. (The terms *standard output* and *standard input* are discussed below.) A *pipeline* is a chain of simpler commands linked in this manner by the shell.

1.1.2 Required Functions and Macros

Four classes of functions are assumed available. They are listed here for quick reference, then discussed more thoroughly when first used. The Appendix contains complete details.

Standard I/O Library.   C statements for input or output are provided by a ''standard I/O library.'' Any source file using this library of functions should have the line

```
#include <stdio.h>
```

(or an *#include* line naming a file containing that line) near the beginning. The library provides the following functions and macros, which the book's programs use for input and output. (The only exception is the *fastfind* program of Section 4.1, which uses system-specific input procedures.)

fopen(), fclose(), fflush()	open, close, or flush an I/O stream
getc(), getchar()	get an input character
gets(), fgets()	get a string of input characters
printf(), fprintf(), sprintf()	formatted output conversion
putc(), putchar()	output a character
puts(), fputs()	output a string of characters
rewind()	return to the beginning of a file

As part of the I/O facilities, the following macros are defined by the *stdio.h* header file.

EOF	an integer returned upon end of file
FILE	the "type" associated with a file
NULL	the null pointer (can point to a character or a FILE)
stderr	FILE pointer for standard error file
stdin	FILE pointer for standard input file
stdout	FILE pointer for standard output file

All six macros are predefined constants; don't try to assign values to them.

Standard String Functions.   The following functions manipulate character strings that are terminated by a null character ('\0'). *Strcat()* and *strcpy()*, the two that create a string, terminate the new string with a null character, but do not check for overflow of the new string. In some C implementations, *index()* is called *strchr()*.

index(s, c)	return the first location of the character *c* in *s*
strcat(s, t)	append a copy of *t* to the end of *s*
strcmp(s, t)	return 0 if and only if *s* equals *t*
strcpy(s, t)	copy *t* to *s* and return *s*
strlen(s)	return the length of *s*

Character-Classification Macros.   Files containing the line

```
#include <ctype.h>
```

can thereafter employ character-testing macros from the list:

isalnum(c)   *c* is one of 'a'–'z', 'A'–'Z', or '0'–'9'
isalpha(c)   *c* is one of 'a'–'z' or 'A'–'Z'
isdigit(c)   *c* is one of '0'–'9'
islower(c)   *c* is one of 'a'–'z'
isprint(c)   *c* is a printing character (not a control character)
isspace(c)   *c* is a space, tab, or newline character
isupper(c)   *c* is one of 'A'–'Z'

For example, the condition

```
if (isspace(c)) ...
```

tests whether *c* is a "whitespace" character.

System-Specific Functions.   The following machine-dependent functions are used; others are introduced in Chapters 2 and 5, as needed.

exit(n)   terminate execution, signaling *n* to the parent process
free(p)   free the memory allocated when *malloc()* returned *p*
malloc(n) allocate *n* bytes and return the address (*NULL* signals failure)

1.1.3 Lib.c—A Library of C Procedures

Let's begin our quick tour of C programs with seven procedures that are used throughout the book.

Savename().   When commands can be combined in pipelines, it is desirable to know which of the constituent commands produced an error message. For example, if the pipeline

```
ls | find | lc
```

produces the message

```
Missing argument.
```

it is unclear which of the commands *ls*, *find*, or *lc* was incorrectly specified; the response

```
find: Missing argument.
```

is more informative.

Most of the programs in this book begin execution with a call like:

```
savename("find");
```

Any subsequent fatal error message will be preceded by the program's name, a colon (:), and a space.

```
#define MAX_NAME 50    /* maximum length of program or file name */
static char prog_name[MAX_NAME+1];    /* used in error messages */
/* savename - record a program name for error messages */
savename(name)
char *name;
{
    char *strcpy();

    if (strlen(name) <= MAX_NAME)
        strcpy(prog_name, name);
}
```

Savename() invokes the standard string function *strlen()* to count the characters in *name*. Another standard string function, *strcpy()*, copies *name* to the array *prog_name[]*, where it can be accessed by procedures in *lib.c* (the file containing *savename()*). *Name* is not copied if it is too long; *prog_name[]* can hold a 50-character name plus the ''null character'' that C uses to mark the end of a string.

Strcpy() is declared to be a function returning a character pointer, even though the returned value is unused; some C compilers demand that the declaration be present. C rules imply that *strlen()* returns an *int* since no declaration states otherwise.

Fatal().   *Fatal()* is used to terminate execution because of an error condition.

```
/* fatal - print message and die */
fatal(msg)
char *msg;
{
    if (prog_name[0] != '\0')
        fprintf(stderr, "%s: ", prog_name);
    fprintf(stderr, "%s\n", msg);
    exit(1);
}
```

Fatal() appends a newline character to the message it is given, then calls the system-specific function *exit()* to terminate execution and make its argument (1 to signal an error) available to the outside world. If *savename()* has deposited the program's name in *prog_name[]*, then the name, a colon, and a space are printed before the message. On the other hand, if *savename()* has not been called, then *progname[0]* is '\0' (because global character arrays are automatically initialized with null characters), so no program name is printed.

Fatalf().   *Fatalf()* works like *fatal()* except that the *msg* string can contain a conversion specification, like %*s*.

```
/* fatalf - format message, print it, and die */
fatalf(msg, val)
char *msg, *val;
{
        if (prog_name[0] != '\0')
                fprintf(stderr, "%s: ", prog_name);
        fprintf(stderr, msg, val);
        putc('\n', stderr);
        exit(1);
}
```

A typical use of *fatalf()* is:

```
        char *name;
        ...
        fatalf("Cannot open %s.", name);
```

which prints a final message of the form

```
            Cannot open thud.c.
```

Although it violates programming etiquette and draws warnings from inter-procedural analyzers like the UNIX *lint* program, programs in this book occasion-ally make calls such as

```
        int k;
        ...
        fatalf("Improper line number: %d.", k);
```

I don't know of any systems where the inconsistently typed second argument causes *fatalf()* to perform improperly. Of course, it is essential that the conversion spec-ification match the second argument; for example,

```
        int k;
        ...
        fatalf("Improper line number: %s.", k);
```

won't work.

Ckopen().   Sometimes there is no graceful way to recover from an unsuccessful attempt to open a file. When the best contingency plan is to print a diagnostic message and terminate execution, programs can call *ckopen()*.

```
/* ckopen - open file; check for success */
FILE *ckopen(name, mode)
char *name, *mode;
{
    FILE *fopen(), *fp;

    if ((fp = fopen(name, mode)) == NULL)
        fatalf("Cannot open %s.", name);
    return(fp);
}
```

Ckopen() needs both the name of the file and a *mode* telling the intended use of the file. For example, setting *mode* to ''*w*'' (the string, not a single character '*w*') informs the operating system that you want to write to the file. *Ckopen()* employs the local *FILE* pointer variable *fp* and invokes the standard I/O function *fopen()*, which returns a *FILE* pointer. The test

```
    if ((fp = fopen(name, mode)) == NULL)
```

calls *fopen()* with *ckopen()*'s arguments, assigns the returned *FILE* pointer to *fp*, then compares it with the *NULL* pointer. Unless *fopen()* signals failure by returning *NULL*, the *FILE* pointer is returned to the calling procedure. If *fopen()* fails, then *ckopen()* calls *fatalf()* with a diagnostic message.

Ckalloc().   A program can ask the operating system for a specified number of bytes of storage by calling *ckalloc()*.

```
/* ckalloc - allocate space; check for success */
char *ckalloc(amount)
int amount;
{
    char *malloc(), *p;

    if ((p = malloc( (unsigned) amount)) == NULL)
        fatal("Ran out of memory.");
    return(p);
}
```

Ckalloc() calls the system-specific function *malloc()* to provide the storage. If *malloc()* indicates failure by returning *NULL*, then *ckalloc()* calls *fatal()* to terminate execution. Otherwise, *malloc()* returns a pointer to a free block of memory, and *ckalloc()* hands that pointer back to the calling procedure.

If the calling program uses the allocated memory to store anything other than characters, it should "cast" (convert) the pointer into the appropriate type. For example, to get storage for an integer, mimic the code fragment:

```
int *int_ptr;
char *ckalloc();
        .
        .
int_ptr = (int *) ckalloc(sizeof(int));
```

Strsame().   Programs rarely want the full power of the standard string function *strcmp()*, which returns a value whose sign is meaningful. (Intuitively, *strcmp(s, t)* < 0 means that *s* would come before *t* in a dictionary.) Most uses merely test whether two strings are the same. The following function lets us write

```
if (strsame(s, t)) {
```

instead of:

```
if (strcmp(s, t) == 0) {
```

The code is trivial:

```
/* strsame - tell whether two strings are identical */
int strsame(s, t)
char *s, *t;
{
      return(strcmp(s, t) == 0);
}
```

An alternative implementation of *strsame()* is considered in Exercise 3.

Strsave().   To "remember" a string of characters, use *strsave()*.

```
/* strsave - save string s somewhere; return address */
char *strsave(s)
char *s;
{
      char *ckalloc(), *p, *strcpy();

      p = ckalloc(strlen(s)+1);   /* +1 to hold '\0' */
      return(strcpy(p, s));
}
```

Strsave() uses *strlen()* to count the characters in *s*. Then *ckalloc()* finds a place to store the string, including the extra byte for '\0'. *Strcpy()* copies *s* into the storage allocated by *ckalloc()*. *Strcpy()* also returns its first argument (the location of the new copy of the string), and that value is returned by *strsave()*.

All code in this book is listed in complete files. (As discussed in the next section, it is imperative to understand how C procedures are grouped into files.) Let us begin with *lib.c*.

EXERCISES

1. How do the examples of common C errors

```
while (i = j)
```

and

```
char c;
while ((c = getchar()) != EOF)
```

affect program behavior?

2. An alternative implementation of *fatalf()* is

```
fatalf(msg, val)
char *msg, *val;
{
        char buf[MAXBUF];

        sprintf(buf, msg, val);
        fatal(buf);
}
```

Discuss the relative merits of the two implementations. Which do you prefer, and why?

3. Does the C preprocessor allow you to implement *strsame()* as a macro? What are the advantages and disadvantages of that approach?

```
/* lib.c - library of C procedures */

#include <stdio.h>

#define MAX_NAME 50        /* maximum length of program or file name */

static char prog_name[MAX_NAME+1];    /* used in error messages */
```

```
/* savename - record a program name for error messages */
savename(name)                                                              savename
char *name;
{
     char *strcpy();

     if (strlen(name) <= MAX_NAME)
          strcpy(prog_name, name);
}

/* fatal - print message and die */
fatal(msg)                                                                  fatal
char *msg;
{
     if (prog_name[0] != '\0')
          fprintf(stderr, "%s: ", prog_name);
     fprintf(stderr, "%s\n", msg);
     exit(1);
}

/* fatalf - format message, print it, and die */
fatalf(msg, val)                                                            fatalf
char *msg, *val;
{
     if (prog_name[0] != '\0')
          fprintf(stderr, "%s: ", prog_name);
     fprintf(stderr, msg, val);
     putc('\n', stderr);
     exit(1);
}

/* ckopen - open file; check for success */
FILE *ckopen(name, mode)                                                    ckopen
char *name, *mode;
{
     FILE *fopen(), *fp;

     if ((fp = fopen(name, mode)) == NULL)
          fatalf("Cannot open %s.", name);
     return(fp);
}

/* ckalloc - allocate space; check for success */
char *ckalloc(amount)                                                       ckalloc
int amount;
{
     char *malloc(), *p;

     if ((p = malloc( (unsigned) amount)) == NULL)
          fatal("Ran out of memory.");
     return(p);
}

/* strsame - tell whether two strings are identical */
int strsame(s, t)                                                          strsame
char *s, *t;
{
     return(strcmp(s, t) == 0);
}
```

```
/* strsave - save string s somewhere; return address */
char *strsave(s)                                                        strsave
char *s;
{
    char *ckalloc(), *p, *strcpy();

    p = ckalloc(strlen(s)+1);   /* +1 to hold '\0' */
    return(strcpy(p, s));
}
```

1.1.4 Lc—Count the Lines and Characters in a File

A typical use of *lc* is the command

```
lc *.c
```

asking for the sizes of all C source files in the current directory. Each output line gives a count of lines and characters, as in

```
238    5572    bldint.c
191    4080    depmod.c
132    3689    macmod.c
113    2816    system.c
 44     900    test.c
214    6330    update.c
932   23387    total
```

(Thus, the file *bldint.c* has 238 lines and 5572 characters, etc.)

Only a half dozen lines of C are needed to read characters, incrementing a counter *nchars* for each one, and incrementing *nlines* whenever a newline character is seen. When these instructions are enclosed in a loop that processes a list of files, the algorithm is

tlines = tchars = 0 /* *initialize totals* */
for each specified file {
    nlines = nchars = 0 /* *initialize counts for this file* */
    for each character in the file {
        ++nchars
        if the character is '\n'
            ++nlines
    }
    print nlines, nchars and the name of the file
    tlines += nlines
    tchars += nchars
}
if there was more than one file
    print tlines, tchars and ''total''

Before the basic algorithm can be packaged as a complete program, two important points about C must be grasped.

When *lc* begins execution, it needs information from the command line. In other words, if you typed

```
lc foo.c thud.c
```

then *lc* needs the strings *"foo.c"* and *"thud.c"*.

This book adopts the more-or-less standard convention that the main program has two arguments; the first tells the number of words on the command line, while the second is an array of pointers to the actual words. With the command

```
lc foo.c thud.c
```

argc (the conventional name for *main()*'s first argument) equals 3, while *argv[0]*, *argv[1]*, and *argv[2]* (the entries in the array of pointers given as *main()*'s second argument) point to the strings *"lc"*, *"foo.c,"* and *"thud.c"*. Not all systems make the command's name available, so later programs don't use *argv[0]*.

Another general point about C programs is illustrated by the code for *lc*. Any program using the standard I/O library automatically starts life with three opened files called *standard input*, *standard output*, and *standard error*. The corresponding *FILE* pointers are denoted *stdin*, *stdout*, and *stderr*. In particular, *lc* reads standard input if no files are specified. (This is why *lc* works in the

```
ls | lc
```

example, mentioned previously.)

Any files that a program opens by calling *fopen()* are automatically closed when the program exits. However, most systems limit the number of files a program can have open at one time. Thus, a program looping over a potentially long list of files should close each one with *fclose()* when the file is no longer needed.

On a machine with 16-bit words, a representable *int* might be bounded by $2^{15} \approx 32,000$, and the total number of characters can easily exceed that limit. Thus, *lc* keeps its counts in *long* variables.

EXERCISES

4. Show how to modify *lc.c* so that *exit()* returns 1 if a file cannot be opened; *lc* should still continue to process files named by later arguments.

PROGRAMMING ASSIGNMENTS

1. Split *lc* into a main routine that loops over file names and a function that handles a single file. Which organization do you prefer?

```
/*
 * lc - count the lines and characters in a file
 *
 *
 * Program description:
 *
 *     A command line has the form:
 *          lc [file1] [file2] ...
 *     If more than one file is named, then totals are printed.  If no files
 *     are named, then standard input is read.
 */

#include <stdio.h>

main(argc, argv)                                                        main
int argc;
char *argv[];
{
     FILE *fopen(), *fp;
     long nchars, nlines, tchars, tlines;
     int c, i;

     tlines = tchars = 0;      /* initialize totals */
     /* for each specified file */
     for (i = 1; i == 1 || i < argc; ++i) {
          if (argc == 1)
               fp = stdin;
          else if ((fp = fopen(argv[i], "r")) == NULL) {
               fprintf(stderr, "lc: cannot open %s\n", argv[i]);
               continue;
          }
          nlines = nchars = 0;      /* initialize counts for this file */
          while ((c = getc(fp)) != EOF) {
               ++nchars;
               if (c == '\n')
                    ++nlines;
          }
          printf("%7ld%7ld", nlines, nchars);
          if (fp != stdin)
               printf(" %s", argv[i]);
          putchar('\n');
          tlines += nlines;
          tchars += nchars;
          if (fp != stdin)
               fclose(fp);
     }
     if (argc > 2)
          printf("%7ld%7ld total\n", tlines, tchars);
     exit(0);
}
```

1.1.5 Tweak—Make a File Look Recently Modified

The file updating tool, named *update* and discussed in Chapter 2, assumes that each file is stamped with the time it was last modified. *Update* is most effective if used with *tweak*, a tool that economically changes the recorded modification time of a file without altering the file's contents.

Suppose you have compiled the C program file *prog.c* and named the executable program *prog*. Now you edit *prog.c* and change a comment line, which makes *prog.c* look younger than *prog*. Thus, *update* would think that *prog.c* should be recompiled to bring *prog* up to date, whereas this work is wasteful because only a comment line was changed. The command

```
tweak prog
```

avoids the unnecessary recompilation by silently setting the modification time of *prog* to the current time. If *update* is now called, it will inspect file modification times, see that *prog* is newer than *prog.c*, and correctly deduce that *prog* is up to date. (In practice, it may also be necessary to *tweak* the object file for *prog.c*.)

Tweak reads the first byte of the file, then writes the byte back. This method works even if the file is an object file or an executable file, rather than a file of text characters. (The approach might fail on a system that is not byte-oriented.) As shown in Chapter 2, it is useful if *tweak* works on empty files, too. In addition, if the file does not exist, then *tweak* trys to create it. This implementation tweaks empty files and nonexistent files by opening the files for writing, then immediately closing them. The basic algorithm is

```
for each specified file
    if you can read and write the file and it contains a byte
        write a byte back to the file
    else
        open the file for writing
```

As implemented, *tweak* has some shortcomings due to limitations of the standard I/O library. In the first place, not all systems will open a file in the read/write mode ''*r+*'', so *tweak* is not completely portable. In addition, *tweak* sometimes takes the wrong action. For example, tweaking a file for which you have *write* permission but not *read* permission discards the file's contents by opening it in mode ''*w*''.

You may well be able to write a system-specific version of *tweak* that does a better job. For example, the UNIX procedure *stat()* checks whether a file exists and sees how many bytes it contains, even if you cannot read or write it. Your *tweak* might even be able to change a file's permission status, do what it wants with the file, then restore the original permission status. (If the code for the UNIX *touch* command is available, consult it for further ideas.) Think about the possibilities if you plan to study Chapter 2 in detail.

```
/*
 * tweak - set a file's last modification time to the current time
 *
 *
 * Program description:
 *
 *     A command line has the form:
 *          tweak file1 [file2] [file3] ...
 *
 *
 * Source files:
 *
 *     lib.c    - library of C procedures
 *     tweak.c  - this file
 */

#include <stdio.h>

main(argc, argv)                                                          main
int argc;
char *argv[];
{
     FILE *fopen(), *fp;
     int c, i;

     savename("tweak");  /* for error messages */
     if (argc == 1)
          fatal("No file was specified.");
     for (i = 1; i < argc; ++i)
          /* if you can read and write the file and it contains a byte */
          if ((fp = fopen(argv[i], "r+")) != NULL && (c = getc(fp)) != EOF) {
               /* write the byte back to the file */
               rewind(fp);
               putc(c, fp);
               fclose(fp);
          } else {          /* open the file for writing */
               if (fp != NULL)       /* the file was empty */
                    fclose(fp);
               if ((fp = fopen(argv[i], "w")) == NULL)
                    fprintf(stderr, "Cannot tweak %s.\n", argv[i]);
               else
                    fclose(fp);
          }
     exit(0);
}
```

1.1.6 Find—Print Lines Containing a Given Substring

Imagine you have just discovered that the procedure *macin()* is being called with an incorrect argument somewhere in your 1000-line program. How can you locate all the lines where *macin()* is mentioned? This is where the *find* tool comes to the rescue. A command like

```
find macin *.c
```

gets the desired information. For example, *find*'s output might begin

```
bldint.c:*     macin(name, definition)      .. file macmod.c
bldint.c:      macin(n, d);
macmod.c:*     macin(name, defn)
macmod.c:/* macin - install a macro name and definition */
macmod.c:macin(name, defn)
update.c:*     macin(name, definition)      .. file macmod.c
update.c:      macin("COMPILE", C_NAME);
update.c:          macin("TARGET", file);
update.c:          macin("YOUNGER", younger);
```

which reveals a missing argument in a call to *macin()* from *update.c*.

The outline of *find* is simple:

> **for** each specified file
> > **for** each line of the file
> > > **if** the line contains the pattern string
> > > > print the line

Find embellishes this basic algorithm. First, *find* prints line numbers, if requested. Moreover, the two-character string ''\n'' at an end of the pattern matches the start or end of a line. For example, the pattern

> \nfound

matches the lines whose first five characters are ''*found*'', while

> found\n

matches the lines ending with ''... *found*''. A ''\n'' pair in the middle of the pattern is not treated as a newline.

Find's efficiency is important since it often scans a large body of text. In a typical application, most input characters differ from the first pattern character. The following algorithm eliminates such positions with just an end-of-line test and a character comparison.

```
main() {
    first__char = the first character of pat (the pattern)
    for each specified file
        scan(file)
}
```

```
        scan(file) {
            for each line of the file
                for each position in the line
                    if the character in that position is first__char
                        if a character-by-character check matches pat
                            print the line·
        }
```

Find implements *scan()* as

```
char *fgets(), *p, *pos, *t;
        ...
/* for each line of the file */
while (fgets(buf+1, MAXTEXT, fp) != NULL) {    /* keeps newlines */
    ++line_number;
    /* for each text position */
    for (pos = buf; *pos != '\0'; ++pos)
        /* quick check for a possible match */
        if (*pos == first_char) {
            /* character-by-character check for complete match */
            p = pat;
            t = pos;
            /* scan for mismatch or end of pattern */
            while (*++p == *++t && *p != '\0')
                ;
            (if *p == '\0' at this point, then a match has been found)
```

Buf[], the character array scanned by *pos*, holds text lines that are preceded and followed by newline characters. The initial newline is installed with

```
buf[0] = '\n';        /* newline character before each line */
```

in *main()*. The newline byte at the end of each line is read in by *fgets()*. Thus, the three-character line ''*abc*'' is stored in *buf[]* as the five-character string ''*NabcN*'', where *N* denotes the newline character. *Main()* reduces character pairs ''\n'' at the ends of *pat* to single newline characters, and the newlines are treated like ordinary characters in the pattern-matching process.

The condition

```
            *pos == first_char
```

means that the first pattern character has been found. If *pat* is ''*abx*'' and the input line is ''*abc*'', this happens when

$$buf: \quad N \quad a \quad b \quad c \quad N$$
$$\uparrow$$
$$pos$$

The *while* statement in the character-by-character check

```
/* character-by-character check for complete match */
p = pat;
t = pos;
/* scan for mismatch or end of pattern */
while (*++p == *++t && *p != '\0')
    ;
(if *p == '\0' at this point, then a match has been found)
```

works as follows. The pointers *p* (to *pat*) and *t* (to *buf*) are incremented to the next characters. The incrementing can be done first because *pat* and *pos* point at matching characters. If *pat* is "*abx*" and the input line is "*abc*", the incrementing produces

$$
\begin{array}{cccc}
 & pat & p & \\
 & \downarrow & \downarrow & \\
 & a & b & x \\
buf: \quad N & a & b & c \quad N \\
 & \uparrow & \uparrow & \\
 & pos & t &
\end{array}
$$

If the addressed characters are equal, then an end-of-pattern test is performed. The loop body is empty because the *while*'s test performs all the necessary computation. The loop terminates if either

$$*p != *t$$

or:

$$*p == '\0'$$

These conditions become true simultaneously if *pat* occurs at a nonsuffix position of *buf[]*, but the test

$$*p == '\0'$$

correctly confirms a match no matter where it occurs.

Chapter 4 covers two other pattern-matching programs. A substantially more efficient version of *find*, called *fastfind*, is given in Section 4.1. Sections 4.2–4.4 present *match*, a program that locates lines matching a class of patterns that is far more flexible than constant character strings. However, there is still a place for *find* in our toolbox because it is much more portable than *fastfind* and is often easier to use than *match*. In particular, several characters, such as

$$+ \quad * \quad [$$

can be used freely in *find*'s pattern strings, but require special care with *match*.

Comments on Find.c.   The use of global variables in *find* should be studied if you are new to C. Variables *nfiles*, *nflag*, *buf[]*, *first_char* and *pat* are used to pass values from the main program to *scan()*. This approach has some small advantages over passing the data as procedure arguments. First, it reduces the number of characters in the program by substituting a single definition of an item for repeated definitions and appearances in argument lists. Second, important program data is prominently displayed.

EXERCISES

5. What does *find* do when it cannot open one of the specified files? What do *lc* and *tweak* do? What do you think they should do?

6. What happens if the pattern string for *find* begins with a minus (−) character? Can *find* search for the character pair ''\n''? How can *find* be modified to handle such patterns?

7. Programs in this book usually read text files as follows:

```
#define MAXTEXT 200
...
char text[MAXTEXT];
...
fgets(text, MAXTEXT, fp);
```

This practice limits the length of lines that can be read with a single call to *fgets()*. How many characters can a line have (not counting '\n')? Explain why *find* declares:

```
char buf[MAXTEXT+1];
```

PROGRAMMING ASSIGNMENTS

2. Give *find* a −*m* option to list the lines *not* containing *pat*.

```
/*
 * find - print lines containing a given substring
 *
 *
 * Program description:
 *
 *    A command line has the form
 *        find [-n] pat [file1] [file2] ...
 * where pat is any string of characters.  A character pair "\n" at the
 * beginning or end of pat matches the beginning or end of a text line.
 * If no file is named, then standard input is read.  If more than one file
 * is named, then each printed line is preceded by its file's name. The
 * optional -n  flag asks that line numbers be printed.
 *
 *
```

```
 * Source files:
 *
 *     find.c     - this file
 *     lib.c      - library of C procedures
 */

#include <stdio.h>
#define MAXTEXT    200

int   nfiles,              /* number of files named on the command line */
      nflag = 0;           /* tells if line numbers should be printed */

char buf[MAXTEXT+1],       /* holds text, with a newline at each end */
     first_char,           /* the first character in the pattern */
     *pat;                 /* the pattern string */

main(argc, argv)                                                                       main
int argc;
char *argv[];
{
     int i, length;

     savename("find");    /* for error messages */

     if (argc > 1 && argv[1][0] == '-')
          if (argv[1][1] == 'n') {
               nflag = 1;
               ++argv;
               --argc;
          } else
               fatal("The only permissible flag is n.");
     if (argc == 1)
          fatal("No pattern was given.");
     pat = argv[1];

     /* handle newline characters at the ends of the pattern */
     if (pat[0] == '\\' && pat[1] == 'n')
          *++pat = '\n';
     if ((length = strlen(pat)) == 0)
          fatal("Pattern length is zero.");
     if (length > 1 && pat[length-2] == '\\' && pat[length-1] == 'n') {
          pat[length-2] = '\n';
          pat[length-1] = '\0';
     }

     buf[0] = '\n';        /* newline character before each line */
     first_char = *pat;
     if ((nfiles = argc - 2) == 0)
          scan("");
     else
          /* for each specified file */
          for (i = 2; i < argc; ++i)
               scan(argv[i]);
     exit(0);
}

/* scan - find lines in file that contain the pattern */
scan(file)                                                                             scan
```

```
char *file;
{
    FILE *fp, *ckopen();
    int line_number = 0;
    char *fgets(), *p, *pos, *t;

    if (nfiles == 0)
        fp = stdin;
    else
        fp = ckopen(file, "r");

    /* for each line of the file */
    while (fgets(buf+1, MAXTEXT, fp) != NULL) {  /* keeps newline */
        ++line_number;
        /* for each text position */
        for (pos = buf; *pos != '\0'; ++pos)
            /* quick check for a possible match */
            if (*pos == first_char) {
                /* character-by-character check for complete match */
                p = pat;
                t = pos;
                /* scan for mismatch or end of pattern */
                while (*++p == *++t && *p != '\0')
                    ;
                if (*p == '\0') {          /* match */
                    if (nfiles > 1)
                        printf("%s:", file);
                    if (nflag)
                        printf("%d:", line_number);
                    fputs(buf+1, stdout);
                    break;              /* try next line */
                }
            }
    }
    if (fp != stdin)
        fclose(fp);
}
```

1.2 ABSTRACT DATA TYPES.

Most of the later programs use ''abstract data types,'' as described in this section. The simple macro processor given here:

- illustrates general points about abstract data types,
- includes a file, *macmod.c*, that is used in the *update* program of Chapter 2, and
- provides useful material for readers learning C.

For a broader survey of abstract data types see *Principles of Software Engineering and Design* by Marvin Zelkowitz, Alan Shaw, and John Gannon (Prentice-Hall, 1979), especially pp. 60–81.

Even medium-sized programs, such as the longer programs in this book, cannot be understood all at once. They must be split into smaller pieces. However, there are many ways of splitting a program. Successful program design depends on creating independent pieces: a good design makes it possible to understand one piece of the program without knowing much about the others.

Programs in this book often hide implementation details of a data structure within a file. Procedures in other files do not depend on the details of the data structure. Thus, those other procedures can be understood without learning about the data structure. Conversely, the data structure can be understood, or changed, without knowledge of the other procedures.

Specifically, with a file containing a main data structure for a later program, several functions can be called from outside the file; these are the *access functions* for the data abstraction. The value (if any) returned by an access function is a simple object, like an integer or a character pointer, not complicated, like a pointer to a structure. All global data and all functions except the access functions are declared *static* to make them invisible from outside the file.

1.2.1 Macro.c—A Macro Processor, Excluding the Symbol Table Module

A small macro processor illustrates how abstract data types are used in later programs. The basic algorithm is

```
for each input line
    if the line begins with the eight characters "#define<space>" {
        split the rest of the line into a name and a definition
        remember the name and the definition
    } else {
        replace each macro name in the line by its definition
        print the resulting line
    }
```

For example, suppose the input is

```
this line comes before abstract is defined
#define abstract not concrete
this line comes after abstract is defined
```

When the macro processor reads the first line, no macros have been defined, so the unaltered line is printed. The second line causes the macro processor to re-member that the eight-character string ''abstract'' (the macro name) should there-after be replaced by the twelve-character string ''not concrete'' (the macro defi-nition). This substitution is made in the third line, so the complete output consists of the two lines

```
this line comes before abstract is defined
this line comes after not concrete is defined
```

The following rules locate the name and definition in a *#define* line.

- The name begins with the first character that follows *#define*, other than space and tab characters.
- The name extends until a space, tab, or newline character is encountered.
- The definition begins with the first character after the name, other than space and tab characters.
- The definition does not include the terminating newline character.

A useful portion of the macro processor can now be written, leaving for later implementation the operations:

1. remember a macro name and definition
2. replace each macro name in a line by its definition

These operations are performed by a "symbol table module" having access functions *macin()* (operation 1) and *macout()* (operation 2).

This symbol table may be implemented in many ways: a simple linear list, hash table, AVL tree, etc. However, when viewed from the file *macro.c*, which contains the body of the macro processor, the symbol table is an *abstract data type*; only the availability of operations *macin()* and *macout()* is known. The exact nature of the concrete data type used to implement the abstract data type is completely hidden from *macro.c*.

One benefit of this design is that *macro.c* can be tested before a specific data structure is chosen for the symbol table. The simple throw-away code in *stubs.c* helps test if *main()* correctly handles its command arguments and if *#define* lines are recognized and split properly. Thus, a static property of the design, namely the use of data abstraction, has a substantial influence on the dynamics of program development.

EXERCISES

1. What does *split()* of *macro.c* do with lines like

```
#define fred
```

and

```
#define<space>
```

that is, *#define* lines where the name and/or definition is absent? What do you think it should do?

2. What is the purpose of declaring *name*, *defn*, *is__define()*, and *split()* of *macro.c* to be *static*? Is it a good idea?

3. When the C preprocessor digests a *#define* statement, it outputs one or more empty lines in place of the macro definition. Why?

PROGRAMMING ASSIGNMENTS

1. Make *macro.c* handle multiline macro definitions. Use the convention that a definition can be continued to the next line by ending it with a backslash character ('\'). Thus, the two lines

```
#define example this is a ve\
ry long definition
```

define ''example'' to be ''this is a very long definition''.

```
/*
* macro - rudimentary macro processor
*
*
* Program description:
*
*    A command line has the form:
*         macro filename
*    Macro definition lines begin with the eight characters "#define<space>".
*    Spaces and tab characters preceding the macro name, or falling between
*    the name and the definition, are discarded and the trailing newline
*    character is removed.
*
*
* Source files:
*
*    lib.c       - library of C procedures
*    macmod.c    - macro symbol table
*    macro.c     - this file
*
*
* External procedure calls:
*
*    macin(name, defn)
*    char *name, *defn;
*         Add the name and definition to the symbol table.  If the name
*         is already defined, then discard the old definition.
*
*    macout(from, to, max_chars)
*    char *from, *to;
*    int max_chars;
*         Copy the first argument to the second, expanding macro names.
*         Macro names begin with a letter (lower or upper case), and
*         contain letters, digits and the underscore (_) character.
*         Macro names used in macro definitions are expanded recursively.
```

```
*          Putting more than max_chars characters into the target string
*          causes a fatal error.
*
*/

#include <stdio.h>
#include <ctype.h>
#define MAXTEXT 200
#define PROG_NAME "macro"

static char *name, *defn;

main(argc, argv)                                                              main
int argc;
char *argv[];
{
     FILE *ckopen(), *fp;
     char *fgets(), text[MAXTEXT], text2[MAXTEXT];

     savename(PROG_NAME);    /* for error messages */
     if (argc != 2)
          fatal("Expecting exactly one file name.");
     fp = ckopen(argv[1], "r");

     /* for each input line */
     while (fgets(text, MAXTEXT, fp) != NULL)
          /* if the line begins with the eight characters "#define<space>" */
          if (is_define(text)) {
               /* split the rest of the line into a name and a definition */
               split(text);
               /* remember the name and the definition */
               macin(name, defn);
          } else {
               /* replace each macro name in the line by its definition */
               macout(text, text2, MAXTEXT);
               /* print the resulting line */
               fputs(text2, stdout);
          }
     fclose(fp);
     exit(0);
}


/* is_define - tell if the first 8 characters are "#define<space>" */
static int is_define(text)                                                    is_define
char *text;
{
     char *s = "#define ";

     while (*s != '\0')
          if (*s++ != *text++)
               return(0);
     return(1);
}

/* split - split #define line into a name and definition */
static split(text)                                                            split
```

```
char *text;
{
      char *end;

      /* skip whitespace after "#define " */
      for (name = text+strlen("#define"); *name == ' ' || *name == '\t'; ++name)
            ;
      /* macro name extends to first whitespace character */
      for (end = name; !isspace(*end); ++end)
            ;
      *end = '\0';    /* mark the end of the name */

      /* skip whitespace to find the definition */
      for (defn = end + 1; *defn == ' ' || *defn == '\t'; ++defn)
            ;
      /* strip the newline from the end of the definition */
      for (end = defn; *end != '\n' && *end != '\0'; ++end)
            ;
      *end = '\0';
}




/*
* stubs.c - test harness for macro.c
*
* Link it with the object versions of macro.c and lib.c.  The input
*
      this line comes before abstract is defined
      #define abstract not concrete
      this line comes after abstract is defined
*
* should produce:
*
      this line comes before abstract is defined
      "abstract" is defined to be "not concrete"
      this line comes after abstract is defined
*/

#include <stdio.h>

/* macin - stub for the procedure that stores the macro's name and definition */
macin(name, defn)                                                                          macin
char *name, *defn;
{
      printf("\"%s\" is defined to be \"%s\"\n", name, defn);
}

/* macout - stub for the procedure that expands macros */
macout(from, to, max_chars)                                                                macout
char *from, *to;
int max_chars;
{
      strcpy(to, from);
}
```

1.2.2 Macmod.c — Symbol Table Module

Before examining implementation details for *macin()* and *macout()*, look at *macmod.c*. Notice that global pointer *start* and functions *expand()* and *search()* are declared *static*:

```
/*
* macmod.c - macro symbol table
...
static struct macro *start = (struct macro *)NULL;
...
static char *expand(from, to, limit)
...
static struct macro *search(name)
```

The *static* declarations limit the scope of the three names to *macmod.c*. This architecture is like a wall with two peepholes. Nothing inside *macmod.c*, neither data nor procedures, is visible from the outside, except though *macin()* and *macout()*. It easy to change the concrete data structure that implements the data abstraction, as illustrated by Programming Assignment 2. Any concrete data structure can be used, just so long as *macin()* and *macout()* work as advertised.

For simplicity, *macmod.c* uses a linked list. Nodes in the list have three fields: a pointer to the name, a pointer to the definition, and a pointer to the next node in the list. The relevant declarations are

```
struct macro {
    char *name;
    char *def;
    struct macro *next;
};

/* start points to the list of macros, which is initially empty */
static struct macro *start = (struct macro *)NULL;
```

After the lines

```
#define abstract not concrete
#define concrete detailed
```

have been processed, the symbol table can be pictured:

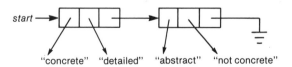

"concrete"   "detailed"   "abstract"   "not concrete"

(Nodes are inserted at the front of the list, so they appear in the reverse of their insertion order.) This data structure leads to simple code for searching the symbol table and inserting new entries. See *search()* and *macin()* in *macmod.c*.

Macro expansion, however, is harder. One minor problem is deciding what counts as a macro name. For instance, does

```
#define A X
A A
```

yield *AA* (this happens if *AA* is considered an indivisible ''word,'' instead of two occurrences of the name *A*) or *XX*? Or perhaps something else? This macro processor produces *AA* because of the way that *expand()* delimits potential macro names. The start of a potential macro name is found by scanning for the first alphabetic character (i.e., a letter *a–z* or *A–Z*). The end of a potential macro name is found by scanning from the start of the name to find the first character that is neither alphanumeric (i.e., a letter or digit *0–9*) nor an underscore (_) character. In brief, macro names follow the C convention for variable names. Only such ''maximal'' strings are looked up in the symbol table.

The following pseudocode loop moves a character pointer *s* down a string, using standard character-classification macros (Section 1.1) to isolate potential macro names.

```
for ( ; ; ) {
    /* find the start of a potential macro name */
    while (!isalpha(*s))
        ++s
    /* find the end of a potential macro name */
    while (isalnum(*s) || *s == '_')
        ++s
}
```

Additional code is needed to generate the output line. As the input string is scanned, characters are copied to the output string. Whenever a potential macro name has been copied, the name is looked up in the symbol table. If the name is found, it is overwritten with the definition, then scanning is resumed.

A macro definition that is copied to the output line may contain the name of another macro, which must be expanded in turn. For example, the input

```
#define abstract not concrete
#define concrete detailed
this line comes after abstract is defined
```

should yield the line:

```
this line comes after not detailed is defined
```

Thus, macro definitions should be subjected to the macro expansion process. To do this, *expand()* calls itself recursively whenever it finds a macro name in its input string.

Expand() guards against infinite recursion in several ways. A procedure argument named *limit* points to the last permissible address for the expanded string, and *expand()* won't copy beyond that point. However, this precaution will not catch infinite recursions like

$$\#define\ A\ A$$
$$A$$

where the target string never grows very long. *Expand()* uses a local variable, *depth*, to bound the chain of recursive calls. *Depth* must be declared *static* so that all instances of *expand()* share the same value, rather than allocate their own variable *depth*. (Make sure you understand how the meaning of *static* differs between external and internal variables.)

The complete recursive macro expander is

```
static char *expand(from, to, limit)
char *from, *to, *limit;
{
    struct macro *mp, *search();
    static int depth = 0;           /* depth of recursion */
    char *potential;

    if (++depth > 100)
        fatal("Infinite recursion while expanding macros.");
    for ( ; ; ) {
        /* find the start of a potential macro name */
        while (!isalpha(*from))
            /* copy characters; check for end of string */
            if ((*to++ = *from++) == '\0') {
                --depth;
                return(to - 1);
            } else if (to >= limit)
                fatal("Line overflow during macro expansion.");
        /* point to the start of a potential macro name */
        potential = to;
        /* find end of potential macro name */
        while (isalnum(*from) || *from == '_') {
            *to++ = *from++;
            if (to >= limit)
                fatal("Line overflow during macro expansion.");
        }
        /* mark end of potential macro name to prepare for search */
        *to = '\0';
        /* if it is a macro name, then expand it */
        if ((mp = search(potential)) != NULL)
            to = expand(mp->def, potential, limit);
    }
}
```

In the example at the bottom of page 29, *expand()* copies the input string to the output string until the first macro name is passed:

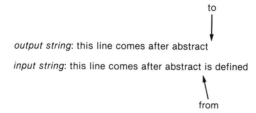

To replace the macro name in the output string by the macro definition, a recursive call

```
expand(mp->def, potential, limit)
```

positions *from* on the definition and *to* on the name:

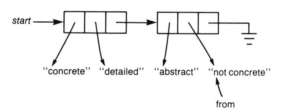

This second instance of *expand()* copies its *from* string to its *to* string until it passes the macro name *concrete*:

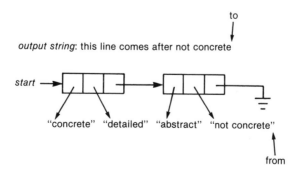

Then a third instance of *expand()* is invoked to expand *concrete*:

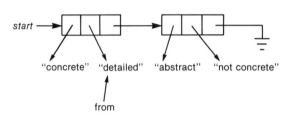

Eventually, this third instance of *expand()* overwrites *concrete* with *detailed* and returns to the second instance. The second instance of *expand()* immediately returns to the first, which finishes the job of copying the input string without further interruption.

EXERCISES

4. What would happen if *macin()* did not check to see if the macro name was already defined?

5. Why does *search()* return a *struct macro* pointer rather than the character pointer *mp−>def*?

6. Explain what *expand()* would do if *potential* were declared

```
static char *potential;
```

Is that declaration desirable?

7. Explain what the macro processor does with the input:

```
#define abstract not concrete
#define concrete not abstract
this line comes after abstract is defined
```

8. The ordering of a definition and a nondefinition line is important, in the sense that a macro name occurring in a nondefinition line preceding the macro's definition is not expanded. Explain how a variation of this rule can avoid the problem of infinite recursion during macro expansion.

9. There are several ways to handle macro definitions that contain macro names. This macro processor performs *late expansion* of macros, in the sense that macro definitions are installed in the symbol table without being checked to see whether they contain macro names. An alternative approach is *early expansion*:

```
for each input line {
        replace each macro name in the line by its definition
        if the line begins with the eight characters "#define<space>" {
                split the rest of the line into a name and a definition
                remember the name and the definition
        } else
                print the resulting line
}
```

Does there exist a set of input lines for which the two approaches produce different outputs?

PROGRAMMING ASSIGNMENTS

2. Rewrite *macmod.c* so that it uses a hash table, and test it with *macro.c*. It is adequate to use the following trivial hash function, though you are welcome to try something fancier.

```
int hash(name)
char *name;
{
        unsigned hashval = 0;

        while (*name != '\0')
                hashval += *name++;
        return (hashval % TABLE_SIZE);
}
```

This approach essentially treats the characters in *name* as integers, computes their sum, divides by the size of the hash table, and returns the remainder.

3. Rewrite *macro.c* and *macmod.c* so that expanded text is written immediately to standard output, rather than being placed in an array. (*Macmod.c* uses the more complicated approach because that capability is needed for the next chapter's *update* program.)

```
/*
 * macmod.c - macro symbol table
 *
 *
 * Entry points:
 *
 *     macin(name, defn)
 *     char *name, *defn;
 *           Add the name and definition to the symbol table.  If the name
 *           is already defined, then discard the old definition.
 *
 *     macout(from, to, max_chars)
```

```
*       char *from, *to;
*       int max_chars;
*           Copy the first argument to the second, expanding macro names.
*           Macro names begin with a letter (lower or upper case) and
*           contain letters, digits and the underscore (_) character.
*           Macro names used in macro definitions are expanded recursively.
*           Putting more than max_chars characters into the target string
*           causes a fatal error.
*
*
* Implementation:
*
*     Macros are stored in a simple linked list.
*/

#include <stdio.h>
#include <ctype.h>

struct macro {
    char *name;
    char *def;
    struct macro *next;
};

/* start points to the list of macros, which is initially empty */
static struct macro *start = (struct macro *) NULL;

/* macin - install a macro name and definition */
macin(name, defn)
char *name, *defn;
{
    struct macro *mp, *search();
    char *ckalloc(), *strsave();

    /* if the macro is not yet defined */
    if ((mp = search(name)) == NULL) {
        /* allocate storage for a node */
        mp = (struct macro *) ckalloc(sizeof(struct macro));
        /* install the name */
        mp->name = strsave(name);
        /* insert the node at the start of the linked list */
        mp->next = start;
        start = mp;
    } else     /* if the macro is being redefined */
        /* free the old definition's storage */
        free(mp->def);
    /* in either case, install the definition */
    mp->def = strsave(defn);
}


/* macout - expand macro names in a string; do not exceed max_chars */
macout(from, to, max_chars)
char *from, *to;
int max_chars;
{
    char *junk, *expand(), *limit;

    limit = &to[max_chars - 1];    /* last permissible address */
    junk = expand(from, to, limit);
}
```

macin (margin note beside `macin(name, defn)`)

macout (margin note beside `macout(from, to, max_chars)`)

```
/*
* expand - recursive procedure to expand macros; do not exceed limit;
*    return pointer to next position in the output string.
*
* The basic algorithm is as follows.  Copy the string beginning at "from"
* to the string beginning at "to".  Check for substrings that are potential
* macro names.  Whenever a potential macro name has been copied, look it
* up in the macro table.  If it is found, then call expand() to overwrite
* the copied macro name with the macro's definition.
*/
static char *expand(from, to, limit)                                              expand
char *from, *to, *limit;
{
    struct macro *mp, *search();
    static int depth = 0;    /* depth of recursion */
    char *potential;

    if (++depth > 100)
        fatal("Infinite recursion while expanding macros.");
    for ( ; ; ) {
        /* find the start of a potential macro name */
        while (!isalpha(*from))
            /* copy characters; check for end of string */
            if ((*to++ = *from++) == '\0') {
                --depth;
                return(to - 1);
            } else if (to >= limit)
                fatal("Line overflow during macro expansion.");
        /* point to the start of a potential macro name */
        potential = to;
        /* find end of potential macro name */
        while (isalnum(*from) || *from == '_') {
            *to++ = *from++;
            if (to >= limit)
                fatal("Line overflow during macro expansion.");
        }
        /* mark end of potential macro name to prepare for search */
        *to = '\0';
        /* if it is a macro name, then expand it */
        if ((mp = search(potential)) != NULL)
            to = expand(mp->def, potential, limit);
    }
}

/* search - look for macro, return pointer to structure */
static struct macro *search(name)                                                 search
char *name;
{
    struct macro *mp;

    /* scan linked list of macros */
    for (mp = start; mp != NULL; mp = mp->next)
        /* if the name is found */
        if (strsame(name, mp->name))
            /* return pointer to the structure */
            return(mp);
    /* if the name is not found, return NULL */
    return(NULL);
}
```

1.3 ISOLATING SYSTEM DEPENDENCIES

A program's construction should allow it to be moved to another operating system or a different hardware environment, if possible. The key is to minimize system-dependent assumptions in the program's design, then isolate system-dependent details during implementation. The program given in this section:

- illustrates general points about handling system dependencies,
- motivates the more complex *update* program of Chapter 2, and
- provides useful material for readers learning C.

The program is used while programming. Suppose your C program has a dozen source files and you have just edited two of them, *file1.c* and *file2.c*. The next step is to compile *file1.c* and *file2.c* and link them with the ten still-valid object files. The required mental process can be described as follows. There is a "base command" for compiling the entire program from scratch. For example, it might be

```
cc -o prog file1.c file2.c file3.c file4.c ...
```

which invokes the C compiler on source files *file1.c*, *file2.c*, ... , links the object files, and names the executable program *prog*. Efficient compilation requires that you remember which of the C source files still have valid object files, i.e., which C source files have not changed since last compiled. Since *file3.o*, *file4.o*, ... (the object files for *file3.c*, *file4.c*, ...) are up to date, the desired command is

```
cc -o prog file1.c file2.c file3.o file4.o ...
```

Effort is needed to remember which object files are valid and to type this long command. Moreover, the likelihood of making an error is high, and the resulting errors are particularly nasty. (Are you likely to make a mistake while naming twelve files? What happens if you actually edit *three* files, but forget one of them?)

Faced with a repetitive and error-prone task on the computer, it is natural to consider writing a software tool. It would be nice to type just

```
compile
```

and sit back while the computer figures out the appropriate command. This section gives a simple software tool that does the job. Chapter 2 gives a much more general and complete solution to the problem.

Can a program produce the proper compilation command? In other words, can a software tool know which object files are out of date? The answer depends on the computer's file system. Many systems can tell a user when a file was last modified. (On UNIX the command is *ls −l*.) If the recorded modification times are relatively accurate, then the crucial information needed for a compilation tool exists; it is just a matter of figuring out how a C program can obtain it.

Compile begins with a base command that tells how to compile the C source files, and replaces a source file name by the corresponding object file name whenever it can. (The user has several ways to specify the base command.) The algorithm is

```
get the base command
for each potential file name, denoted s__name
    if s__name is the name of a C source file {
        o__name = the corresponding object file name
        if modtime(o__name) > modtime(s__name)
            replace s__name by o__name
    }
execute the modified command
```

For each C file named in the base command, *compile* builds the associated object file name and invokes a system-dependent function, *modtime()*, that tells when a file was last modified. If the object file is younger than the source file, then its name replaces the source file name in the base command.

For *compile* to be most effective, the host computer must satisfy several assumptions.

1. *Compile* must be able to tell which words in the base command are the names of C source files. (This assumption is not terribly restrictive; even if the file system and C compiler do not enforce naming conventions on C source files, such conventions are a good idea.)

2. It must be possible to derive the name of a C object file from the source file's name by some systematic transformation (such as changing the suffix ''.c'' to ''.o'').

3. The file system must associate with each file a ''time stamp'' indicating when the file was last modified. Moreover, it must be possible for a program to read a time stamp. For best results, time stamps should be accurate to within a second or better.

4. There must be some way for a user program to execute a command (e.g., invoke the C compiler).

Even among systems that satisfy these assumptions, details vary widely. How can a C source file be spotted from its name? What is the transformation for deriving object file names? How does a program get the modification time of a file? Can a user program invoke the C compiler, or must the program be content to write a command file that the user submits? *Compile* isolates the answers to these questions in low-level procedures and highly visible macros. The specific answers given are appropriate for UNIX.

The design and construction of *compile* curtails system dependencies. For example, *compile* does not depend on the name of the C compiler; the compiler can be named *cc*, *ccom*, or whatever. In fact, *compile* treats the base command as an arbitrary string of characters that may contain the names of C files.

In addition, *compile* avoids the assumption that an object file name is just as long as the source file name. On some systems, the object file's name can be longer (in one case, *file.rel* is the object version of *file.c*). To simplify porting to such systems, the procedure *bldname()* constructs the final command by copying pieces of the base command to another array, instead of merely changing characters in the base command.

```
#define O_SUFFIX   ".o"   /* suffix for C object file names */
#define S_SUFFIX   ".c"   /* suffix for C source file names */

/*
 * bldname - construct an object file name from the name of a C source file;
 * return NULL for names not belonging to C files   (UNIX only)
 */
char *bldname(s_name)
char *s_name;
{
     static char o_name[CMD_SIZE];

     if (!strsame(s_name+strlen(s_name)-strlen(S_SUFFIX), S_SUFFIX))
         return(NULL);
     strcpy(o_name, s_name);
     /* strip off S_SUFFIX */
     o_name[strlen(o_name) - strlen(S_SUFFIX)] = '\0';
     strcat(o_name, O_SUFFIX);
     return(o_name);
}
```

S_SUFFIX and *O_SUFFIX* can be changed to have different lengths. In particular, the expression

```
     s_name+strlen(s_name)-strlen(S_SUFFIX)
```

computes a pointer to the suffix portion of a source file name, regardless of suffix length.

Of course, there is a limit to program portability. With *compile*, file time stamps are critical. It is possible to write a *compile*-like tool for computers that lack them, but the cost in program complexity and usefulness is high. See the hints in Programming Assignment 1.

Even where *compile* works as designed, there are several limitations to its usefulness:

1. Sometimes, object files appear up to date when, in fact, they are not. For example, if the only modified file is *defs.h*, and the line

```
#include "defs.h"
```

appears in every C source file, then *compile* will incorrectly believe that no compilation is needed.

2. It is useful to automate all sorts of commands, not just C compilations. For example, one might want to print listings of just the files modified since the last listings were made, without remembering which files have changed.

The program discussed in Chapter 2 addresses these deficiencies.

EXERCISES

1. What does *compile* do if a named C source file does not exist? What do you think it should do?

2. How can *compile* be adapted to a system where file names in the command line are separated by commas instead of blanks?

3. How can *compile* be adapted to a system where compilation of a C file produces an assembler language file (say, with a name given a ''.s'' suffix) which is translated by an assembler to produce the ''.o'' file?

PROGRAMMING ASSIGNMENTS

1. Get *compile* running on your computer. If files are not automatically stamped with an accurate modification time, or if those time stamps cannot be read by a C program, then try to devise an alternative approach that provides roughly the same capabilities as *compile*. (*Hints:* Some file systems maintain ''version numbers'' that can be read by user programs. On such systems, *compile* could keep its own file telling the version numbers of source and object files when *compile* was last called. However, efficiency is then lost if the C compiler is called directly by the user; when *compile* finds that both the source and object files have been modified since it was last called, it has no choice but to recompile. With even more primitive file systems, *compile* could keep a file of its actions that also records uses of your text editor, though this may be difficult to arrange.)

2. As written, *compile* issues a command even if all object files are up to date. Modify *compile* to correct this deficiency. Should *compile* check the time stamp on the executable program?

3. Modify *compile* to detect commands longer than *CMD_SIZE*. Is the precaution worth the effort?

```
/*
 * compile.c - automatic generation of an efficient compilation command
 *
 *
 * Program description:
 *
 *    A command line has the form:
 *        compile [-filename] [base command]
```

```
*     If there is no command argument, then the base command is the first line
*     of the file named COMMAND.  Otherwise, there must be only one argument;
*     if it begins with '-' then what follows names a file containing the base
*     command; if it does not begin with '-' then it is the base command. If
*     a C source file named in the base command is older than its object file,
*     then the object file's name replaces the source file's name. The
*     resulting command is executed.
*
*
* Source files:
*
*     compile.c - this file
*     lib.c     - library of C procedures
*
*
* Portability:
*
*     The macros O_SUFFIX and S_SUFFIX must give the file name suffixes that
*     characterize C object and source files.
*
*     The macro TIME_TYPE must give the type of time stamps on files.
*
*     The function
*         TIME_TYPE modtime(file)
*         char *file;
*     must return the file's modification time (0 for nonexistent files).
*
*     The function
*         execute(command)
*         char *command;
*     must execute the command (probably a compilation command).  The call
*     need not return control to the calling program.
*/

#include <stdio.h>
#include <ctype.h>

#define CMD_SIZE        500             /* maximum command length */
#define DEFAULT_FILE    "COMMAND"       /* default home of base command */
#define O_SUFFIX        ".o"            /* suffix for C object file names */
#define S_SUFFIX        ".c"            /* suffix for C source file names */
#define TIME_TYPE       long            /* type of time stamps on files */

main(argc, argv)                                                            main
int argc;
char *argv[];
{
    FILE *ckopen(), *fp;
    TIME_TYPE modtime();
    char *b, base_cmd[CMD_SIZE], *bldname(), *fgets(), *filename, *n,
        new_cmd[CMD_SIZE], *o_name, *s_name;

    savename("compile");

    /* get the base command */
    if (argc > 1 && argv[1][0] != '-')
        b = argv[1];
    else {
        if (argc == 1)
            filename = DEFAULT_FILE;
```

```
            else /* argv[1][0] == '-' */
                 filename = &argv[1][1];
         fp = ckopen(filename, "r");
         if (fgets(base_cmd, CMD_SIZE, fp) == NULL)
                 fatal("No base command could be found.");
         fclose(fp);
         /* trim off the newline character */
         base_cmd[strlen(base_cmd)-1] = '\0';
         b = base_cmd;
    }

    /* for each potential file name */
    for (n = new_cmd; *b != '\0'; ) {
         /* copy leading white space */
         while (isspace(*b))
                 *n++ = *b++;
         /* copy the name after remembering where it starts */
         for (s_name = n; *b != '\0' && !isspace(*b); )
                 *n++ = *b++;
         *n = '\0';
         /* if s_name is the name of a C source file */
         if ((o_name = bldname(s_name)) != NULL &&
           modtime(o_name) > modtime(s_name))
                 /* overwrite s_name with o_name */
                 for (n = s_name; *o_name != '\0'; )
                         *n++ = *o_name++;
    }
    *n = '\0';
    puts(new_cmd);        /* tell what is about to happen */
    execute(new_cmd);
    exit(0);
}


/*
 * bldname - construct an object file name from the name of a C source file;
 * return NULL for names not belonging to C files   (UNIX only)
 */
char *bldname(s_name)                                                         bldname
char *s_name;
{
    static char o_name[CMD_SIZE];

    if (!strsame(s_name+strlen(s_name)-strlen(S_SUFFIX), S_SUFFIX))
         return(NULL);
    strcpy(o_name, s_name);
    /* strip off S_SUFFIX */
    o_name[strlen(o_name) - strlen(S_SUFFIX)] = '\0';
    strcat(o_name, O_SUFFIX);
    return(o_name);
}

/* modtime - return file's modification time -- 0 for nonexistent files (UNIX only) */
#include <sys/types.h>
#include <sys/stat.h>
TIME_TYPE modtime(file)                                                       modtime
char *file;
{
    struct stat buf;

    return( stat(file, &buf) >= 0 ? buf.st_mtime : 0 );
}
```

```
/* execute - cause a command to be executed  (UNIX only) */
execute(command)
char *command;
{
      system(command);
}
```

2

A FILE UPDATING TOOL

The *compile* program of Section 1.3 performs a limited but useful task: if some source files of a C program have been modified, *compile* may economically and correctly regenerate the executable program. Although *compile* is inadequate for certain problems described in Sections 1.3 and 2.1, its capabilities are worth extending. This chapter develops a tool, called *update*, that performs a wider range of updating chores. *Update* is closely akin to the UNIX *make* command, as described in the paper "Make—a program for maintaining computer programs" by Stuart I. Feldman (*Software—Practice and Experience*, April 1979, pp. 255–265).

An *update* user specifies (1) which files should be regenerated after some files are modified and (2) the commands needed to regenerate those files. These specifications are placed in a file named *UPDATE*. Section 2.1 explains the syntax for writing the specifications and presents *bldint.c*, the part of *update* that reads and digests the user's *UPDATE* file.

Section 2.2 discusses the complex considerations underlying *update()*, the core procedure that determines which files need updating. The section includes:

> *update.h*—header file of symbolic constants used in *update*,
>
> *update.c*—main program and *update()* procedure, and
>
> *system.c*—*update*'s system-dependent procedures.

Section 2.3 covers the remaining source file, *depmod.c*, which maintains *update*'s record of the *UPDATE* file. Earlier code defines the needed access functions, which are easy to write.

Sections 2.1–2.3 follow the "outside-in" order that I wrote *update*, first de-

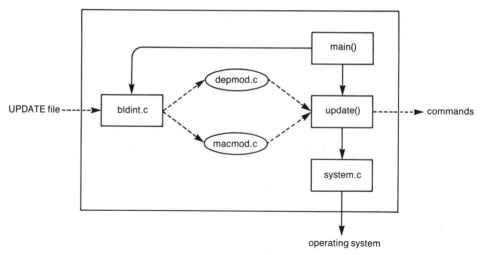

Figure 2.1 Structure of *update*.

termining what is in *UPDATE*, then exploring ramifications of the update rule, and finally implementing the main data structure. Figure 2.1 gives a high-level picture of *update*. The files *depmod.c* and *macmod.c* (Section 1.2) are best thought of as data repositories, rather than processing modules. The distinction is displayed by drawing data modules as ellipses and processing modules as rectangles. Data flow is indicated by dashed lines, control flow by solid lines. (The data structures are implemented as abstract data types so, to be completely precise, data flow is realized by control flow.)

Update is a rather complicated tool. New users must learn the small language described in Section 2.1. Moreover, the subtle behavior discussed in Section 2.2 occasionally surprises even experienced users. However, the reward for mastering *update* is a substantially improved programming environment.

2.1 A GENERAL APPROACH TO FILE DEPENDENCY

As a first step toward improving on the *compile* program of Section 1.3, consider a situation where *compile* is inadequate. After seeing how to properly handle that situation, we will turn to more ambitious tool capabilities.

Consider updating a C program whose source files contain *#include* lines. Section 1.1 mentions two such included files, namely the standard header files *stdio.h* and *ctype.h*. In addition, programmers often put macro definitions and declarations of external variables in a file that is included (using *#include*) in the appropriate source files. *Update.h* of the next section is such a header file.

Imagine the following program arrangement. The file *defs.h* defines macros that are used in several files. Each of the source files, *file1.c*, *file2.c*, and *file3.c* contains the line

<code>#include "defs.h"</code>

The corresponding object files, *file1.o*, *file2.o*, and *file3.o*, are linked with *lib.o*, a compiled file of library procedures, and the executable program is called *prog*. Thus, the "base command" for *compile* would be

<code>cc -o prog file1.c file2.c file3.c lib.o</code>

Compile is inadequate to manage updating when *defs.h* is changed. Suppose *prog* is generated (perhaps by *compile*), *defs.h* is edited, and a *compile* command is issued. Because *compile* has no way of knowing about *defs.h*, it will think that the ".o" files are up to date and, therefore, will not recompile the source files.

What tool capabilities are needed to properly recompile *prog*? The tool must be told to recompile all three source files whenever *defs.h* is changed. Thus, two lists are associated with each object file: (1) the files for which a change necessitates regeneration of the object file, and (2) the commands that regenerate the object file. The first list is required because it names a file, *defs.h*, that cannot be deduced from the second list.

A clean and general conceptual model for file updating is needed before designing *compile*'s successor. Divide files into two categories: *primary* and *derived* files. Primary files are created "by hand," e.g., C source and header files. Derived files are generated by executing programs. For example, object files and executable files are derived by running compilers and linkers. (The distinction between primary and derived files is not always clear-cut. Section 2.2 mentions a program for regenerating files that were originally constructed by hand. For now, ignore such complications.)

The general conceptual model must capture crucial file relationships. A derived file *f* is said to *depend on* file *g* (either primary or derived), or, equivalently, *g* is a *precursor* of *f*, if *f* should be regenerated whenever *g* is changed. Thus, with the hypothetical C program, *file1.o* depends on *defs.h* and *file1.c*. (There is a natural tendency to say that the source files depend on *defs.h*. Be sure you understand why the object files, rather than the source files, are said to depend on *defs.h*.)

Figure 2.2 pictures these dependencies. Arrows point from a file to its pre-

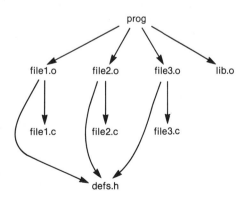

Figure 2.2 Dependency graph for files of a hypothetical program.

cursors. Such a *dependency graph* shows which derived files must be regenerated after some primary files are modified. Combined with commands for updating files, the graph determines the updating process:

THE RULE FOR UPDATING FILES

Associate with every derived file *f*:

1. the list of *f*'s precursors, and
2. a list of commands.

Suppose some primary files have been modified. The process of updating a file is defined recursively as follows. First, update the file's precursors. If the file is now older than any of its precursors, or if it does not yet exist, then execute the file's list of commands.

The Basic File Updating Tool.   Our goal is a software tool that (1) reads a file named *UPDATE* containing precursors and commands of derived files, (2) gets the modification times of files, and (3) generates an economical set of commands to update a given file. The syntax for specifying precursor and command lists in *UPDATE* is illustrated by

```
prog -> file1.o file2.o file3.o lib.o
        cc -o prog file1.o file2.o file3.o lib.o
```

The first line states that *prog* depends on *file1.o*, *file2.o*, *file3.o* and *lib.o*. The "−>" notation for dependency relations is appropriately reminiscent of dependency graph edges, as in Fig. 2.2. The second line gives the command for updating *prog*. *Update* interprets it as a command because it begins with a tab character.

The following example is a complete *UPDATE* file for compiling and linking the hypothetical program; in it the command

```
cc -c file.c
```

compiles *file.c* and creates *file.o*.

```
prog -> file1.o file2.o file3.o lib.o
        cc -o prog file1.o file2.o file3.o lib.o

file1.o -> defs.h file1.c
        cc -c file1.c
```

```
file2.o -> defs.h file2.c
      cc -c file2.c

file3.o -> defs.h file3.c
      cc -c file3.c
```

Figure 2.1.1   First sample *UPDATE* file

Update is invoked with

`update <name>`

where *name* appears on the left of an *UPDATE* dependency line. The command *update* (without any file name) updates the first file named on a dependency line (*prog* in the sample *UPDATE* file).

For example,

`update file1.o`

triggers the following events. First, *update* reads *UPDATE* and discovers the entry

```
file1.o -> defs.h file1.c
      cc -c file1.c
```

describing when and how to update *file1.o*. The dependency line tells *update* to update *defs.h* and *file1.c* before *file1.o*. However, the remainder of *UPDATE* (and *update*'s implicit dependency rules, as described below) specify no precursors or commands for *defs.h* and *file1.c* (they are primary files), so *update* processes *file1.o*. The file system is queried for the modification times of *file1.o*, *defs.h*, and *file1.c*. If either of *defs.h* or *file1.c* is younger than *file1.o*, or if *file1.o* does not exist, then the command *cc −c file1.c* is executed.

In the same example, the command

`update`

applies the updating rule to *prog*. After *UPDATE* is read, the listed precursors of *prog*, namely *file1.o*, *file2.o*, *file3.o*, and *lib.o*, are recursively updated. For each of the first three, *update* performs the steps described in the previous paragraph. For *lib.o*, *update* does no work because *lib.o* has no precursors or commands. (Assume that *lib.c* is contained in some other directory.) If *prog* is either older than one of its precursors or nonexistent, then the command

`cc -o prog file1.o file2.o file3.o lib.o`

is executed.

Shorthand Notations.   *Update* extends the basic tool capabilities in two directions. First, it provides notational conveniences that simplify *UPDATE* files. Later enhancements allow *update* to accomplish new tasks. The added notational conventions are

1. *Continued lines.* A convention for ''continued'' lines allows long lines to appear in *UPDATE*. Any *UPDATE* line ending with a backslash character (\) is joined to the following line, as in

```
prog -> file1.o file2.o\
        file3.o lib.o
```

Update replaces the backslash character and any trailing whitespace characters by a single blank. Thus, the above *UPDATE* entry is equivalent to the single line

```
prog -> file1.o file2.o file3.o lib.o
```

2. *Comments.* C-style comment lines are permitted in *UPDATE*.
3. *Macros.* C-style macros without arguments are allowed. For example, in the above *UPDATE* file for *prog*, repetition of the string

```
file1.o file2.o file3.o
```

can be avoided by defining

```
#define OBJECTS file1.o file2.o file3.o
```

and substituting the word *OBJECTS* for occurrences of the longer string.
4. *Multiple dependents.* Dependency lines can have several file names to the left of '' − >''. The line

```
file1.o file2.o file3.o -> defs.h
```

shows that three object files depend on *defs.h*.
5. *Multiple occurrence as a dependent.* A derived file can appear on the left of several dependency lines, as with *file1.o* in

```
file1.o file2.o file3.o -> defs.h
file1.o -> file1.c
       cc -c file1.c
```

Precursors are recursively updated in the order they appear in *UPDATE*. Similarly, commands are executed in order of appearance. Suppose *UPDATE* contains

```
der1 -> pre1   pre2
       com1
       com2
der1 der2 -> pre3
       com3
```

The process of updating *der1* begins by updating *pre1*, *pre2*, and *pre3* in that order. If any of them is then younger than *der1*, or if *der1* does not exist, then *com1*, *com2*, and *com3* are executed in that order.

6. *Implicit rules. Update* knows that changing a ''.o'' suffix to ''.c'' produces the name of a potential precursor. This ''implicit dependency rule'' makes it unnecessary for *UPDATE* to contain entries like

```
file1.o -> file1.c
    cc -c file1.c
```

Whenever *update* regenerates *file1.o*, it automatically applies the *cc* command, provided that *file1.c* exists and that *UPDATE* contains no commands for *file1.o*. On the other hand, commands for *file1.o* contained in *UPDATE* will override the implicit rule. (Programming Assignment 1 of Section 2.3 asks you to extend *update* so that *UPDATE* can specify other implicit rules.)

Given these six additional features, the *UPDATE* file for *prog* might contain

```
/* UPDATE file for prog, a hypothetical program */
#define OBJECTS file1.o file2.o file3.o
#define ALL OBJECTS lib.o

prog -> ALL
     cc -o prog ALL

OBJECTS -> defs.h
```

Figure 2.1.2   Second sample *UPDATE* file

With this *UPDATE* file, the command

```
update file1.o
```

triggers the following events. First, *update* reads *UPDATE* and discovers that *file1.o* appears on the left of the second dependency line (once the macro *OBJECTS* is expanded). Then, *update* applies the rule for constructing source file names from object file names, producing ''file1.c''. If *file1.c* exists, then *update* infers the entry

```
file1.o -> defs.h file1.c
    cc -c file1.c
```

Finally, *update* gets modification times of *file1.o*, *defs.h*, and *file1.c*, and decides if *file1.o* needs updating.

Further Embellishments.   Two extensions to *update* are given below; others appear as Programming Assignments 1–4 in Section 2.3. The first extension makes it easy to change the intrinsic rule for compiling C files. Users may want to compile with a flag that generates optimized code or code tailored for debugging. *UPDATE* macros provide the following solution:

7. *The COMPILE macro.* The macro *COMPILE* is automatically initialized to ''*cc −c*''. An *UPDATE* line

```
#define COMPILE ...
```

changes the implicit rule for compiling C programs. (The line affects all default compilations, regardless of where it appears in *UPDATE*.) If *UPDATE* contains no commands for *file.o*, and if *file.c* exists, then the updating command for *file.o* is produced by submitting

```
COMPILE file.c
```

to the macro expander.

The macros discussed so far are ''static'': once defined, they maintain their defined value until explicitly changed. Certain ''dynamic'' macros are also useful.

8. *The YOUNGER macro. YOUNGER* is a *dynamic macro*, meaning it is automatically redefined for each derived file. Its value is the list of all precursors found to be younger than the dependent file. Thus, the file is updated if *YOUNGER* is a non-empty string. *YOUNGER* helps specify commands that operate on recently changed files. (To support dynamic macros, macros in updating commands are expanded just before command execution. On the other hand, macros in dependency lines are expanded as *UPDATE* is read.)

The following *UPDATE* file illustrates most of *update*'s capabilities:

```
/* UPDATE file for prog, a hypothetical program */
#define COMPILE cc -c -g
#define PRIMARIES defs.h file1.c file2.c file3.c
#define OBJECTS file1.o file2.o file3.o
#define ALL OBJECTS lib.o

prog -> ALL
        cc -g -o prog ALL
```

```
OBJECTS -> defs.h

print -> PRIMARIES
      pr YOUNGER
      tweak print

test ->
      prog data > output
      fcomp output answers
      rm output
```

Figure 2.1.3   Third sample *UPDATE* file

In this example, the *COMPILE* macro is defined to invoke the C compiler with the $-g$ flag. (One compiler then generates information used by a symbolic debugger.) The dynamic macro *YOUNGER* helps keep program listings up to date. An empty file named *print* is kept solely for its time stamp. The command *update print* causes *update* to print (with the *pr* command) all primary files younger than *print*. The *tweak* command from Section 1.1 then makes *print*'s time stamp current. Thus, the next *update print* command will list all primary files changed in the interim. (It is preferable to *tweak print* and run *pr* in the background, if your system permits. This lets you get back to work right away.)

UPDATE names the "derived file" *test*, though no such file exists. Since it is nonexistent, its commands are always executed as a consequence of the updating rule. Thus, the command *update test* triggers the following events. First, *prog* is applied to *data*, and the output is collected in the file *output*. Then the program *fcomp* compares the output with the contents of *answers* to determine if they differ. (*Fcomp* is given in Section 3.2.) Finally, *output* is removed. This use of *test* illustrates the general tactic of associating an arbitrary command sequence in *UPDATE* with a nonexistent "dependent" file. (Names can be chosen freely; the only file name with special meaning for *update* is *UPDATE*.)

The following table lists the files associated with the hypothetical program. Keep the list in mind as you study the examples.

header file	*defs.h*
source files	*file1.c, file2.c* and *file3.c*
object files	*file1.o, file2.o, file3.o* and *lib.o*
executable file	*prog*
empty file	*print*
test data	*data*
true solutions	*answers*
trial solutions	*output*

Built-In Macros.   In summary, three macro names are reserved and should not be used for other purposes.

1. COMPILE: *Update* initializes this macro to "cc −c" before the *UPDATE* file is read. The user may redefine it.
2. YOUNGER: A dynamic macro that should be used only in commands (not in "−>" lines). The user should not redefine it.
3. TARGET: A dynamic macro that should be used only in commands. The value of *TARGET* is the name of the file currently being updated. The user should not redefine it. (This macro is used internally by *update*, but occasionally it has other uses. See Exercises 2 and 3 of Section 3.3.)

Comments on Bldint.c.   Given the syntax for *UPDATE* files, the part of *update* that reads *UPDATE* can be written. In other words, we are ready to discuss the box labeled *bldint.c* in Fig. 2.1. Procedures in *bldint.c* call procedures

```
prein(file, precursor)
char *file, *precursor;
```

and

```
cmdin(file, command)
char *file, *command;
```

to store precursors and commands. (*Prein()* and *cmdin()* are implemented in Section 2.3.) Given the *UPDATE* entry

```
file1.o -> file1.c
     cc -c file1.c
```

update first calls *prein()* with *file* = "file1.o" and *precursor* = "file1.c", then calls *cmdin()* with *file* = "file1.o" and *command* = "cc −c file1.c".

This portion of *update* also installs the names and definitions of static macros in the macro table and expands macros in dependency lines. This is done with procedures

```
macin(name, definition)
char *name, *definition;
```

and

```
macout(line1, line2, maxchars)
char *line1, *line2;
int maxchars;
```

described in Section 1.2.

For example, the *UPDATE* file

```
#define LEFTS l1 l2
#define RIGHTS r1 r2
#define CMD_MAC don't expand yet
LEFTS -> RIGHTS
        CMD_MAC
```

results in the calls

Function	First Argument	Second Argument
macin()	"LEFTS"	"l1 l2"
macin()	"RIGHTS"	"r1 r2"
macin()	"CMD_MAC"	"don't expand yet"
macout()	"LEFTS − > RIGHTS"	returned as "l1 l2 − > r1 r2"
prein()	"l1"	"r1"
prein()	"l2"	"r1"
prein()	"l1"	"r2"
prein()	"l2"	"r2"
cmdin()	"l1"	"CMD_MAC"
cmdin()	"l2"	"CMD_MAC"

Macros in commands are not expanded when *UPDATE* is read because commands can contain dynamic macros (like *YOUNGER*), whose definitions are determined (and repeatedly changed) during the updating process.

Bldint.c applies the following detailed steps to lines in *UPDATE*. First, comments are removed, and lines ending with a backslash character are joined to the following line using the rule: the '\', and all blanks, tabs, and newlines on either side are replaced by a single blank. The terminating '\n' is removed. Each resulting line is classified as a macro definition line, command, or dependency line using the rules:

1. A line beginning with '#' is a macro definition line. The next six characters must be "*define*", followed by one or more blanks and tabs. Then comes the macro name, terminated by a blank, tab, or end of line. Blanks and tabs after the macro name are skipped, and whatever remains on the line is the definition.

2. A line beginning with a tab character gives a command, and leading blanks and tabs are removed. The command is associated with each name that appears to the left of "− >" in the closest preceding dependency line. (The code for handling dependency lines makes the names available.)

3. A line not beginning with '#' or a tab character is a dependency line. After macros are expanded, the line must contain the character pair "− >". To the left and right of "− >" are lists of names separated by one or more

blanks or tabs. Each file named on the left side depends on each file on the right.

Test.c, a test harness used for developing *update*, lets you experiment with *bldint.c*. It provides a main program and procedure stubs that print the dependency information and commands extracted from *UPDATE* by *bldint.c*.

EXERCISES

1. Tell what happens if the dependency line

```
      prog -> file1.o file2.o file3.o lib.o
```

in the first sample *UPDATE* file is replaced by the ''complete'' dependency line

```
prog -> file1.o file2.o file3.o lib.o file1.c file2.c file3.c defs.h
```

2. To reduce clutter when listing the names of files in a directory, the UNIX *ls* command ordinarily ignores file names that begin with '.'. Explain the advantage of the *UPDATE* entry

```
               print -> .print
               .print -> PRIMARIES
                    pr YOUNGER
                    tweak .print
```

3. Explain in detail why *YOUNGER* must be a dynamic macro.
4. What modification to Fig. 2.1 would depict the existence of dynamic macros?
5. Can dynamic macros be allowed in dependency lines? Explain.

```
/*
 * bldint.c - build internal form of the UPDATE file
 *
 *
 * Entry point:
 *
 *     int bldint()
 *         Read the UPDATE file and record the information.  Return
 *         a count of the syntax errors in UPDATE.
 *
 *
 * External procedure calls:
 *
 *     cmdin(file, command)                        .. file depmod.c
 *     char *file, *command;
 *         Record a command of a file.
 *
```

```
*      macin(name, definition)                         .. file macmod.c
*      char *name, *definition;
*           Record a macro name and definition.
*
*      macout(line1, line2, maxchars)                  .. file macmod.c
*      char *line1, *line2;
*      int maxchars;
*           Expand macros while copying line1 to line2.  At most
*           maxchars characters are copied.
*
*      prein(file, precursor)                          .. file depmod.c
*      char *file, *precursor;
*           Record a precursor of a file.
*/

#include "update.h"

static FILE *U_file;           /* UPDATE file */
static int line_nbr = 0;       /* current position in UPDATE file */

/*
* bldint - classify UPDATE lines; return error count
*
* Macro definition lines begin with '#'; commands are preceded by a tab
* character; the rest are dependency lines.
*/
int bldint()                                                             bldint
{
     FILE *ckopen();
     int errors = 0;
     char dependents[CMD_SIZE], line[CMD_SIZE], line2[CMD_SIZE];
     /*
     * dependents[] holds the names on the left of the most recent dependency
     * line, separated by '\0' characters and terminated with two '\0's.  The
     * dependents are determined by blddep() and used by bldcmd().
     */

     U_file = ckopen(U_NAME, "r");   /* U_NAME is "UPDATE" */
     dependents[0] = '\0';
     while (inline(line) != EOF)
          switch (*line) {
               case '#':
                    errors += bldmac(line);
                    break;
               case '\t':
                    errors += bldcmd(line, dependents);
                    break;
               default:
                    macout(line, line2, CMD_SIZE);
                    errors += blddep(line2, dependents);
          }
     fclose(U_file);
     return(errors);
}

/* bldmac - process a macro definition line; return error count */
static int bldmac(line)                                                 bldmac
char *line;
{
     char *d, *n = line + 7; /* 7 = length of "#define" */
```

```
        if (!isspace(*n))
            return(improper("macro definition"));
        *n++ = '\0';
        if (!strsame(line, "#define"))
            return(improper("macro definition"));
        /* find start of name */
        while (isspace(*n))
            ++n;
        if (*n == '\0')
            return(improper("macro definition"));
        /* find end of name */
        for (d = n+1; !isspace(*d) && *d != '\0'; ++d)
            ;
        if (isspace(*d))
            *d++ = '\0';
        /* find start of definition */
        while (isspace(*d))
            ++d;
        macin(n, d);
        return(0);
}


/* bldcmd - process a command; return error count */
static int bldcmd(line, dependents)                                    bldcmd
char *line, *dependents;
{
        if (dependents[0] == '\0')
            return(improper("command"));
        /* strip blanks and tabs from front of command */
        while (isspace(*line))
            ++line;
        /* for each dependent file ... */
        for ( ; *dependents != '\0'; dependents += strlen(dependents)+1)
            cmdin(dependents, line);
        return(0);
}


/* blddep - process a dependency line; return error count */
static int blddep(line, dependents)                                    blddep
char *line, *dependents;
{
        char *e, *f = dependents, *p = line;

        /* copy names on left of "->", separate with '\0'. */
        while (*p != '\0' && (p[0] != '-' || p[1] != '>'))
            if (isspace(*f++ = *p++)) {
                f[-1] = '\0';
                while (isspace(*p))
                    ++p;
            }
        f[1] = f[0] = '\0';
        if (*p == '\0')
            return(improper("dependency line"));

        p += 2;         /* skip "->" */

        /* for each name on the right of "->", record all precursor relations */
        for ( ; ; ) {
            /* find start of name */
            while (isspace(*p))
                ++p;
```

```
            if (*p == '\0')
                break;
            /* find end of name */
            for (e = p+1; !isspace(*e) && *e != '\0'; ++e)
                ;
            if (isspace(*e))
                *e = '\0';
            else
                e[1] = '\0';            /* terminate on next iteration */
            /* for each name to the left of "->" ... */
            for (f = dependents; *f != '\0'; f += strlen(f) + 1)
                prein(f, p);            /* record the dependency */
            p = e + 1;
        }
        return(0);
}


/*
 * inline - input an UPDATE line; return its last character ('\n' or EOF)
 *
 * Comments are removed; continued lines (those ending with '\') are collected;
 * the terminating '\n' is removed; lines containing only whitespace are ignored.
 */
static int inline(line)                                                              inline
char *line;
{
        int c = U_char();
        char *line_start = line, *s;

        while (c != EOF && line - line_start < CMD_SIZE)
            switch (c) {
                case '/':               /* possible comment */
                    if ((c = U_char()) == '*') {
                        skip_comment();
                        c = U_char();
                    } else
                        *line++ = '/';
                    break;
                case '\\':              /* possible continued line */
                    if ((c = U_char()) == '\n') {
                        /* back up over white space */
                        while (line > line_start && isspace(line[-1]))
                            --line;
                        *line++ = ' ';
                        while (isspace(c = U_char()))
                            ;
                    } else
                        *line++ = '\\';
                    break;
                case '\n':
                    for (s = line_start; s < line; ++s)
                        if (!isspace(*s)) {
                            *line = '\0';
                            return(c);
                        }
                    /* ignore lines containing only white space */
                    line = line_start;
                    c = U_char();
                    break;
```

```
                default:
                        *line++ = c;
                        c = U_char();
                }
        if (line - line_start >= CMD_SIZE)
                fatalf("%s line exceeds maximum length", U_NAME);
        *line = '\0';
        return(c);
}

/* U_char - get character from UPDATE file; count lines */
static int U_char()                                                  U_char
{
        int c;

        if ((c = getc(U_file)) == '\n')
                ++line_nbr;
        return(c);
}

/* skip_comment - discard a comment */
static skip_comment()                                            skip_comment
{
        int new_c = '\0', old_c = '\0';

        while (old_c != '*' || new_c != '/') {
                old_c = new_c;
                if ((new_c = U_char()) == EOF)
                        fatalf("EOF in %s comment", U_NAME);
        }
}

/* improper - report syntax error in UPDATE line; return error increment */
static int improper(type)                                          improper
char *type;
{
        fprintf(stderr, "Improper %s at line %d of %s.\n",
                type, line_nbr, U_NAME);  /* U_NAME is "UPDATE" */
        return(1);
}


/*
 * test.c - test driver for update's front end.
 *
 * Link it with the object versions of bldint.c, macmod.c and lib.c.
 * The UPDATE file
 *
        /* This UPDATE file tests update's front end * /
        #define LEFTS  l1 l2
        #define RIGHTS r1 r2
        #define CMD_MAC  don't expand yet
        LEFTS -> RIGHTS
                CMD_MAC
 *
 * should produce:
 *
        l1 depends on r1
        l2 depends on r1
        l1 depends on r2
        l2 depends on r2
```

```
    l1 is updated by the command: CMD_MAC
    l2 is updated by the command: CMD_MAC
*/

main()                                                              main
{
    int errors;

    if ((errors = bldint()) > 0)
        printf("%d errors in dependency file\n", errors);
}

/* prein - stub for the procedure that stores dependency information */
prein(file, precur)                                                 prein
char *file, *precur;
{
    printf("%s depends on %s\n", file, precur);
}

/* cmdin - stub for the procedure that stores commands */
cmdin(file, cmd)                                                    cmdin
char *file, *cmd;
{
    printf("%s is updated by the command: %s\n", file, cmd);
}
```

2.2 A CLOSER LOOK AT THE UPDATE ALGORITHM

At the heart of *update* lies a rather complicated procedure, *update()*, that determines which files should be updated. This section incorporates ideas from Section 2.1 into an outline of *update()*, then discusses the additional considerations behind *update()*'s final design.

Recall the rule for updating a file: first, update the file's precursors; if the file now has a younger precursor or is nonexistent, then update the file. This update procedure accesses a function *modtime(file)* that returns a file's modification time (0 for nonexistent files). An outline of *update()* follows readily from this rule and the need for implicit rules (''.o'' files depend on ''.c'' files) and *YOUNGER* (the dynamic macro).

```
update(file)
{
    install implicit precursors and commands for file

    /* bring precursor files up to date */
    for each of file's precursors
        update(precursor)

    /* compare modification times */
    m_time = modtime(file)
    YOUNGER = '' ''
```

```
        for each of file's precursors
            if modtime(precursor) > m__time
                append precursor's name to YOUNGER

    /* update file if necessary */
    if YOUNGER ≠ '' '' or m__time == 0 {
        install YOUNGER in the macro table
        for each of file's commands {
            expand macros in the command
            execute the command
        }
    }
}
```

Figure 2.2.1   Outline of *update()*

The command

$$update\ a$$

calls *update(a)* to perform a *depth-first search* of the dependency graph, beginning at *a*. Suppose the dependency graph is

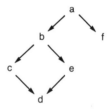

where precursors of a file are ordered left to right. Calls to the outlined *update()* have the order

$$a\ b\ c\ d\ e\ d\ f$$

This order is called "depth-first" because the search moves deeper in the graph as long as possible, instead of fanning out.

Modification 1.   The detection and handling of invalid data remain to be treated. Upon encountering an argument, *file*, where

  (i) *file* does not exist,
 (ii) *file* has no known precursors, and
(iii) *file* has no known commands,

update() terminates execution with the message

```
Don't know how to update <file's name>.
```

Simultaneous occurrence of any two of the conditions (i)–(iii) is normal and does not cause execution to terminate. Conditions (i) and (ii) arise with the use of fictitious files, such as *test* in the third sample *UPDATE* file of Section 2.1. (*Test* names a set of commands in the *UPDATE* file, but doesn't name an actual file.) Primary files satisfy conditions (ii) and (iii). Conditions (i) and (iii) occur with an *UPDATE* entry whose only purpose is to perform several updating tasks simultaneously. For example, the third sample *UPDATE* file has the entry *prog* that reconstructs the executable file and the entry *test* that tests it. An *UPDATE* entry

```
try -> prog test
```

where *try* is not the name of an existing file (condition (i)) and *try* has no updating commands (condition (iii)) provides a command, *update try*, that regenerates and tests the program.

Modification 2.   *Update()* uses the following strategy to avoid both (i) multiple updates of a file that is the precursor of several files and (ii) infinite looping on dependency graphs containing cycles.

```
update(file)
{
    mark file as active
    for each of file's precursors
        if the precursor is not yet reached
            update(precursor)
    m_time = modtime(file)
    for each of file's precursors
        if precursor is not active and modtime(precursor) > m_time
            record that file is out-of-date
    if file is out-of-date or m_time == 0
        execute file's commands
    mark file as processed
}
```

Figure 2.2.2   *Update*'s node-marking strategy

(Marks do not affect the actual files, but instead are recorded in *update*'s internal record of the file's status. Thus, all *active* and *processed* marks disappear when *update* terminates.)

A node is marked *active* when first encountered and marked *processed* when the search backtracks from the node. This strategy detects common precursors (files that are a precursor of several files). In a case like

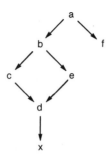

(*d* is the common precursor) *update()* records when *d* has been processed and does not traverse the edge $e \rightarrow d$. Henceforth, pictures of dependency graphs will use dashed arrows to indicate edges that do not generate calls to *update()*, like this

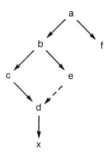

The solid edges (the ones corresponding to *update()* calls) form the *depth-first search tree*. Notice that this separation of dependency edges into solid and dashed edges depends on where the depth-first search begins; with the above graph, the command

update e

would induce a solid (depth-first tree) edge from *e* to *d*.

A file's commands are executed after the search explores all edges leaving that node. Therefore, the ordering of files according to potential command execution gives a *postorder* listing of the depth-first search tree. In the above example, the order is

x d c e b f a

Active nodes are distinguished from processed nodes so that cycles in the dependency graph are treated properly. Suppose

- *prog* is an executable program,
- *source* is the source file for *prog*, and

- *versions* is a file containing archived versions of *source* that are maintained by a version control tool (see Section 3.3).

The precursor of *prog* is *source*, the precursor of *source* is *versions* (since *source* can be derived by running a program that extracts it from *versions*) and the precursor of *versions* is *source* (since *versions* is updated by executing a program that installs the contents of *source*). If *prog* and *source* do not exist, then a call to *update(prog)* yields the depth-first search:

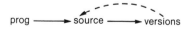

prog ──────► source ──────► versions

The call to *update(prog)* calls *update(source)*, which calls *update(versions)*. After *versions* is found to be current, *source* is extracted from *versions* and compiled to produce *prog*. If *source* is then edited, a second update of *prog* yields the same depth-first search, and the call to *update(versions)* again avoids calling *update(source)* because *source* is active. The critical point is that the modification times of *source* and *versions* are not compared during the update decision for *versions*, so the installation commands associated with *versions* are not executed. In brief, even though *source* is younger than *versions*, *versions* will not be updated if the depth-first search starts at *prog* or *source*. However, once the edit-compile-test iteration brings *prog* to the desired state, the command to update *versions* will perform the search

versions ──────► source

and run the commands that install the contents of *source* in *versions*. In general, the updating decision for a file ignores the precursors that are ancestors of the file in the depth-first search tree.

Modification 3.   The last addition to *update()* extends the capabilities discussed in Section 2.1 and enhances portability. Sometimes *update* will not actually execute the commands that it generates.

- A user may want *update* merely to list the commands it deems necessary. Visual inspection of the commands before they are run might avoid an expensive disaster. With *update*, this "no-execution" option is specified with a −*n* flag in the command line.
- There are computer systems where command execution cannot be interleaved with execution of *update*. Instead, commands are written to a file and executed later.

When updating commands are not executed concurrently with *update*, *mod-time()* cannot be used to see whether *precursor* was modified. For such *off-line updating problems*, *update()* will assume that the precursor is modified if and only if (i) the precursor has one or more commands and (ii) these commands are executed. This can be done by dividing the processed files into two categories, *changed* and *unchanged*. Thus, at any point in the update process, every file falls into exactly one of the categories: (i) not yet reached by the depth-first search, (ii) active, (iii) changed or (iv) unchanged. With off-line updating, *precursor* will be considered younger than *file* if either *modtime(precursor)* > *modtime(file)* or *precursor* is marked *changed*.

The following update algorithm incorporates all three modifications:

1. It checks for error conditions.
2. Nodes are marked so that (i) a file is updated at most once, even if it is a precursor of several files, and (ii) cycles in the dependency graph are treated properly.
3. Off-line updating is provided.

```
update(file)
{
        install implicit precursors and commands for file

        /* check for error conditions */
        if file does not exist, has no precursors, and has no commands
                fatal "Don't know how to update file."
        mark file as active

        /* bring precursor files up to date */
        for each of file's precursors
                if the precursor is not yet reached
                        update(precursor)

        /* compare modification times */
        m_time = modtime(file)
        YOUNGER = '' ''
        for each of file's precursors
                if precursor is not active and modtime(precursor) > m_time
                or the precursor is changed and updating is off line
                        append precursor's name to YOUNGER

        /* update file if necessary */
        if (YOUNGER ≠ '' '' or m_time == 0)
        and file has one or more commands {
                install YOUNGER in the macro table
                for each of file's commands {
                        expand macros in the command
                        print the command
```

```
                if updating is not off line
                     execute the command
            }
        mark file as changed
    } else
        mark file as unchanged
}
```

Figure 2.2.3 Complete *update()* procedure

A straightforward implementation of *update()* is given in *update.c*. Also listed are *update.h*, which is the program's header file, and the file *system.c* containing *update*'s system-specific procedures.

Off-Line Updating.   The following example, from *The UNIX Programming Environment* by Brian W. Kernighan and Rob Pike (Prentice-Hall, 1984), pp. 265–266, illustrates differences between off-line and on-line (normal) updating. The example has been simplified to expose the aspects of interest here.

In *update*'s notation, the *UPDATE* file is

```
#define SOURCES      hoc.y code.c init.c symbol.c
#define OBJECTS      hoc.o code.o init.o symbol.o

hoc -> OBJECTS
    cc -o hoc OBJECTS

hoc.o -> hoc.y
    < some commands that generate hoc.o from hoc.y --
    as a side-effect, they generate a file named y.h >

code.o init.o symbol.o -> x.h

x.h -> y.h
    if x.h ≠ y.h, then copy y.h to x.h
```

If *hoc.y* is modified, then *update* will execute the commands to generate *hoc.o*. As a side-effect, these commands generate a header file, *y.h*, that is included in *code.c*, *init.c*, and *symbol.c*. Ordinarily, the new contents of *y.h* will be identical to the previous contents, though the time stamp on *y.h* will have changed. To avoid unnecessary recompilations, a copy of *y.h* is kept in *x.h*. Regeneration of *hoc.o* from *hoc.y* triggers recompilation of *code.c*, *init.c*, and *symbol.c* only if *x.h* changes.

This *UPDATE* file illustrates the two conditions when off-line updating can differ from on-line updating. First, problems can arise if a file's commands do not always modify the file. Suppose that *hoc* is brought up to date, then *y.h* is touched by the *tweak* command. The command

```
update -n
```

performs a depth-first search of the dependency graph in Fig. 2.3. *Update* will assume that *x.h* would be modified by its updating command and will generate the report

```
if x.h ≠ y.h, then copy y.h to x.h
cc -c code.c
cc -c init.c
cc -c symbol.c
cc -o hoc hoc.o code.o init.o symbol.o
```

Only the first command would actually be executed by *update*.

This example also illustrates problems caused by commands that have side-effects on other files. Suppose that *hoc* is brought up to date, then *hoc.y* is modified. Off-line updating of *hoc* discovers that *hoc.y* is younger than *hoc.o* and reports that *hoc.o*'s commands should be executed. However, given only *UPDATE* and the implicit rules, *update* cannot anticipate that updating *hoc.o* has the side-effect of modifying *y.h*. Thus, off-line updating lists just the commands of *hoc.o* and *hoc*. On-line updating also executes the command of *x.h* and may recompile *code.c*, *init.c*, and *symbol.c*.

Strands and Update Graphs.   To help picture the conditions when off-line and on-line updating differ, let us adorn the dependency graph with *strands* that represent the effects of updating commands. If commands of file *u* can alter the time stamp of file *v*, then a dotted arrow will be drawn from *u* to *v*. A depen-

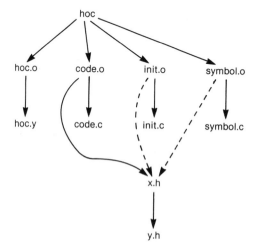

Figure 2.3 Dependency graph for the *hoc* example.

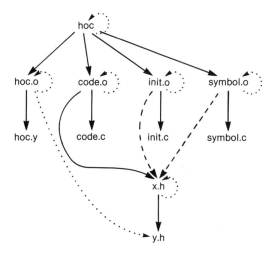

Figure 2.4 Update graph for the *hoc* example.

dency graph with these added strands will be called an *update graph*. Figure 2.4 gives the update graph for the *hoc* example. Keep in mind that the solid and dashed edges in an update graph depict precursor information, while the dotted edges mirror the updating commands.

Strands can represent several kinds of effects on time stamps: *u*'s commands might set *v*'s time stamp to 0 by removing *v*, or they might set it to an essentially arbitrary time by assigning the name ''*v*'' to some other file with a *move* or *rename* command. However, the strands in the *hoc* example represent ''touches'' that stamp a file with the current time. Each strand from a ''.*o*'' file to itself is a *must-touch loop*, i.e., successful command execution always sets the time stamp to the current time. On the other hand, *x.h* has only a ''may-touch'' loop.

In essence, off-line updating assumes that each derived file has a must-touch loop, and certain kinds of side-effects cause trouble. To be precise, off-line and on-line updating generate the same commands if

 (i) every node with one or more commands has a must-touch loop, except possibly the root of the depth-first search tree, and

 (ii) there are no strands *u* · · · > *v* such that either (a) *v* follows *u* in postorder or (b) *v* is a precursor of a node that follows *u* in postorder.

See Exercise 4 for a formal model of file updating that facilitates a rigorous proof of this fact.

Taking *u* to be the node *init.o* in Fig. 2.3, conditions (i) and (ii) disallow strands to any nodes except *init.o*, *hoc.y*, *code.c*, *init.c*, and *y.h*. Except for a loop on *init.o*, strands to these nodes are permitted because their time stamps affect only updating decisions that are made before *init.o* is updated. Other strands affect updating decisions made after the side-effect occurs. For example, a strand from *init.o* to *x.h* would mean that *init.o*'s commands can alter the time stamp on *x.h*, thereby affecting the update decision for *symbol.o*.

The − i Flag.   Since occasional inconsistency between off-line and on-line updating is unavoidable, *update* provides an "interactive" (−*i*) option. When invoked with the −*i* flag, *update* records the commands announced in no-execution mode; the user has the option of executing exactly those commands. An alternative implementation could let the user pick a subset of the listed commands. However, the extra flexibility seems to be more trouble for the user than it is worth.

The TARGET Macro.   There is an interaction between *update()* and *execute()* that needs to be explained. Before *update()* executes a file's commands, it installs the file's name in the macro table as the definition of *TARGET*. The UNIX version of *execute()* removes the *TARGET* file from the file system if the command's execution results in an error condition. This is done because some UNIX commands modify the file they are trying to produce even if they cannot successfully complete the job, which can confuse *update*. For example, suppose *update* is trying to regenerate *prog*, but some function call references a nonexistent procedure. The UNIX linker modifies the *prog* file, notices the missing function, prints a diagnostic message, and dies. However, from *update*'s perspective, *prog* is now up to date. The same situation occurs if the linker is interrupted (e.g., by pressing the <*break*> key) when it is almost done. Unfortunately, problems arise if *TARGET* is removed whenever the command returns an error status flag. See Programming Assignment 3 in Section 2.3.

EXERCISES

1. The update decision is made by

```
m__time = modtime(file)
for each of file's precursors
    if precursor is not active and modtime(precursor) > m__time
        record that file is out of date
if file is out of date or m__time == 0
    execute file's commands
```

If *file* does not exist, then *m__time* is 0 so *file* appears older than all of its precursors. This suggests that the test

```
if file is out of date or m__time == 0
```

can be simplified to:

```
if file is out of date
```

Is this change correct? Explain.

2. Suppose the object file *ofile* has an existing source file, *sfile*. The following rules are applied by *implicit()* in *system.c* to add implicit precursors and updating commands:
   (i) Add *sfile* to *ofile*'s precursor list.
   (ii) If *ofile* has no known commands, then add the default compile command to its command list.
   Why does rule (ii) check for known commands? Why doesn't rule (i) check for known precursors?

3. Can the *UPDATE* file for the *hoc* example be modified so that the strand from *hoc.o* to *y.h* does not mislead off-line updating? In particular, consider the following modifications:
   (a) Add the dependency line

   ```
   y.h -> hoc.y
   ```

   This makes *hoc.y* a precursor of *y.h* but does not associate any commands with *y.h*.
   (b) Change the line

   ```
   hoc.o -> hoc.y
   ```

   to

   ```
   hoc.o y.h -> hoc.y
   ```

   This makes *hoc.y* a precursor of *y.h* and associates the same commands with *hoc.o* and *y.h*.
   (c) Change the line

   ```
   x.h -> y.h
   ```

   to

   ```
   x.h -> hoc.y y.h
   ```

   Which of these three modified *UPDATE* files correctly specify how to update *hoc*? For which ones will off-line updating correctly predict whether *x.h* will be updated? In each case, explain how the complete sequence of commands predicted off line can differ from the sequence executed on line. (*Hint:* Consider what happens with (c) if *hoc* is brought up to date, then *hoc.y* and *x.h* are *tweak*ed, in that order.)

4. Show that on-line and off-line updating are equivalent if the update graph satisfies:
   (i) every node with one or more commands has a must-touch loop, except possibly the root, and
   (ii) there are no strands $u \cdots > v$ such that either (a) v follows u in postorder or (b) v is a precursor of a node that follows u in postorder.
   The intuitive meaning of "equivalent" is that they generate identical command sequences. All factors affecting the update decisions must be fixed. Just as the contents of the files *x.h* and *y.h* affect the command sequence in the *hoc* example, so can factors such as the time of day or system load. For example, if *update* detaches the commands

for a file so that they run in parallel, then the completion of those processes might affect the update decision for a postorder successor. Such subtleties make it difficult to treat the notion of "equivalent update procedures" informally, so the following formal model of file updating is appropriate.

An *update problem* is an update graph in which each node and strand has been assigned a nonnegative integer, called a *time*. The integer assigned to *file* represents the time returned by *modtime(file)*. The integer assigned to a strand, $u \cdots > v$, represents the effect of u's commands on v's time stamp; if u is updated (u's commands are executed), then the time on each strand $u \cdots > v$ is attached to v, replacing v's former time. In this model, a *must-touch loop* is a strand $u \cdots > u$ whose attached time must exceed the time on every node. Two update procedures are *equivalent for an update problem* if they update the same nodes. Two update procedures are *equivalent for an update graph* if they are equivalent for every conceivable update problem (assignment of times to nodes and strands) on the given update graph.

Consider the update problem:

With on-line updating, v will be updated (because it is older than u), setting w's time to 6. Thus, on-line updating updates v and x (but not y since there are no touch loops). With off-line updating, v and y are updated.

For this Exercise, prove that on-line and off-line updating are equivalent, in the formal sense, for any update graph satisfying conditions (i) and (ii). The paper "Side-effects in automatic file updating" by Webb Miller and Eugene W. Myers (*Software—Practice and Experience*, Sept. 1986, pp. 809–20) covers several results of this type.

5. (Difficult) Stripped of details involving error checks, implicit rules, and macros, the update algorithm used by the UNIX *make* command is

```
make(file)
{
    mark file as active
    m_time = modtime(file)
    for each of file's precursors {
        if the precursor is neither active nor processed
            make(precursor)
        if precursor is not active and pseudo_time[precursor] > m_time
            record that file is out of date
    }
    if file is out of date or m_time == 0 {
        execute file's commands
        m_time = modtime(file)
        if m_time == 0 or updating is off line
            m_time = current_time()
```

```
            }
            pseudo__time[file] = m__time
            mark file as processed
    }
```

Figure 2.2.4   The *make* command's update algorithm

Make() differs from *update()* in two main ways. The first difference is *make()*'s use of the *current__time()* function. If *file* does not exist after its commands are executed, then the current time is used as its time stamp in all later decisions. The rationale for this addition is to support fictitious files (like *test* in Section 2.1). If a fictitious file is updated, then it will look younger than other files, so files that depend on the fictitious file will be updated.

Make() and *update()* also schedule calls to *modtime()* differently. While *update()* samples *file*'s modification time *after* processing all precursors, *make()* samples it *before* processing the precursors. Also, *update()* samples a precursor's modification time after processing *all* precursors, whereas *make()* samples it either (a) the instant that the precursor becomes active (if it is not updated) or (b) just after the precursor is processed (if it is updated).

(a) Show that *make()* and *update()* are equivalent (in the sense of Exercise 4) for an update graph if
  (i) every node with precursors, except possibly the root, has commands and a must-touch loop,
  (ii) there are no strands $u \cdot \cdot \cdot > v$ such that either (a) v is a proper ancestor of u in the depth-first search tree, or (b) v precedes u in postorder and v is a precursor of some node that follows u in postorder.

(b) (Requires access to the source code for UNIX.) Examine a number of existing *makefiles* (*UPDATE* files for *make*) to see how often, in practice, update graphs fail to satisfy conditions (i) or (ii) of part (a).

```
/* update.h - macro definitions for the update program */

#include <stdio.h>
#include <ctype.h>

#define NO              0
#define YES             1

#define C_NAME          "cc -c"   /* default compilation command */
#define CMD_SIZE        500       /* maximum length of line in UPDATE file */
#define CONCURRENT      YES       /* concurrent execution of commands? */
#define NAME_SIZE       100       /* maximum length of file name */
#define PROG_NAME       "update"  /* program name (for error messages) */
#define TIME_TYPE       long      /* type of time stamps on files */
#define U_NAME          "UPDATE"  /* name of the dependency file */

/* file status */
#define NOT_REACHED     0         /* not yet encountered */
#define ACTIVE          1         /* being processed */
#define CHANGED         2         /* processed; needed updating */
#define UNCHANGED       3         /* processed; did not need updating */
```

```
/*
 * update.c - automatic file updating
 *
 *
 * Program description:
 *
 *     A command line has the form:
 *         update [-i] [-n] [name]
 *     Update consults the dependency description file named UPDATE, and
 *     applies intrinsic rules relating C language source files and object
 *     files, then deduces a minimal set of commands for updating the named
 *     file.  If no name is given, then update uses the first name that appears
 *     in the UPDATE file.  With the -n (no execution) option the commands are
 *     merely printed, not executed. With the -i (interactive) option the
 *     commands are printed and the user is asked whether the commands should
 *     be executed; a response beginning with 'y' triggers command execution.
 *
 *
 * Source files:
 *
 *     bldint.c  - build internal form of the UPDATE file
 *     depmod.c  - data structure for dependencies
 *     lib.c     - library of C procedures
 *     macmod.c  - macro symbol table
 *     system.c  - system-dependent procedures for the update program
 *     update.c  - main program and core updating procedure
 *     update.h  - macro definitions for the update program
 *
 *
 * Portability:
 *
 *     The macro TIME_TYPE in update.h must give the type of time stamps on
 *     files.
 *
 *     The macro C_NAME in update.h must give the default C compile command,
 *     without the source file's name.
 *
 *     The macro CONCURRENT in update.h must be defined as NO if commands
 *     cannot be executed concurrently by update.
 *
 *     The functions execute(), implicit(), and modtime() in system.c must be
 *     implemented in a manner appropriate for the host system.
 *
 *
 * External procedure calls:
 *
 *     int bldint()                       .. file bldint.c
 *         Read the UPDATE file and record the information.  Return
 *         a count of the syntax errors in UPDATE.
 *
 *     cmdin(file, command)               .. file depmod.c
 *     char *file, *command;
 *         Record a command for a file.
 *
 *     char *cmdout(file, n)              .. file depmod.c
 *     char *file;
 *     int n;
 *         Return file's n-th command (NULL if there aren't n commands).
 *
```

```
*       execute(command)                    .. file system.c
*       char *command;
*           Cause the specified command to be executed.
*
*       implicit(file)                      .. file system.c
*       char *file;
*           Add any implicit dependency relations and commands for the
*           named file to update's internal record of UPDATE.
*
*       macin(name, definition)             .. file macmod.c
*       char *name, *definition;
*           Record a macro name and definition.
*
*       macout(line1, line2, maxchars)      .. file macmod.c
*       char *line1, *line2;
*       int maxchars;
*           Expand macros while copying line1 to line2.  At most
*           maxchars characters are copied.
*
*       TIME_TYPE modtime(file)             .. file system.c
*       char *file;
*           Return file's modification time (0 for nonexistent files).
*
*       char *preout(file, n)               .. file depmod.c
*       char *file;
*       int n;
*           Return file's n-th precursor (NULL if there aren't n precursors).
*
*       statin(file, status)                .. file depmod.c
*       char *file;
*       int status;
*           Record the status of a file.
*
*       int statout(file)                   .. file depmod.c
*       char *file;
*           Return file's current status.
*
*       char *topname()                     .. file depmod.c
*           Return the first file named in UPDATE.
*/

#include "update.h"

static int did_work = NO, iflag = NO, nflag = NO, off_line;

main(argc, argv)                                                    main
int argc;
char *argv[];
{
    TIME_TYPE modtime();
    int cn, i;
    char *cmdout(), *command, *name, *topname();

    savename(PROG_NAME);         /* for error messages */

    for (i = 1; i < argc && argv[i][0] == '-'; ++i)
        if (argv[i][1] == 'i')
            iflag = YES;
```

```
        else if (argv[i][1] == 'n')
            nflag = YES;
        else
            fatalf("Illegal option: %c.", argv[i][1]);
    if (i < argc-1)
        fatalf("Correct usage: %s -i -n name.", PROG_NAME);
    macin("COMPILE", C_NAME);
    if (bldint() > 0)
        fatalf("Improper %s file.", U_NAME);
    if (i == argc) {
        /* default to first name in UPDATE */
        if ((name = topname()) == NULL)
            fatalf("No file names are given in %s.", U_NAME);
    } else
        name = argv[i];
    off_line = (iflag == YES || nflag == YES || !CONCURRENT);
    update(name);
    if (!did_work)
        printf("%s is up to date\n", name);
    else if (iflag == YES) {
        printf("execute? ");
        if (getchar() == 'y')
            for (cn = 1; (command = cmdout("", cn)) != NULL; ++cn) {
                printf("%s\n", command);
                execute(command);
            }
    }
    exit(0);
}


/*
 * update - recursive procedure to update a file
 *
 * The procedure begins by recursively updating the precursors of
 * the named file.  If the file is then older than one or more of its
 * precursors, or if it does not exist, then the commands associated
 * with the file are executed.
 *
 */
static int update(file)
char *file;                                                          update
{
    TIME_TYPE m_time, modtime();
    int cn, pn, status;
    char cmdbuf[CMD_SIZE], *cmdout(), *command, *precursor, *preout(),
        younger[CMD_SIZE];

    implicit(file);      /* install implicit precursors and commands */

    /* check for error conditions */
    /* if file does not exist, has no precursors, and has no commands .. */
    if (modtime(file) == 0 && preout(file, 1) == NULL && cmdout(file, 1) == NULL)
        fatalf("Don't know how to update %s.", file);
    statin(file, ACTIVE);

    /* bring precursor files up to date */
    for (pn = 1; (precursor = preout(file, pn)) != NULL; ++pn)
        if (statout(precursor) == NOT_REACHED)
            update(precursor);
```

```
        /* compare modification times */
        m_time = modtime(file);
        younger[0] = '\0';
        for (pn = 1; (precursor = preout(file, pn)) != NULL; ++pn) {
            status = statout(precursor);
            if (status != ACTIVE && modtime(precursor) > m_time
               || status == CHANGED && off_line) {
                if (strlen(younger) + strlen(precursor) + 1 >= CMD_SIZE)
                    fatalf("'%s' has too many younger precursors.",
                        file);
                if (younger[0] != '\0') /* omit the first time */
                    strcat(younger, " ");
                strcat(younger, precursor);
            }
        }

        /* update file if necessary */
        if ((younger[0] != '\0' || m_time == 0) && cmdout(file, 1) != NULL) {
            /* install name of file being updated */
            macin("TARGET", file);
            /* install macro of younger precursors */
            macin("YOUNGER", younger);
            for (cn = 1; (command = cmdout(file, cn)) != NULL; ++cn) {
                /* expand macros */
                macout(command, cmdbuf, CMD_SIZE);
                printf("%s\n", cmdbuf);
                if (iflag == YES)
                /* associate command with empty file name */
                    cmdin("", cmdbuf);
                else if (nflag == NO)
                    execute(cmdbuf);
            }
            did_work = YES;
            statin(file, CHANGED);
        } else
            statin(file, UNCHANGED);
}


/*
 * system.c - system-dependent procedures for the update program   (UNIX version)
 *
 *
 * Entry points:
 *
 *     execute(command)
 *     char *command;
 *         Cause the specified command to be executed.
 *
 *     implicit(file)
 *     char *file;
 *         Add any implicit dependency relations and commands for the
 *         named file to update's internal record of UPDATE.
 *
 *     TIME_TYPE modtime(file)
 *     char *file;
 *         Return file's modification time (0 for nonexistent files).
 *
 *
 *
```

```
* External procedure calls (not counting system-specific functions):
*
*     cmdin(file, command)                .. file depmod.c
*     char *file, *command;
*          Record a command of a file.
*
*     char *cmdout(file, n)               .. file depmod.c
*     char *file;
*     int n;
*          Return file's n-th command (NULL if there aren't n commands).
*
*     macout(line1, line2, maxchars)      .. file macmod.c
*     char *line1, *line2;
*     int maxchars;
*          Expand macros while copying line1 to line2.  At most
*          maxchars characters are copied.
*
*     prein(file, precursor)              .. file depmod.c
*     char *file, *precursor;
*          Record a precursor of a file.
*/

#include "update.h"
#include <sys/types.h>
#include <sys/stat.h>

/* execute - execute a command; if unsuccessful, remove target file and die */
execute(command)                                                                    execute
char *command;
{
     TIME_TYPE modtime();
     char target[NAME_SIZE];

     if (system(command) != 0) {
         /* get name of file being updated */
         macout("TARGET", target, NAME_SIZE);
         /* if target exists, remove it */
         if (modtime(target) != 0) {
              fprintf(stderr, "Error.  %s deleted.\n", target);
              unlink(target);
         }
         exit(1);
     }
}

/* implicit - install implicit dependency relations and commands */
implicit(ofile)                                                                     implicit
char *ofile;
{
     TIME_TYPE modtime();
     char *bldsrc(), *cmdout(), command[CMD_SIZE], *getnam(), sfile[NAME_SIZE];

     /* if ofile is an object file and the source file exists */
     if (strlen(ofile) >= NAME_SIZE) {
         ofile[NAME_SIZE] = '\0';
         fatalf("The name '%s...' is too long.", ofile);
     }
     if (bldsrc(ofile, sfile) != NULL && modtime(sfile) != 0) {
         prein(ofile, sfile);
         /* install the default command if none is known */
```

```
            if (cmdout(ofile, 1) == NULL) {
                sprintf(command, "COMPILE %s", sfile);
                cmdin(ofile, command);
            }
        }
}

/* modtime - return file's modification time (0 for nonexistent files) */
TIME_TYPE modtime(file)                                                             modtime
char *file;
{
        struct stat buf;

        return(stat(file, &buf) >= 0 ? buf.st_mtime : 0);
}

/*
 * bldsrc - construct a source file name from the name of a C object file;
 * return NULL for names not belonging to C object files.
 */
#define O_SUFFIX            ".o"
#define S_SUFFIX            ".c"
static char *bldsrc(ofile, sfile)                                                   bldsrc
char *ofile, *sfile;
{
        if (!strsame(ofile + strlen(ofile) - strlen(O_SUFFIX) , O_SUFFIX))
            return(NULL);
        strcpy(sfile, ofile);
        /* strip off O_SUFFIX */
        sfile[strlen(sfile) - strlen(O_SUFFIX)] = '\0';
        strcat(sfile, S_SUFFIX);
        return(sfile);
}
```

2.3 STORING THE DEPENDENCY INFORMATION

The remaining module of *update* stores and parcels out dependency information. A review of earlier code reveals a need for

cmdin()	record a command of a file
cmdout()	return a file's n^{th} command
prein()	record a precursor of a file
preout()	return a file's n^{th} precursor
statin()	record the status of a file
statout()	return a file's current status
topname()	return the first file name in *UPDATE*

The file *depmod.c* implements these functions with a simple data structure:

```
* Implementation:
*
*      File information is stored in a simple linked list of "filenodes", where
*      each file has two lists (precursors and commands) of linked "listnodes".
       ...
struct listnode {
    char *string;
    struct listnode *next;
};

struct filenode {
    char *name;                      /* file's name */
    struct listnode *pres;           /* precursors */
    int pre_nbr;                     /* number of precursors */
    struct listnode *cmds;           /* commands */
    int cmd_nbr;                     /* number of commands */
    int status;                      /* file's status */
    struct filenode *link;           /* link to the next file */
};

static char *first_file = NULL;       /* first file name to be recorded */
static struct filenode *begin = NULL; /* points to the list of files */
```

Filenodes are simply inserted at the beginning of the list, since order is unimportant. Precursors and commands are also inserted at the fronts of lists, but counts are kept to help locate the nth one inserted.

The *UPDATE* file

```
f1  ->  p1  p2
        c1
f2  ->  p3
        c2
        c3
```

would produce the calls

Function	First Argument	Second Argument
prein()	"f1"	"p1"
prein()	"f1"	"p2"
cmdin()	"f1"	"c1"
prein()	"f2"	"p3"
cmdin()	"f2"	"c2"
cmdin()	"f2"	"c3"

Given the additional calls

Function	First Argument	Second Argument
statin()	"f1"	0
statin()	"f2"	3

depmod.c would store

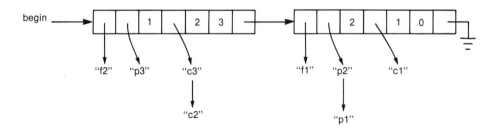

Once the data structure can be visualized, *depmod.c* is easy to read. For instance, consider *preout()*.

```
/* preout - return file's n-th precursor */
char *preout(file, n)
char *file;
int n;
{
      struct filenode *lookup(), *p;
      struct listnode *scan;
      int steps;

      if ((p = lookup(file)) == NULL || p->pres == NULL || p->pre_nbr < n)
            return(NULL);
      steps = p->pre_nbr - n;
      for (scan = p->pres; steps-- > 0; scan = scan->next)
            ;
      return(scan->string);
}
```

Suppose the data structure is as pictured above and consider the call *preout(''f1'', 1)*. *Lookup()* returns a pointer, *p*, to the second (and last) *filenode* in the list pointed to by *begin*. Since $p->pre\_nbr = 2$, *steps* is computed as 1; from the *listnode* pointed to by $p->pres$, one ''step''

$$scan = scan->next$$

is needed to reach the desired precursor.

Porting Update to Non-UNIX Systems.   To facilitate the job of porting *update*, system-dependent procedures have been isolated in *system.c*. However, for operating systems that differ extensively from UNIX, the job may be difficult or impossible. The main hurdles are

- The file system may not provide modification times that can be read by a user program.

- The operating system may not permit a system program to be executed under the control of a user program.

If files lack a time stamp, it may suffice to maintain an additional file, essentially a "pseudodirectory," that provides these times for *update*. However, provisions must then be made to change the appropriate pseudodirectory entry each time a file in *update*'s environment is touched (for example, by a text editor), since the pseudodirectory will not be maintained automatically by the system. It is unnecessary to record actual times; a system clock can be simulated with an integer counter. When a file is modified, the counter's current value serves as the file's "modification time" and the counter is incremented. That is, the clock "ticks" each time an event occurs.

Even if one program cannot directly execute another, it may be possible to execute a sequence of commands taken from a file (e.g., the *batch* facility in MS-DOS and the *submit* facility in CP/M). In such cases, *update* could create an appropriate command file instead of executing commands immediately. This approach works smoothly if *update* is invoked from a command file that next executes the command file that *update* creates. If possible, target files should still be removed whenever updating commands fail, for reasons discussed at the end of Section 2.2. (Incidently, the use of command files may be the easiest way to see that the pseudodirectory entry for a source file is modified whenever the file is edited; the editor can be called from a command file that also calls a little program to record the editor's arguments.)

If *update* is modified so that it keeps a file to record its actions, then a subtle complication arises. As written, *update* can call itself recursively (an *UPDATE* file can contain an *update* command) and can be interrupted if it is executing the wrong commands. However, if *update* maintains a history of its actions, then either event might cause *update* to mangle its history file.

Performance.   Detailed performance statistics for *update* seem irrelevant. In typical applications, *update* generates commands faster than the commands could be typed.

If necessary, *update* can be made more efficient. If *bldint.c* is taking too much time, then a "compiled" version of *UPDATE* could be maintained. (If *UPDATE* is younger than its binary version, then *update* would have to "recompile" *UPDATE*.) To speed up the rest of *update*'s operation, replace the data structure in *depmod.c*.

EXERCISES

1. *Prein()* does not check whether the precursor is already on the file's precursor list. Would it be wise to avoid duplicate entries?

PROGRAMMING ASSIGNMENTS

1. Allow *UPDATE* to contain ''generic'' entries like

```
%.o -> %.p
     pc -c %.p
```

The special symbol '%' is a ''wild card'' that can be replaced by any string of characters, so long as all occurrences in one *UPDATE* entry are replaced by the same string. Generic dependency lines can be limited to two file-name patterns, each containing at most one '%'; you don't have to handle lines like

```
%.o -> %.c %.p
```

and

```
%.o% -> %.c
```

As it stands, *update* knows the rule

```
%.o -> %.c
     cc -c %.c
```

The *UPDATE* entry for ''.*p*'' suffixes should make *update* treat ''.*p*'' files like it treats ''.*c*'' files. In other words, when processing a file whose name ends in the two characters ''.*o*'', construct a new file name by changing '*o*' to '*p*'. If the ''.*p*'' file exists, then the ''.*o*'' file depends on the ''.*p*'' file and (unless it already has commands) is generated by the *pc* command.

For example, consider the *UPDATE* file

```
%.o -> %.p
     pc -c %.p

prog -> file1.o file2.o file3.o file4.o
     pc -o prog file1.o file2.o file3.o file4.o

file1.o -> file1.p
     pc -c -w file1.p
```

If *file1.p*, *file2.p*, and *file3.p* are younger than *prog*, then the command *update prog* would trigger the commands

```
pc -c -w file1.p
pc -c file2.p
pc -c file3.p
pc -o prog file1.o file2.o file3.o file4.o
```

Note that *file1.p* will twice be installed as a precursor of *file1.o* (once when *UPDATE* is read; once when *file1.o* is updated), but the default updating command

```
pc -c file1.p
```

will not be installed.

Your modified *update* should handle arbitrary sets of commands and longer suffixes, or even generic rules not based on meaningful file name suffixes. (Prefixes like "*c*." might be used.) Consider a language that is translated into C by a macro processor named *macpro*, then compiled. Let *macpro* input files be distinguished by a "*.mac*" suffix and let *macpro* generate the corresponding "*.c*" file. The appropriate generic rule is

```
%.o -> %.mac
    macpro %.mac
    cc -c %.c
    rm %.c
```

Alternatively, one could use

```
%.c -> %.mac
    macpro %.mac
```

Coupled with *update*'s intrinsic rule for "*.c*" files, this would achieve much the same effect. (The existence of generic rules in *UPDATE* should not affect *update*'s intrinsic rule for C files.) The difference is that the second approach requires that "*.c*" files be kept.

There is yet another wrinkle. Suppose you are updating *foo.o*, where suffix rules are given for

```
%.o -> %.x
```

and

```
%.x -> %.y
```

In addition, suppose *foo.y* exists but *foo.x* does not. Using the process described above, *update* would not realize that suffix rules apply to *foo.o*. Is this what you want to happen? If your program tries to detect such chains of dependencies, beware of "cycles" in the generic rules.

2. Write a procedure that generates the dependency lines implied by *#include* statements. For example, if *file.c* contains the line

```
#include "defs.h"
```

then the line

```
file.o -> defs.h
```

should be produced. Call your procedure from *update* if a certain flag appears in the command line. Handle nested include statements (an include line in an included file) and ignore included system files like *stdio.h*. (However, the user may want to replace system files, so a line like

```
#include "stdio.h"
```

might refer to a user file.)

The example discussed in Section 2.1 illustrates the basic motivation behind this assignment. Recall the *UPDATE* file

```
#define OBJECTS file1.o file2.o file3.o
#define ALL OBJECTS lib.o

prog -> ALL
        cc -o prog ALL

OBJECTS -> defs.h
```

The last line gives dependencies that can be inferred automatically. If it were not initially typed, then a command like

```
update -#include
```

could produce the lines

```
file1.o -> defs.h
file2.o -> defs.h
file3.o -> defs.h
```

which could be collected and appended to *UPDATE*.

To do this, *update* can perform the following actions. The call *update(file1.o)* in turn calls *implicit(file1.o)*, which deduces that *file1.o* depends on *file1.c*. Because the −*#include* flag is present, no time stamps are checked and no compilation commands are generated. Instead, *update* reads *file1.c*, discovers the line

```
#include "defs.h"
```

and emits the first line of output. The other two lines are produced in a similar fashion.

A second example illustrates the points made about nested include statements and system header files. Let *UPDATE* contain

```
prog -> a.o b.o c.o
     cc -o prog a.o b.o c.o
```

where *a.o*, *b.o* and *c.o* are C object files. In addition, suppose the included files are In *a.c* and *b.c*:

```
#include <stdio.h>
#include "x.h"
```

In *c.c*:

```
#include <ctype.h>
#include "y.h"
```

In *x.h*:

```
#include "z.h"
```

In *y.h* and *z.h*:

```
No included files.
```

Then the output of the command

```
update -#include prog
```

should be

```
a.o -> x.h
a.o -> z.h
b.o -> x.h
b.o -> z.h
c.o -> y.h
```

The following list discusses some of the subtleties with this assignment. Handle as many as you can.

(a) Although a file may be included in several files, your program should read the included file only once. Thus, in the preceding example, *x.h* should be read just once.

(b) Nontext files (such as object files and executable files) can masquerade as primary files, as with *lib.o* in Fig. 2.2. Your program should not scan such files for *#include* lines. (*Hint:* Every byte *c* in a text file should satisfy:

```
isprint(c) || c == '\n' || c == '\t'
```

With ASCII characters and 8-bit bytes, the probability of this being satisfied by the first ten bytes of a "random" binary file is $(97/256)^{10}$, or about 1 in 16,000. Of course, the first few bytes of a nontext file may not be ''random,'' and experiments should be performed with any proposed method of detecting nontext files.)

(c) The *#include* lines within *#ifdef* or *#ifndef* blocks may be inactive. Your program could invoke the C preprocessor to remove inactive lines. For example, suppose that *fake.c* contains

```
#define FOO
#ifdef FOO
#include "x.h"
#else
#include "y.h"
#endif
```

If the C preprocessor is run on *fake.c* (on UNIX, this is done with the command *cc −E fake.c*) the output mentions *x.h* but not *y.h*. (In fact, using the C preprocessor may greatly simplify the solution of this programming assignment.)

(d) The C preprocessor's syntax for include lines is not universal. For example, lines like

```
include 'defs.h'
```

are required for the UNIX Fortran 77 compiler. Effort is needed to make this modification to *update* work smoothly with program files for several languages.

(e) If you extend *update* to allow generic rules (Programming Assignment 1), then the following problem may arise. Suppose you have a rule for creating ''.c'' files from ''.x'' files. That is, files whose names end in ''.x'' are assumed to contain input for some preprocessor that produces C source files. How should you interpret the line

```
#include "defs.h"
```

in file *foo.x*? If the x-preprocessor processes this line, then *foo.c* depends on *defs.h*. On the other hand, if the x-preprocessor merely passes the line on to the C compiler, then *foo.o* depends on *defs.h*. How is your program going to know which case holds? Ideas can be found in the paper ''Automatic generation of Make dependencies'' by Kim Walden (*Software—Practice and Experience*, June 1984, pp. 575–585).

3. UNIX users will find that the approach taken by *execute()* of *system.c* is sometimes inadequate. The UNIX *system()* procedure occasionally returns a nonzero value even when the command was successfully executed. For example, this happens when *rm* (remove) cannot find a named file, when *diff* (file comparison) is applied to two files whose contents differ, and when *grep* (pattern matching) finds no lines matching the specified pattern. (The file-comparison and pattern-matching programs in Chapters 3 and 4 terminate with the call *exit(0)*, which circumvents the problem.) Under such conditions, you may not want *update* to unlink the *TARGET* file and cease execution. The assignment is to let the user signify that a nonzero system status value should be ignored. For example, a '!' character at the front of a command in *UPDATE* might instruct *update* to ignore the command's returned status.

4. Make it possible to provide macro definitions as arguments of the *update* command. For example, the command

```
update "#define VERSION UNIX"
```

(quotation marks may be needed when a command argument contains blanks) or

```
update VERSION=UNIX
```

can define a macro just as if the line

```
#define VERSION UNIX
```

appeared in *UPDATE*. Think about the appropriate time to install the definitions in the macro table. If a macro is defined in *UPDATE* and defined to be something different in the *update* command, which definition should apply? Should a macro definition be ignored if the macro name is already defined? Will your approach work for macros in both dependency lines and commands in *UPDATE*?

```
/*
 * depmod.c - data structure for dependencies
 *
 *
 * Entry points:
 *
 *      cmdin(file, command)
 *      char *file, *command;
 *          Record a command of a file.
 *
 *      char *cmdout(file, n)
 *      char *file;
 *      int n;
 *          Return file's n-th command (NULL if there aren't n commands).
 *
 *      prein(file, precursor)
 *      char *file, *precursor;
 *          Record a precursor of a file.
 *
 *      char *preout(file, n)
 *      char *file;
 *      int n;
 *          Return file's n-th precursor (NULL if there aren't n precursors).
 *
 *      statin(file, status)
 *      char *file;
 *      int status;
 *          Record the status of a file.
 *
 *      int statout(file)
 *      char *file;
 *          Return file's current status.
 *
```

```
*     char *topname()
*          Return the first file name to be recorded.
*
*
* Implementation:
*
*     File information is stored in a simple linked list of "filenodes", where
*     each file has two lists (precursors and commands) of linked "listnodes".
*/

#include "update.h"

struct listnode {
    char *string;
    struct listnode *next;
};

struct filenode {
    char *name;                     /* file's name */
    struct listnode *pres;          /* precursors */
    int pre_nbr;                    /* number of precursors */
    struct listnode *cmds;          /* commands */
    int cmd_nbr;                    /* number of commands */
    int status;                     /* file's status */
    struct filenode *link;          /* link to the next file */
};

static char *first_file = NULL;         /* first file name to be recorded */
static struct filenode *begin = NULL;   /* points to the list of files */

/* cmdin - record a command of a file */
cmdin(file, command)                                                    cmdin
char *file, *command;
{
    struct filenode *install(), *lookup(), *p;
    struct listnode *new;
    char *ckalloc(), *strsave();

    if ((p = lookup(file)) == NULL)
        p = install(file);
    new = (struct listnode *) ckalloc(sizeof(struct listnode));
    new->string = strsave(command);
    new->next = p->cmds;
    p->cmds = new;
    ++(p->cmd_nbr);
}

/* cmdout - return file's n-th command */
char *cmdout(file, n)                                                   cmdout
char *file;
int n;
{
    struct filenode *lookup(), *p;
    struct listnode *scan;
    int steps;

    if ((p = lookup(file)) == NULL || p->cmds == NULL || p->cmd_nbr < n)
        return(NULL);
    steps = p->cmd_nbr - n;
```

```
    for (scan = p->cmds; steps-- > 0; scan = scan->next)
        ;
    return(scan->string);
}

/* prein - record a precursor of a file */
prein(file, precursor)                                                    prein
char *file, *precursor;
{
    struct filenode *install(), *lookup(), *p;
    struct listnode *new;
    char *ckalloc(), *strsave();

    if ((p = lookup(file)) == NULL)
        p = install(file);
    new = (struct listnode *) ckalloc(sizeof(struct listnode));
    new->string = strsave(precursor);
    new->next = p->pres;
    p->pres = new;
    ++(p->pre_nbr);
}

/* preout - return file's n-th precursor */
char *preout(file, n)                                                     preout
char *file;
int n;
{
    struct filenode *lookup(), *p;
    struct listnode *scan;
    int steps;

    if ((p = lookup(file)) == NULL || p->pres == NULL || p->pre_nbr < n)
        return(NULL);
    steps = p->pre_nbr - n;
    for (scan = p->pres; steps-- > 0; scan = scan->next) .
        ;
    return(scan->string);
}

/* statin - record the status of a file */
statin(file, status)                                                      statin
char *file;
int status;
{
    struct filenode *lookup(), *p;

    if ((p = lookup(file)) != NULL)
        p->status = status;
}

/* statout - return file's current status */
int statout(file)                                                         statout
char *file;
{
    struct filenode *lookup(), *p;

    if ((p = lookup(file)) != NULL)
        return(p->status);
    else
        return(NOT_REACHED);
}
```

```
/* topname - return the first file name to be recorded */
char *topname()                                                            topname
{
     return(first_file);
}

/* lookup - search the linked list of files */
static struct filenode *lookup(file)                                       lookup
char *file;
{
     struct filenode *p;

     for (p = begin; p != NULL; p = p->link)
          if (strsame(file, p->name))
               return(p);
     return(NULL);
}

/* install - install a file in the linked list */
static struct filenode *install(file)                                      install
char *file;
{
     struct filenode *new;
     char *ckalloc(), *strsave();

     if (first_file == NULL)
          first_file = strsave(file);
     new = (struct filenode *) ckalloc(sizeof(struct filenode));
     new->name = strsave(file);
     new->cmds = new->pres = NULL;
     new->cmd_nbr = new->pre_nbr = 0;
     new->status = NOT_REACHED;
     /* install the node at the front of the list */
     new->link = begin;
     begin = new;
     return(begin);
}
```

3

FILE COMPARISON PROGRAMS

A file comparison program determines instructions for converting one given file into another. These instructions may be couched in terms of lines, e.g., by telling which lines must be inserted, deleted, or moved. Alternatively, individual bytes may be identified. Byte-oriented comparisons are useful with nontext files, for example, compiled programs which are not divided into lines.

The programs in this chapter generate instructions that operate on whole lines. Since lines are treated as indivisible objects, it suffices to think in terms of files whose lines consist of single symbols. Thus, an illustrative example might insert and delete symbols in the string *abcabba* to produce *cbabac* instead of inserting and deleting lines in a particular seven-line file to get a six-line file.

Another ground rule is that these programs require random access. Specifically, the programs of Sections 3.1 and 3.2 assume that the two files fit simultaneously in memory.

File comparison algorithms have a number of potential uses, beside merely producing an edit script (sequence of edit instructions) to help the user understand the evolution of a program or document. For example, the edit script might be text editor instructions that avoid the expense of storing two nearly identical files. It suffices to save just one of the files and a (presumably short) file containing instructions like

```
replace lines 6-8 by the line "*s++ = *t++;"
```

that generate the other file. Section 3.3 discusses a ''version control system'' that uses this idea to economically store multiple versions of a text file.

The list of uses for file comparison techniques is long and varied. One of the earliest algorithms was invented simultaneously by biologists, who are interested in determining how many amino acids need to be deleted and inserted to convert one protein to another, and by speech processing experts, who want to automatically compare spoken words with known words. These algorithms also cope with spelling mistakes in information retrieval systems. Another use is for video redisplay, where the problem is to update the screen with the fewest possible display-modification commands.

The ability to generate shortest possible edit scripts depends critically on the repertoire of instructions that are allowed in the scripts. If the only permitted instructions either delete a symbol or interchange two adjacent symbols, then it is computationally infeasible to produce a shortest edit script for converting one given string to another. For a clarification of this point see *Computers and Intractability: A Guide to the Theory of NP-Complete Problems* by Michael R. Garey and David S. Johnson (W. H. Freeman, 1979), especially pp. 230–231.

Section 3.1 shows how to find a minimal script of append and copy instructions. Such scripts are well suited to certain applications, such as version control. Alternatively, the algorithm of Section 3.2 determines a minimal script of insert and delete instructions. Users may find insert/delete scripts more informative than append/copy scripts.

Section 3.3 outlines the facilities provided by version control systems, an important and interesting application of file comparison techniques. Code for a version control system is not given in this book. Possible capabilities and implementations for such a tool are sketched to provide the ingredients for a large programming project. Constructing a nontrivial program from scratch reinforces lessons that cannot be learned by merely reading and revising code. Readers are encouraged to sift through the ideas presented in Section 3.3, then design and build a version control system.

3.1 USING APPEND AND COPY INSTRUCTIONS

Consider the problem of finding a shortest edit script that constructs a given string B, consisting of the n symbols $B[1], \ldots, B[n]$, from another given string A, consisting of the m symbols $A[1], \ldots, A[m]$. For this section, the allowed edit instructions have the form

Append x.

where x is a symbol, or

Copy the k symbols beginning at position i.

which places a copy of the string $A[i]A[i+1] \ldots A[i+k-1]$ as the next portion of *B*. For example, the string *B* = *acab* is constructed from *A* = *ab* by the edit script

> Copy symbol 1.
> Append *c*.
> Copy the two symbols beginning at position 1.

(The instruction "Copy symbol 1" is shorthand for "Copy the one symbol beginning at position 1.")

Assume that copying a symbol is always preferable to appending it. This makes sense when comparing files, since an instruction like

> Copy line 6.

is generally much shorter than an instruction like

> Append "The quick brown fox . . .".

The assumption implies that the only symbols appended to *B* are the ones not found in *A*.

Example: The example

$$A = abcabba$$
$$B = cbadabc$$

sets the stage for the general algorithm. *B* is systematically constructed from left to right. Each step picks the instruction that adds the most symbols to *B*. As it turns out, this strategy is optimal. (Exercise 2 discusses an "improved" strategy that is, in fact, worse.)

Producing *B[1]* requires that *A[3]* be copied, since *A[3]* is the only *c* in *A*. Moreover, the instruction to copy *c* can copy only one symbol, since *A[4]* = *a* ≠ *b* = *B[2]*. Thus, the first instruction must be

> Copy symbol 3.

B[2] = *b* can be produced by copying *A[2]*, *A[5]*, or *A[6]*. Picking *A[6]* allows two symbols to be copied with one instruction since *A[7]* = *a* = *B[3]*. Thus, the second instruction is

> Copy the two symbols beginning at position 6.

The only way to produce the next symbol, *B[4]* = *d*, is

> Append *d*.

B[5] = *a* appears in three positions of *A*. Picking *A[1]* is best because three symbols can be copied at once. This finishes the job of producing *B*, so the resulting edit script is

Copy symbol 3.
Copy the two symbols beginning at position 6.
Append *d*.
Copy the three symbols beginning at position 1.

The Algorithm.   The general plan follows readily from the example. If *j* is fixed, then a longest match between substrings *B[j]B[j+1]* . . . and *A[i]A[i+1]* . . . is found by considering each position in *A* where *A[i]* equals *B[j]*. For each such *i*, the loop

```
for (k = 1; A[i+k] == B[j+k]; ++k)
    ;
```

computes the number of symbols that can be copied from *A* to *B* in one instruction. Pick the value of *i* that maximizes *k*, record the instruction

Copy the *k* symbols beginning at position *i*.

then raise *j* by *k* and repeat the process. If *B[j]* appears nowhere in *A*, record the instruction

Append *B[j]*.

then raise *j* by 1 and repeat the process. In more formal terms, this gives

```
for (j = 1; j ≤ n; j += max(k__best,1)) {
    /* find the best way to constuct B[j] */
    k__best = 0
    for i such that A[i] == B[j] {
        /* how long is the match beginning at A[i]? */
        for (k = 1; A[i+k] == B[j+k], ++k)
            ;
        if k>k__best {
            k__best = k
            i__best = i
        }
    }
    if k__best == 0
        print "Append B[j]."
    else
        print "Copy the k__best symbols beginning at position i__best."
}
```

Figure 3.1.1   The *bdiff* algorithm

Optimality of the Edit Script.   The *bdiff* algorithm always produces an optimal append/copy script. In other words, if *B* can be constructed from *A* by *N* instructions of the form

> Append *x*.

or

> Copy the *k* symbols beginning at position *i*.

then the algorithm produces at most *N* instructions.

An example illustrates the reason for optimality. Suppose that $B = cbadabc$ can be constructed from A by two copy instructions, e.g., copying cba and $dabc$. How do we know that the algorithm will produce at most two instructions? Since the algorithm first copies the longest prefix of B that appears in A, it copies at least three symbols. For example, suppose that it copies $cbad$. To find its second instruction, the algorithm searches A for the longest initial segment of abc (the remaining portion of B). But, abc appears in A (we know this since there exists an instruction that copies $dabc$), so the algorithm generates just one more copy instruction.

Comments on Bdiff.c and Next.c.   The file *bdiff.c* implements the *bdiff* algorithm. The output's appearance is improved by appending consecutive lines as with

```
Append:
    The quick brown fox jumped
    over the lazy dog.
```

instead of

```
Append:
    The quick brown fox jumped
Append:
    over the lazy dog.
```

Single lines are copied with

```
Copy line 6.
```

instead of

```
Copy the 1 lines beginning at line 6.
```

The only nontrivial implementation decision concerned the pseudocode statement

> **for** i such that A[i] = = B[j]

The implementation of *bdiff.c* is independent of that decision. It merely requires an access function, named *next__match()*, where the loop

```
while ((i = next_match(...)) > -1) {
```

returns all the positions in *A* that match *B[j]*. The leading comments of *bdiff.c* specify *next__match()* more precisely.

Implementation decisions about *next__match()* are hidden in the file *next.c*. In brief, lines of *A* are installed in a hash table. With *j* set, the code computes *B[j]*'s hash value (where *B[j]* is the jth line of the second file), searches through the set of lines of *A* with that hash value, and picks out those that are identical to *B[j]*.

Efficiency.   The following empirical data support the claim that *bdiff* is quite efficient. In this experiment *bdiff* was only about three times slower than a trivial program run on the same data. Moreover, the figures justify the use of hashing to implement *next__match()*.

	Problem 1	Problem 2
bdiff with hashing	2.6	2.8
bdiff with a linear search	3.0	6.7

Table entries give *bdiff*'s execution time divided by the execution time of *lc*, the program of Section 1.1 that merely counts the characters and lines in its input. Problem 1 involved two 1000-line C source files, where the resulting edit script contained 10 copy instructions and appended no lines. Problem 2 involved two 1000-line C source files, where the edit script contained 10 copy instructions and appended 50 lines. The first *bdiff* program is the one that appears at the end of the section. For the second, *next.c* was replaced by an implementation of *next__ match()* using linear search.

The *bdiff* algorithm was first discussed by Walter F. Tichy in ''The string-to-string correction problem with block moves'' (*ACM Transactions on Computer Systems*, Nov. 1984, pp. 309–321). The paper rigorously verifies optimality of the generated append/copy script. In addition, it describes a complicated data structure that outperforms hashing if the problem is sufficiently large and gives a way to construct *B* from *A* when memory is scarce.

EXERCISES

1. Suppose there exists a sequence of *N* instructions of the form

Insert *x* after symbol *i*.

or

Delete symbol *i*.

that converts *A* to *B*. For example, the instructions

Insert *a* after symbol 2.
Delete symbol 5.

convert $A = abcdef$ to $B = abacdf$. Show that the *bdiff* algorithm constructs *B* from *A* in at most $2N + 1$ instructions.

2. Consider the following strategy for generating append/copy scripts. Find the longest string of symbols that appears (consecutively) in both *A* and *B*, and generate the command to copy that string from *A*. In other words, maximize the portion of *B* that can be constructed in a single instruction. Then recursively repeat the process using *A* and the remaining portions of *B*. *Append* instructions are used when necessary. Unlike the *bdiff* algorithm, this strategy does not generate the edit instructions in order.

   For example, consider the problem of constructing $B = dcdbcda$ from $A = abcd$. The longest common substring of *A* and *B* is *bcd*, so the algorithm generates the instruction

Copy the 3 symbols beginning at position 2.

This leaves the problem of constructing *dcd* (the first three symbols of *B*) and *a* (the last symbol of *B*). If *dcd* is attacked first, the algorithm locates *cd* (the longest substring common to *A* and *dcd*) and generates the instruction

Copy the 2 symbols beginning at position 3.

This leaves the problem of producing the first and last symbols of *B*. Eventually, the following edit script is produced:

Copy symbol 4.
Copy the 2 symbols beginning at position 3.
Copy the 3 symbols beginning at position 2.
Copy symbol 1.

   Show that this strategy sometimes produces an unnecessarily long edit script.

3. Discuss the value of replacing the algorithm's statement

for i such that A[i] == B[j]

by

for i such that A[i] == B[j] && i + k__best ≤ m && j + k__best ≤ n

For a striking example, consider the case where both *A* and *B* are a string of 1000 *x*'s.

4. Does the implementation of *next_match()* in *next.c* allow a calling program to reread the list of lines in *A* that match a given line in *B*? Explain.

5. Under what conditions can the integer addition performed by the line

```
hashval += *s++;
```

in *hash()* produce an overflow? What are the disadvantages of declaring *hashval* to be type *int*?

PROGRAMMING ASSIGNMENTS

1. Modify *bdiff* so that both files are hashed, and use comparison of hash values as a quick check on whether a match extends more than one line. Measure performance to see whether this modification improves *bdiff* 's efficiency.

```
/*
 * bdiff - a file comparison program
 *
 *
 * Program description:
 *
 *     A command line has the form:
 *         bdiff file1 file2
 *
 *     Bdiff produces a shortest sequence of instructions of the form
 *         Append the line ...
 *     or
 *         Copy the k lines beginning at line i.
 *     that produces file2 from file1.
 *
 *
 * Source files:
 *
 *     bdiff.c    - the main program
 *     lib.c      - library of C procedures
 *     next.c     - produce the next matching line of a file
 *
 *
 * Portability:
 *
 *     File1 and file2 must fit simultaneously in memory.
 *
 *
 * External procedure calls:
 *
 *     int next_match(j, A, B, m)          .. file next.c
 *     int j, m;
 *     char *A[], *B[];
 *         Return the number of the next line of file1 that matches line
 *         j of file2.  A[] and B[] point to the lines of the two files,
 *         and m is the number of lines in the first file.  The loop
 *             while ((i = next_match(j, A, B, m)) > -1)
 *         generates all matching lines.
 */
```

```
#include <stdio.h>
#define MAXFILE         2000        /* maximum file length (in lines) */
#define MAXTEXT         200         /* maximum line length */
#define PROG_NAME       "bdiff"     /* name of this program */

static char *A[MAXFILE], *B[MAXFILE];   /* lines of file1 and file2 */

main(argc, argv)
int argc;
char *argv[];
{
    int appending = 0, i, i_best, j, k, k_best, m, n;

    savename(PROG_NAME);        /* for error messages */
    if (argc != 3)
        fatal("Two file names are required.");

    /* read file1 and file2 */
    m = in_file(argv[1], A);
    n = in_file(argv[2], B);

    for (j = 0; j < n; j += (k_best > 0) ? k_best : 1 ) {
        /* find the best way to construct B[j] */
        k_best = 0;
        /* for i such that A[i] == B[j] and a new k_best is possible */
        while ((i = next_match(j, A, B, m)) > -1 && i+k_best<m && j+k_best<n) {
            /* how long is the match beginning at A[i]? */
            for (k = 1; i+k<m && j+k<n && strsame(A[i+k],B[j+k]); ++k)
                ;
            if (k > k_best) {
                k_best = k;
                i_best = i;
            }
        }
        if (k_best == 0 && !appending) {
            printf("Append:\n");
            appending = 1;
        } else if (k_best > 0)
            appending = 0;
        if (k_best == 0)
            printf("  %s", B[j]);
        else if (k_best == 1)
            printf("Copy line %d.\n", i_best+1);
        else
            printf("Copy the %d lines beginning at line %d.\n",
                k_best, i_best+1);
    }
    exit(0);
}

/* in_file - read in a file and return a count of the lines */
static int in_file(filename, P)
char *filename, *P[];
{
    FILE *fp, *ckopen();
    int lines = 0;
    char text[MAXTEXT], *fgets(), *strsave();

    fp = ckopen(filename, "r");
```

main

in__file

```
    while (fgets(text, MAXTEXT, fp) != NULL) {
        if (lines >= MAXFILE)
            fatalf("'%s' contains too many lines.", filename);
        P[lines++] = strsave(text);
    }
    fclose(fp);
    return(lines);
}

/*
* next.c - produce the next matching line of a file
*
*
* Entry point:
*
*    int next_match(j, A, B, m)
*    int j, m;
*    char *A[], *B[];
*        Return the number of the next line of file1 that matches line
*        j of file2.  A[] and B[] point to the lines of the two files,
*        and m is the number of lines in the first file.  The loop
*            while ((i = next_match(j, A, B, m)) > -1)
*        generates all matching lines.
*
*
* Implementation:
*
*    Hashing is used.  For fixed j, search the list of all lines of
*    file1 having the same hash value as line j of file2.
*/

#include <stdio.h>
#define HASHSIZE 1000    /* number of hash buckets */

struct line {        /* stored line of file1 */
    int line_number;
    struct line *link;
};

struct line *hashtab[HASHSIZE];

int next_match(j, A, B, m)                                        next_match
int j, m;
char *A[], *B[];
{
    static struct line *try;    /* remembers what to try next */
    static int last_j = -1;     /* remembers j from the last call */
    int found;

    if (last_j == -1)        /* the first call */
        make_hash(A, m);
    if (j != last_j) {       /* new line of file2 */
        last_j = j;
        try = hashtab[hash(B[j])];
    }

    /* scan the lines of file1 having the same hash value */
    for ( ; try != NULL; try = try->link)
        if (strsame(A[try->line_number], B[j]) ) {
```

```
                    round = try->line_number;
                    try = try->link;
                    return(found);
            }
        return(-1);
}

/* hash - a simple hash function for character strings */
static int hash(s)                                                              hash
char *s;
{
    unsigned hashval = 0;

    /*
     * Treat the characters as small integers, add them up, divide by the
     * hash table size, and return the remainder.
     */
    while (*s != '\0')
        hashval += *s++;
    return(hashval % HASHSIZE);
}

/* make_hash - initialize the hash table */
static make_hash(A, m)                                                      make__hash
char *A[];
int m;
{
    struct line *new;
    int hash(), hashval;
    char *ckalloc();

    /*
     * Treat lines in reverse order.  Install each one at the front of the
     * linked list of lines having the same hash value.  Thus lines in each
     * list will appear in ascending order.
     */
    while (--m >= 0) {
        new = (struct line *) ckalloc (sizeof(struct line));
        new->line_number = m;
        hashval = hash(A[m]);
        new->link = hashtab[hashval];
        hashtab[hashval] = new;
    }
}
```

3.2 USING INSERT AND DELETE INSTRUCTIONS

The edit scripts considered in this section contain only instructions of the form

Insert x after symbol i.

or

Delete symbol i.

An algorithm is developed to produce a shortest possible insert/delete script for converting one string to another.

Consider the example at the start of the previous section, where $A = ab$ and $B = acab$. Either of the scripts

> Insert *a* after symbol 0.
> Insert *c* after symbol 0.

("Insert after symbol 0" means to place at the front of the string) or

> Insert *c* after symbol 1.
> Insert *a* after symbol 1.

is a shortest possible insert/delete script converting A to B. Notice that if several symbols are inserted after the same symbol of the initial string, then they appear in the second string in the order they are inserted. Also, since there may be several shortest edit scripts, it is proper to say "*a* shortest edit script" instead of "*the* shortest edit script".

Copy instructions are unnecessary because these edit scripts transform one string to another instead of constructing the second string from scratch. In effect, substrings can be copied from the first string to the second by leaving them alone. Conversely, the edit scripts considered in the previous section "delete" a symbol by not copying it.

Sometimes an insert/delete script is shorter than any append/copy script for the same strings, as with the above example. An even simpler example is provided by the case $A = B$: the optimal insert/delete script has zero instructions, while the optimal append/copy script has one. (A more general result is given as Exercise 1 of the previous section.) On the other hand, it is common for append/copy scripts to be shorter, sometimes dramatically so, than corresponding insert/delete scripts. For example, if A has m symbols and B is produced by

> Copy all of A.
> Copy all of A.

then an optimal insert/delete script has m instructions.

The length of a shortest insert/delete script for two strings is called the *edit distance* between the strings. For instance, the edit distance between *abcabba* and *cbabac* is 5. This is confirmed by showing that (i) there exists an edit script of length five that converts the first string to the second, and (ii) no edit script of length less than five performs the conversion. Part (i) is easy; for example, the following edit script works.

1. Delete the leading *a* (to give *bcabba*).
2. Delete the first *b* (to give *cabba*).
3. Delete the first remaining *b* (to give *caba*).
4. Insert a *b* after the *c* (to give *cbaba*).
5. Insert a *c* at the end (to give *cbabac*).

Part (ii) is harder. A little thought shows that no edit script of length two or four can convert a string of length seven to a string of length six. (See Exercise 1.) Single edit instructions (i.e., edit scripts of length 1) can be ruled out by trying all the possibilities. For an edit script of length three to work, it would have to consist of two deletions and one insertion, but a minute or two of trial and error will convince you that no such edit script converts *abcabba* to *cbabac*.

An Inadequate Approach. Determination of an insert/delete script for strings *A* and *B* begins with a symbol-by-symbol scan to find the first position where they disagree. Once the mismatch is found, it is natural to search forward for matching symbols. Nonmatching symbols in *A* are to be deleted, while nonmatching symbols in *B* are to be inserted. For example, consider $A = abcdfg$ and $B = abdefg$. $A[1], B[1]$ and $A[2], B[2]$ match, but a mismatch occurs at position 3. A forward scan discovers that $A[4] = d = B[3]$, which suggests adding

Delete symbol 3.

to the edit script. The next pair of symbols to be compared, namely $A[5] = f$ and $B[4] = e$, do not match, but looking ahead reveals that $B[5] = f$. In terms of converting *A* to *B*, this suggests adding the instruction

Insert *e* after position 4.

Regardless of the strategy for resynchronizing after a mismatch, this simple approach is inadequate because the generated edit script can be unnecessarily long. To see what goes awry, let the first string consist of *n* repetitions of the six symbols *axxbxx* and let the second string be derived by adding *bxx* to the front of the first string. Most simple resynchronization strategies will match *x*'s. For the case $n = 1$, the matching looks like

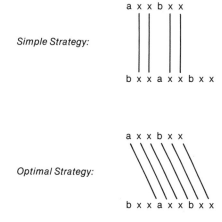

In the general case, the simple strategy produces an edit script of length $4n + 3$. (For each of the n segments, a and b are deleted, then inserted in the opposite order; bxx is inserted at the end.) On the other hand, the optimal edit script merely inserts bxx at the front.

File comparison programs commonly require that several consecutive lines match before resynchronization. In the above example, the edit script of length $4n + 3$ is produced even if resynchronization requires that two contiguous symbols must match. But, if three symbols must match before resynchronization is achieved, then the optimal script is found. Nonetheless, the example can be modified to illustrate the suboptimality of any resynchronization strategy that looks for k aligning symbols. Moreover, for large k more time is required and matching substrings of length less than k are missed.

The failure of simple file comparison algorithms is more than just a theoretical curiosity; it can easily happen in practice. Imagine adding a procedure to the top of a program source file and comparing with the original file. Where is the first point that lines of the files match? Quite possibly the match occurs at the ends of the first procedures in each file, where there is (for example) a blank line. If the file comparison program resynchronizes at this point by, in effect, removing the first procedure from each file, then we are back where we started: *file2* is just *file1* with an additional procedure tacked on the front. Thus, the algorithm may report that the two files are entirely different, except for blank lines.

Computing the Edit Distance.   The algorithm developed below always produces a shortest insert/delete script. It performs quite efficiently if file differences are small (i.e., for the majority of practical applications); it is time consuming only when the files are quite different. The algorithm was first described by

W. Miller and E. W. Myers in "A file comparison program" (*Software—Practice and Experience*, Nov. 1985, pp. 1025–1040).

All the information needed to compute the edit distance between A and B can be determined by comparing every element of A with every element of B. Thus, denoting the length of A by m and the length of B by n, $m \times n$ comparisons suffice. On the other hand, it is not so obvious how to order the comparisons and how to record the information obtained. The following systematic method uses three rules to build up a solution from the solutions for prefixes (i.e., initial segments) of the given strings. However, the discussion of inadequate approaches shows that we cannot be sure of what subproblems need to be solved until the final solution is in hand. Those approaches fail because they start generating edit instructions before the two files are completely known.

Let $D[i,j]$ be the edit distance between the first i symbols of A, denoted $A[1:i]$, and the first j symbols of B, denoted $B[1:j]$. $D[i,j]$ makes sense even when i or j is zero; for example, $D[i,0]$ is the edit distance between a string of i symbols and a string of 0 symbols, which obviously equals i. Arrange these values as a matrix with $1 + m$ rows (one row giving the values $D[0,j]$ and one row for each entry of A) and $1 + n$ columns (one column giving the values $D[i,0]$ and one for each entry of B). Continuing the example where $A = abcabba$ and $B = cbabac$, the values are

0	1	2	3	4	5	6	
1	2	3	2	3	4	5	a
2	3	2	3	2	3	4	b
3	2	3	4	3	4	3	c
4	3	4	3	4	3	4	a
5	4	3	4	3	4	5	b
6	5	4	5	4	5	6	b
7	6	5	4	5	4	5	a
	c	b	a	b	a	c	

Consider the entry $D[5,4]$, which lies at the intersection of row 5 and column 4. (Row and column numbers start with 0.) $D[i,j]$ is defined as the edit distance between *abcab* (the string labeling rows 1–5) and *cbab* (the string labeling columns 1–4). For these particular strings, $D[i,j] = 3$ because

Insert *c* after symbol 0.
Delete symbol 1.
Delete symbol 3.

changes *abcab* to *cbab*, but no shorter insert/delete script works.

The above matrix exhibits several useful patterns that appear for any choice of the two input strings (not just *abcabba* and *cbabac*). The ith row (for any i) begins with i, and adjacent values differ by 1. The same is true of columns. Diagonals, however, have a different structure. To make this precise, label the diagonals of D as

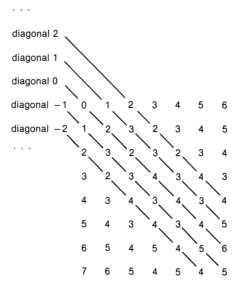

The values along diagonal k begin with $|k|$, then jump to $|k| + 2$, then to $|k| + 4$, and so on. This fact follows from the observation (soon to be justified) that all occurrences of a given value d are on diagonals $-d$, $-d + 2, \ldots, d - 2$ and d. That is, the entries with value d lie on alternate diagonals in a band of half-width d, centered around diagonal 0.

The algorithm uses three rules to systematically fill in the D matrix. With each value $D[i,j]$, the algorithm associates an edit script of length $D[i,j]$ that converts $A[1:i]$ to $B[1:j]$. Operation begins by finding all the 0's in D. These are clearly just the values $D[i,i]$ where $A[k] = B[k]$ for all $k \le i$. In other words, the algorithm starts by finding identical prefixes of A and B. The algorithm then applies the rules to determine all entries in D that equal 1. Then it fills in the 2's, then the 3's, an so on. This continues until the "southeast" value $D[m,n]$ is determined, which solves the original problem.

Rule 1: "Move Right".   Suppose that:

(i) $D[i,j-1]$ (the value just to the left of $D[i,j]$) is known.

(ii) An edit script of length $D[i,j-1]$ that converts $A[1:i]$ to $B[1:j-1]$ is known.
(iii) $D[i,j]$ is unknown.

Then $D[i,j] = D[i,j-1] + 1$, and adding the command "Insert $B[j]$ after symbol i" to the edit script of (ii) produces a shortest edit script converting $A[1:i]$ to $B[1:j]$.

If the algorithm has determined $D[i,j-1]$ but not $D[i,j]$, then $D[i,j]$ must be greater than $D[i,j-1]$. Consequently, $D[i,j]$ must equal $D[i,j-1] + 1$, since the rule shows how to construct a script of this length.

As an example, consider $D[3,3]$, the edit distance from *abc* to *cba* in the sample problem. Suppose that (i) $D[3,2]$, the edit distance from *abc* to *cb*, is known to be 3, that (ii)

> Delete symbol 1.
> Delete symbol 2.
> Insert *b* after symbol 3.

is a shortest edit script converting *abc* to *cb*, and that (iii) $D[3,3]$ has not been filled in. Rule 1 asserts $D[3,3] = 4$, and appending the command "Insert *a* after symbol 3" to the edit script given in (ii) yields a shortest edit script converting *abc* to *cba*.

Edit instructions refer to symbol positions in the *original* string. Thus, the second delete command in the script above removes the *b* in *abc* and not the *c*. Also, a sequence of insertions after the same position are assumed to occur in order. Thus, the first insert command in the script above places a *b* after the *c* in *abc* and the second "Insert after symbol 3" places an *a* after the *b* just inserted.

Rule 2: "Move Down".   Suppose that:

(i) $D[i-1,j]$ (the value just above $D[i,j]$) is known.
(ii) An edit script of length $D[i-1,j]$ that converts $A[1:i-1]$ to $B[1:j]$ is known.
(iii) $D[i,j]$ is not known.

Then $D[i,j] = D[i-1,j] + 1$, and adding the command "Delete symbol i" to the edit script of (ii) produces a shortest edit script converting $A[1:i]$ to $B[1:j]$.

Again consider $D[3,3]$ in the sample problem; $D[3,3]$ is the edit distance from *abc* to *cba*. Suppose that (i) $D[2,3]$, the edit distance from *ab* to *cba*, is known to be 3, that (ii)

> Delete symbol 1.
> Insert *c* after symbol 1.
> Insert *a* after symbol 2.

is a shortest edit script converting ab to cba, and that (iii) $D[3,3]$ has not been filled in. Rule 2 then asserts $D[3,3] = 4$, and appending the command "Delete symbol 3" to the edit script given in (ii) yields a shortest edit script converting abc to cba.

Rule 3: "Slide Down the Diagonal".   Suppose that:

(i) $D[i-1,j-1]$ (the value just above and to the left of $D[i,j]$) is known.

(ii) An edit script of length $D[i-1,j-1]$ that converts $A[1:i-1]$ to $B[1:j-1]$ is known.

(iii) $A[i] = B[j]$.

Then $D[i,j] = D[i-1,j-1]$, and the edit script of (ii) is a shortest edit script converting $A[1:i]$ to $B[1:j]$.

Consider $D[5,4]$ in the sample problem. Rule 3 says that any edit script of length $D[4,3]$ for $abca$ and cba, such as

> Delete symbol 1.
> Delete symbol 2.
> Insert a b after symbol 3.

is an edit script of length $D[5,4]$ for $abcab$ and $cbab$.

To illustrate how the rules are used, suppose that the 0's, 1's, and 2's have been filled in the sample D matrix:

0	1	2	.	.	.	.	
1	2	.	2	.	.	.	a
2	.	2	.	2	.	.	b
.	2	.	.	.	.	.	c
.	.	.	.	.	.	.	a
.	.	.	.	.	.	.	b
.	.	.	.	.	.	.	b
.	.	.	.	.	.	.	a
	c	b	a	b	a	c	

Apply Rules 1–3 to see how far 3's extend down diagonal 1. Rules 1 and 2 place 3's in every unfilled position that is immediately to the right of, or immediately below, a 2. This puts 3's in positions [1,2], [2,3], and [3,4]. Rule 3 then fills a 3 in the [4,5] location, since row and column labels match and a 3 lies immediately to the northwest. Similar reasoning fills in the 3's shown in diagonals -3, -1, and 3:

```
0  1  2  3  .  .  .
1  2  3  2  3  .  .  │ a
2  3  2  3  2  3  .  │ b
3  2  3  .  3  .  3  │ c
.  3  .  3  .  3  .  │ a
.  .  3  .  3  .  .  │ b
.  .  .  .  .  .  .  │ b
.  .  .  .  .  .  .  │ a
   ─────────────────
   c  b  a  b  a  c
```

As this illustrates, the algorithm fills d values in the D matrix by moving right or down from a $d-1$ entry and then making a sequence of diagonal moves. It follows that d values are placed only on diagonals $-d$, $-d+2$, . . . , $d-2$, d. As already mentioned, 0's go on diagonal 0. The 1's are filled in by either moving down from diagonal 0 to diagonal -1, or moving right from diagonal 0 to diagonal 1, then sliding down a diagonal. For the 2's, the algorithm moves right or down from diagonals ± 1, from which it can reach only diagonals -2, 0, and 2, then slides diagonally. Continuing inductively verifies the general pattern.

For efficiency, not all the entries of D are explicitly computed and stored. It suffices to record only those d entries nearest the bottom of D in each relevant diagonal (i.e., diagonals $-d$, $-d+2$, . . . , $d-2$, d). Moreover, since the diagonals containing $(d-1)$'s alternate with diagonals containing d's, a single array, $last\_d[]$, can simultaneously indicate both the lowest d entries and the lowest $d-1$ entries used to compute them. Thus, row $last\_d[k]$ contains the most recent value filled in diagonal k.

Assuming that $last\_d[k-1]$ and $last\_d[k+1]$ correctly indicate the positions of the last $(d-1)$'s on diagonals $k-1$ and $k+1$, how is the last d on diagonal k located? The first problem is to find a value of d on diagonal k. One possibility is to move right from the last $d-1$ on diagonal $k-1$ to row $last\_d[k-1]$ on diagonal k. The alternative is to move down from the last $d-1$ in diagonal $k+1$ to row $last\_d[k+1]+1$ on diagonal k. The algorithm selects the more advantageous of the two moves. Thus, if $last\_d[k+1] \geq last\_d[k-1]$ it moves down; otherwise, it moves right. (Special care is needed for $k = \pm d$, i.e., for the diagonals that have $(d-1)$'s on only one side.) Once on diagonal k, the algorithm slides as far as permitted by Rule 3.

Return to the problem of filling 3's in diagonal 1 of the sample problem. Just after the 2's have been filled in, $last\_d[0] = 2$ and $last\_d[2] = 2$. Moving right from diagonal 0 would yield a 3 in row 2 of diagonal 1, whereas moving down from diagonal 2 yields a 3 in row 3. Hence the algorithm moves down to position [3,4], slides down diagonal 1 to row 4, and sets *last__d[1]* to 4.

Given this method of determining edit distances, producing a corresponding edit script is straightforward. An edit script denoted *script[k]* is associated with each *last__d[k]*, and updated according to Rules 1–3. The algorithm is

```
/* find a d on diagonal k. */
if (k == -d || (k ≠ d && last__d[k+1] ≥ last__d[k-1])) {
    /*
    * Moving down from the last d-1 on diagonal k+1
    * puts you farther along diagonal k than does
    * moving right from the last d-1 on diagonal k-1.
    */
    row = last__d[k+1] + 1
    script[k] = script[k+1] with the instruction
            "Delete the row^th symbol" appended
} else {
    /* move right from the last d-1 on diagonal k-1 */
    row = last__d[k-1]
    script[k] = script[k-1] with the instruction
            "Insert B[row+k] after the row^th symbol" appended
}

col = row + k     /* column where row intersects diagonal k */

/* slide down the diagonal */
while ( row<m && col<n && A[row+1] == B[col+1])
        ++row, ++col
last__d[k] = row
```

Figure 3.2.1   Locating the last d on diagonal k

The test

```
if (k == -d || (k ≠ d && last__d[k+1] ≥ last__d[k-1])) {
```

takes special care with the cases $k = \pm d$. When k is $-d$, the algorithm is considering the lowest diagonal that contains d's. The diagonal above it (diagonal $k + 1$) contains one or more $d - 1$'s, but the diagonal just below (diagonal $k - 1$) contains none, and *last__d[k-1]* is not defined. The purpose of the clause "k == -d" is to guarantee that the move down rule will be applied. Similarly, the clause "k ≠ d" guarantees that the move right rule is applied when k equals d.

The next step is to enclose the above algorithm fragment in loops that vary d and k appropriately. Perhaps the first pair of looping statements that one might try is

```
for (d = 1; ; ++d)
    for (k = -d; k ≤ d; d += 2)
```

However, an alternative approach keeps array references in bounds and further restricts the algorithm's "search band." Suppose *row* reaches m on diagonal k, meaning that the algorithm has hit the bottom of the D matrix. It is pointless to fill in values to the left of diagonal k, since they cannot contribute to $D[m,n]$. The algorithm arranges that diagonal $k + 1$ will be the lowest diagonal that is considered when d is incremented. This is done using bounds, *lower* and *upper*, for the range of diagonals considered at each iteration. Normally, *lower* is decremented by one and *upper* is incremented by one in each iteration. However, if the bottom row is reached, *lower* is set to $k + 2$ so that the default decrement sets it correctly to $k + 1$. *Upper* is set similarly if the rightmost column is reached.

```
/* initialize: 0 entries in D indicate identical prefixes */
row = min (i: A[i+1] ≠ B[i+1])
last_d[0] = row
script[0] = NULL
lower = (row == m) ? 1 : -1
upper = (row == n) ? -1 : 1
if lower > upper
    Report that the files are identical and terminate execution.

/* for each value of the edit distance . . . */
for (d = 1; d ≤ max_d; ++d) {
    /* for each relevant diagonal . . . */
    for (k = lower; k ≤ upper; k += 2) {

        locate the last d on diagonal k, as above

        if row == m && col == n
            Print the edit script pointed to by script[k]
            and terminate execution.
        if row == m
            /* hit last row; don't look to the left */
            lower = k + 2
        if col == n
            /* hit last column; don't look to the right */
            upper = k - 2
    }
    --lower
    ++upper
}
Print a message indicating that the edit distance is greater than max_d.
```

Figure 3.2.2   The *fcomp* algorithm

The algorithm terminates after *max_d* iterations of the outer loop. To avoid seeing (and paying for) differences that are too large to be useful, *max_d* can be set to a small value. If *max_d* is set to $m + n$, the algorithm will find the difference regardless of its size.

Comments on Fcomp.c.   In C, all arrays have origin 0, so *last_d[]* cannot be declared to have subscripts ranging from -2000 to 2000. Thus, the program does things in a slightly different way than expressed in the above algorithm. A bound *MAXFILE* is set on m and n, and subscripts k for *last_d[]* and *script[]* are limited to the range 0 to $2 \times MAXFILE$. The subscript $k = MAXFILE$ corresponds to diagonal 0 and, in general, a subscript k corresponds to diagonal $k-ORIGIN$, where *ORIGIN* is defined as *MAXFILE*.

The function *put_scr()* that prints the final edit script tries to produce a nicely tailored listing. Instead of

```
Deleted line 10:
    *s = *t;
Deleted line 11:
    ++s;
Deleted line 12:
    ++t;
Inserted after line 12:
    *s++ = *t++;
```

it generates:

```
Changed lines 10-12:
    *s = *t;
    ++s;
    ++t;
To:
    *s++ = *t++;
```

Efficiency.   At worst, the algorithm must determine all of D, hence its running time can be proportional to $m \times n$ (the product of the sizes of A and B). This is to be expected, since the paper "Bounds on the complexity of the longest common subsequence problem" by A. V. Aho, D. S. Hirschberg and J. D. Ullman (*Journal of ACM*, Jan. 1976, pp. 1–12) shows that every file comparison algorithm meeting certain general conditions occasionally takes time proportional to $m \times n$.

The algorithm's advantage is efficient performance when the output is small compared to m and n. Since the algorithm stops as soon as $D[m,n]$ is filled in, only diagonals $-d$ to d are considered, where $d = D[m,n]$. Thus, the running time is proportional to the number of entries in those diagonals, which is less than $(2d + 1)$

$\times$ *min(m,n)*. Moreover, the expected running time is proportional to *min(m,n)* + d^2 under appropriate assumptions about the distribution of the input. This fact is proved by Eugene W. Myers in "An O(ND) difference algorithm and its variations" (*Algorithmica*, 1986, pp. 251–266). The paper also shows that when *d* is large compared with *m* and *n*, execution time can be roughly halved by simultaneously working toward the middle of the *D* matrix from both the [0,0] position and the [*m,n*] position.

The UNIX *diff* program uses an algorithm much like that described by James W. Hunt and Thomas G. Szymanski in "A fast algorithm for computing longest common subsequences" (*Communications of ACM*, May 1977, pp. 350–353). Its performance depends heavily on the number *r* of positions [*i,j*] in *D* where *A[i]* equals *B[j]*; *r* may be large in cases where *d* is small. To see how disastrous this dependence on *r* can be, *fcomp* and *diff* were run with *file1* consisting of 1000 blank lines and *file2* consisting of *file1* with a single nonblank line added to both ends. This choice makes *d* = 2 and *r* = one million. *Fcomp* took about one half second of computer time (on a VAX 11/780), while *diff* took over 2.5 minutes.

To turn the tables, *fcomp* and *diff* were run on a pair of 1000-line files having no lines in common. This choice makes *d* = 2000 and *r* = 0. *Fcomp* ran out of memory after one minute (and reported that the edit distance was at least 617), while *diff* solved the problem in about 8 seconds. (This failure of *fcomp* can be avoided; in the paper cited above, Gene Myers shows how the algorithm can be modified to run in space proportional to *m* + *n*.) Thus, there exist pathological cases where *fcomp*'s performance is much worse than *diff*'s, and vice versa.

For a more realistic comparison, *fcomp* and *diff* were run on a number of 1000-line C source files with values *d* between 5 and 50. Values of *r* fell in the range 10,000–30,000. (If one out of every 10 lines is blank, then pairs of blank lines, one from each file, contribute 10,000 to *r*.) On these problems, *fcomp* typically ran about four times faster than *diff*. The only examples breaking this trend were cases when all differences between the two files fell in a small range of lines. *Diff* begins operation by stripping away matching prefixes and suffixes of the files. For example, if all differences between two files occur in lines 201–300, *diff* quickly reduces the problem to that of comparing two 100-line files, then applies its main algorithm. For such problems, *fcomp* ran roughly two to three times faster than *diff*.

It is notoriously difficult to judge the relative merits of two programs since performance often depends critically on programming details. The effect of coding differences was investigated using a precursor of *fcomp* from an early draft of this chapter. (The current algorithm was used as soon as it was discovered.) This program implements *diff*'s underlying algorithm in the spirit of *fcomp*; in particular, files are stored with *ckalloc()*. Using it in place of *diff* removed the most serious coding difference between *fcomp* and *diff*. To conserve space, *diff* stores internally only the lines' hash values. This strategy spends extra time computing hash values and reading files twice, but speeds the process of comparing lines. This earlier version of *fcomp* was also less efficient by a factor of roughly four, so *fcomp*'s performance superiority stems from its algorithm, not its implementation.

EXERCISES

1. Show that an edit script converting $A[1:i]$ to $B[1:j]$ has even length if and only if $|i-j|$ is even. Relate this fact to the values that appear in the D matrix.

2. Apply *fcomp*'s algorithm by hand to *abcabba* and *cbabac*. In particular, verify that the following values of *last_d[k]* are computed. Rows correspond to values of d, columns to values of k.

	-4	-3	-2	-1	0	1	2	3
0					0			
1				1		0		
2			3		2		2	
3		5		5		4		3
4	7		7		5		4	
5				7				

3. How many distinct edit scripts of length 2 have the effect of replacing symbol 3 by z? Which script is found by *fcomp*'s algorithm?

4. *Fcomp* generates the edit script in reverse order, then flips pointers just before printing the script. Can the edit instructions be linked in the proper order as they are initially generated? Explain.

5. Prove correctness of *fcomp*'s algorithm by fleshing out the following inductive argument showing that stage d finds all d entries in the D matrix. In effect, an argument about *all* edit scripts is required. Scripts that insert and subsequently delete a given symbol are not optimal and can be ignored. For the remaining scripts, assume without loss of generality that the instructions are ordered according to the affected position in A. Scripts produced by *fcomp*'s algorithm have this property.

   Let S be a shortest edit script of length d for $A[1:i]$ and $B[1:j]$. For the induction basis, $d = 0$, it follows that $i = j$ and $A[k] = B[k]$ for all $k \leq i$. The algorithm correctly fills in these entries in its initialization step. Proceeding inductively, suppose $d > 0$ and let R be the first $d - 1$ instructions of S. The algorithm's strategy is correct if R is a shortest script for a position $[p,q]$ from which $[i,j]$ can be reached by a move right or down, perhaps followed by some diagonal moves. Suppose the last instruction of S is "Delete symbol k", where k is between 1 and i. Then the last $i - k$ symbols of $A[1:i]$ must match the last $i - k$ symbols of $B[1:j]$. S must also be a shortest script converting $A[1:k]$ to $B[1:j-(i-k)]$; otherwise the shorter script would be a shorter script for $A[1:i]$ and $B[1:j]$ (a contradiction). Also, R must be a shortest script converting $A[1:k-1]$ to $B[1:j-(i-k)]$; otherwise the shorter script plus the instruction "Delete symbol k" would improve upon S (a contradiction). But, position $[i,j]$ can be reached from position $[k-1, j-(i-k)]$ by a move down and a sequence of diagonal moves. The other case is that the last instruction of S is "Insert x after symbol k", where k is between 1 and i, and x is arbitrary. The above reasoning shows that R is a shortest script converting $A[1:k]$ to $B[1:j-(i-k)-1]$, where position $[i,j]$ can be reached from position $[k,j-(i-k)-1]$ by a move right and a sequence of diagonal moves. This completes the inductive proof.

6. A *subsequence* of a given string is any string obtained by deleting zero or more symbols from the given string. A *longest common subsequence* of two strings is both (i) a subsequence of both strings and (ii) as long as any other common subsequence. For example, *caba* is a longest common subsequence of *abcabba* and *cbabac*, as is *baba*.

   A *trace* for two strings connects occurrences of each symbol in a common subsequence. The trace is *maximal* if the subsequence is a longest common subsequence. For example,

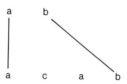

and

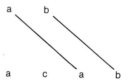

are the two maximal traces corresponding to the unique longest common subsequence *ab* of $A = ab$ and $B = acab$. Adapt *fcomp*'s algorithm to compute a maximal trace for two strings.

7. Suppose S is a trace (Exercise 6) for A and B, and T is a trace for B and C. The set of connections $a—b—c$, where S connects a and b, and T connects b to c, is a *three-way trace* for A, B, and C. Such a three-way trace connects occurrences of each symbol in some common subsequence of A, B, and C.

   For example,

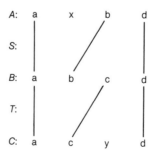

determines the three-way trace

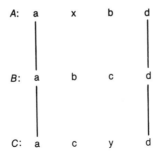

connecting occurrences of symbols in the common substring *ad* of *A*, *B*, and *C*. A connection in *S* is ignored if it does not link to a connection in *T*, and vice versa.

Show that the three-way trace need not be maximal (in the obvious sense) even if *S* and *T* are maximal traces.

PROGRAMMING ASSIGNMENTS

1. Modify *fcomp* so that it automatically requests confirmation, as with

    ```
    The files differ in over 20 lines.  Shall I continue?
    ```

    if the two files are substantially different.

2. (Suggested by Gene Myers.) *Fcomp* can be sped up (by a factor of around two on a Berkeley UNIX system) using the following ideas. Read each file with a single system-dependent input call. This avoids all calls to *fgets()* and *malloc()*. Hash lines and replace every call to *strsame()* by a simple comparison of pointers. The hash function should be tuned for efficiency; characters in a line can be grouped by fours, treated as integers, and added.

3. Using a system timing utility (such as the UNIX profiling command, *prof*), find where *fcomp* spends its time. Then make *fcomp* more efficient. For example, if storage allocation with *ckalloc()* is relatively expensive, then write a procedure that gets large blocks of storage from the operating system and hands out small pieces.

4. Give *fcomp* the −*e* option for producing a script of instructions for some text-editing program. In essence, the goal is for the commands

    ```
    fcomp -e file1 file2 > script
    remove file2
    edit file1 < script
    ```

    to reproduce *file2*. The first line sends the output of the command

    ```
    fcomp -e file1 file2
    ```

to the file *script*. The last line applies an editor to *file1*, taking editing instructions from *script*.

Be warned that some editors use current line numbers, which change as the file is modified. Thus, inserting a line increments the line numbers of subsequent lines. It may be useful to observe what happens if a file is edited from back to front.

5. Design and implement a command

$$\text{merge file1 file2 file3}$$

that incorporates into *file1* the changes leading from *file2* to *file3*. Suppose *file2* is the UNIX version of a source file, and *file1* is the version for another operating system. If a bug is fixed by manually editing *file2* to produce *file3*, then *merge* might be able to automatically incorporate the corrections into *file1*.

Thinking in terms of strings of symbols, consider

$$\textit{file1}: \quad a \quad x \quad b \quad c \quad d$$

$$\textit{file2}: \quad a \quad b \quad c \quad d$$

$$\textit{file3}: \quad a \quad b \quad d$$

Deleting *c* changes *file2* to *file3*, so *merge* should delete *c* from *file1*, producing *axbd*.

A number of merge-algorithms seem plausible. Christopher Fraser gives some useful ideas in the paper "Maintaining program variants by merging editor scripts" (*Software—Practice and Experience*, Oct. 1980, pp. 817–821).

The UNIX *diff3* command suggests an alternative approach. In essence, *diff3* applies *fcomp* twice; once to *file1* and *file3*, and once to *file2* and *file3*. In both cases, a maximal trace (Exercise 6) is inferred from the generated edit script, and a three-way trace is (implicitly) constructed as in Exercise 7. In the above example, this gives

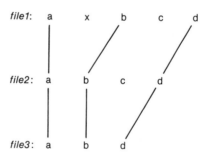

If adjacent connections are separated by one or more symbols, then the three substrings lying between the connections are joined, as in

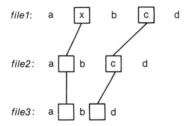

Each joined triple of substrings

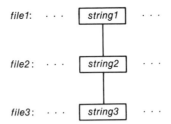

isolates a region where changes have been made. The regions can be treated separately, perhaps by

```
if string3 ≠ string2
    if string1 == string2
        replace string1 by string3
    else if string1 ≠ string3
        warning "overlapping changes; resolve by hand"
```

If you opt for the *diff3* approach, then think about the following questions. Can anomalous behavior result from the use of a nonmaximal trace? (See Exercise 7.) Is it ever a good idea to split connected substrings? For example, with

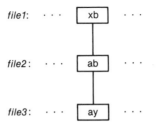

the above algorithm fragment warns of overlapping changes, but with

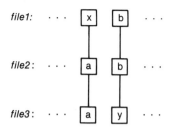

the algorithm changes the *xb* in *file1* to *xy*.

Regardless of the merge algorithm you pick, think carefully about when to warn of "overlapping changes". However, keep in mind that two sets of changes can interact regardless of how far apart they occur. Suppose *file1* differs from *file2* by the addition of a global variable *i* that is accessed in several procedures, while *file3* adds a local variable *i* to some procedure. Merging these changes could produce an incorrect program.

```
/*
 * fcomp - a file comparison program
 *
 *
 * Program description:
 *
 *    A command line has the form:
 *        fcomp [-n] file1 file2
 *
 *    Fcomp produces a shortest sequence of instructions of the form
 *        Insert the line "..." after line i.
 *    or
 *        Delete line i.
 *    that changes file1 to file2.  If an integer n is specified, then only
 *    sequences of at most n instructions are considered.
 *
 *
 * Source files:
 *
 *    fcomp.c   - this file
 *    lib.c     - library of C procedures
 *
 *
 * Portability:
 *
 *    File1 and file2 must fit simultaneously in memory.
 */

#include <stdio.h>
#define DELETE      1
#define INSERT      2
#define MAXFILE     2000            /* maximum file length (in lines) */
#define MAXTEXT     200             /* maximum line length */
#define ORIGIN      MAXFILE         /* subscript for diagonal 0 */
#define PROG_NAME   "fcomp"         /* name of this program */

/* edit scripts are stored in linked lists */
struct edit {
    struct edit *link;              /* previous edit instruction */
```

```
      int op;                          /* INSERT or DELETE */
      int line1;                       /* line number in file1 */
      int line2;                       /* line number in file2 */
};

char *A[MAXFILE], *B[MAXFILE];         /* lines of file1 and file2 */

main(argc,argv)                                                                main
int argc;
char *argv[];
{
      int  col,                        /* column number */
           d,                          /* current edit distance */
           lower,                      /* left-most diagonal under consideration */
           k,                          /* current diagonal */
           m,                          /* number of lines in file1 */
           max_d,                      /* bound on size of edit script */
           n,                          /* number of lines in file2 */
           row,                        /* row number */
           upper;                      /* right-most diagonal under consideration */

      /* for each diagonal, two items are saved: */
      int last_d[2*MAXFILE+1];         /* row containing the last d */
      struct edit *script[2*MAXFILE+1]; /* corresponding edit script */

      struct edit *new;
      char *malloc();

      savename(PROG_NAME);     /* for error messages */
      if (argc > 1 && argv[1][0] == '-') {
          max_d = atoi(&argv[1][1]);
          ++argv;
          --argc;
      } else
          max_d = 2*MAXFILE;
      if (argc != 3)
          fatal("Two file names are required.");
      /* read in file1 and file2 */
      m = in_file(argv[1], A);
      n = in_file(argv[2], B);

      /* initialize: 0 entries in D indicate identical prefixes */
      for (row = 0; row < m && row < n && strsame(A[row], B[row]); ++row)
          ;
      last_d[ORIGIN] = row;
      script[ORIGIN] = NULL;
      lower = (row == m) ? ORIGIN + 1 : ORIGIN - 1;
      upper = (row == n) ? ORIGIN - 1 : ORIGIN + 1;
      if (lower > upper) {
          puts("The files are identical.");
          exit(0);
      }

      /* for each value of the edit distance ... */
      for (d = 1; d <= max_d ; ++d) {
          /* for each relevant diagonal ... */
          for (k = lower; k <= upper; k += 2) {
              /* get space for the next edit instruction */
              new = (struct edit *) malloc(sizeof(struct edit));
              if (new == NULL)
                  exceeds(d);
```

```
                    /* find a d on diagonal k */
                    if (k == ORIGIN-d || k != ORIGIN+d && last_d[k+1] >= last_d[k-1]) {
                        /*
                         * Moving down from the last d-1 on diagonal k+1
                         * puts you farther along diagonal k than does
                         * moving right from the last d-1 on diagonal k-1.
                         */
                        row = last_d[k+1]+1;
                        new->link = script[k+1];
                        new->op = DELETE;
                    } else {
                        /* move right from the last d-1 on diagonal k-1 */
                        row = last_d[k-1];
                        new->link = script[k-1];
                        new->op = INSERT;
                    }
                    /* code common to the two cases */
                    new->line1 = row;
                    new->line2 = col = row + k - ORIGIN;
                    script[k] = new;

                    /* slide down the diagonal */
                    while (row < m && col < n && strsame(A[row],B[col])) {
                        ++row;
                        ++col;
                    }
                    last_d[k] = row;

                    if (row == m && col == n) {
                        /* hit southeast corner; have the answer */
                        put_scr(script[k]);
                        exit(0);
                    }
                    if (row == m)
                        /* hit last row; don't look to the left */
                        lower = k+2;
                    if (col == n)
                        /* hit last column; don't look to the right */
                        upper = k-2;

                }
            --lower;
            ++upper;
        }
        exceeds(d);
}

/* in_file - read in a file and return a count of the lines */
static int in_file(filename, P)
char *filename, *P[];
{
        FILE *fp, *ckopen();
        int lines = 0;
        char text[MAXTEXT], *fgets(), *strsave();

        fp = ckopen(filename, "r");
        while (fgets(text, MAXTEXT, fp) != NULL) {
            if (lines >= MAXFILE)
                fatalf("'%s' contains too many lines.", filename);
            P[lines++] = strsave(text);
```

in_file

```
      }
      fclose(fp);
      return(lines);
}

/* put_scr - print the edit script */
put_scr(start)                                                                              put_scr
struct edit *start;
{
      struct edit *a, *ahead, *b, *behind, *ep;
      int change;

      /* reverse the pointers */
      ahead = start;
      ep = NULL;
      while (ahead != NULL) {
          behind = ep;
          ep = ahead;
          ahead = ahead->link;
          ep->link = behind;  /* flip the pointer */
      }

      /* print instructions */
      while (ep != NULL) {
          b = ep;
          if (ep->op == INSERT)
                  printf("Inserted after line %d:\n", ep->line1);
          else {    /* DELETE */
                  /* look for a block of consecutive deleted lines */
                  do {
                      a = b;
                      b = b->link;
                  } while (b!=NULL && b->op==DELETE && b->line1==a->line1+1);
                  /* now b points to the instruction after the last deletion */
                  change = (b!=NULL && b->op==INSERT && b->line1==a->line1);
                  if (change)
                      printf("Changed ");
                  else
                      printf("Deleted ");
                  if (a == ep)
                      printf("line %d:\n", ep->line1);
                  else
                      printf("lines %d-%d:\n",ep->line1, a->line1);
                  /* print the deleted lines */
                  do {
                      printf("   %s", A[ep->line1-1]);
                      ep = ep->link;
                  } while (ep != b);
                  if (!change)
                      continue;
                  printf("To:\n");
          }
          /* print the inserted lines */
          do {
              printf("   %s", B[ep->line2-1]);
              ep = ep->link;
          } while (ep != NULL && ep->op == INSERT && ep->line1 == b->line1);
      }
}
```

```
/* exceeds - report that the edit distance exceeds d; terminate execution */
exceeds(d)                                                                          exceeds
int d;
{
     printf("At at least %d %s inserted or deleted.\n", d,
         (d == 1) ? "line was" : "lines were" );
     exit(1);
}
```

3.3 PROGRAMMING PROJECT: A VERSION CONTROL SYSTEM

A few years after the first UNIX was developed at Bell Telephone Laboratories, a variant called "The Programmer's Workbench" appeared outside of the research environment. PWB/UNIX addresses problems that arise when dozens of programmers develop and maintain multiple versions of a program. Perhaps the most popular facility added for PWB/UNIX was *SCCS*, the Source Code Control System.

SCCS keeps track of versions of an ordinary text file. Such a text file, hereafter called a *working file*, typically contains either a document or program source. A working file may exist in several versions, e.g., variants that arise as program bugs are fixed and capabilities added, or program versions for different machines.

SCCS condenses all versions of a working file into a single *version file* associated with the working file. Versions of the working file can be extracted from the version file, and new versions of the working file can be installed in the version file. SCCS automatically records such version attributes as creation date and time, author's login name, and explanatory comments. Moreover, extracted versions of the working file can be automatically stamped with identifying information.

Lines appearing in several versions of the working file are not duplicated. Instead, only one complete "master" version is stored in the version file, together with the attribute lists (installation date and time, author's name, explanatory comments, etc.) and edit scripts that record the changes between successive versions. (Each set of changes is traditionally called a "delta.") Version control systems work best when file changes are minor and infrequent. For such files, a little additional file storage allows the user to back up any point in the file's development. The only appreciable space overhead, beyond that needed for the master version of the working file, is for the attribute lists and edit scripts.

While a "production" version control system like SCCS might require 10,000 lines of C, the basic capabilities can be provided in 500–1000 lines. The reader is encouraged to design and build such a stripped-down tool; experience has proven it to be an excellent programming project.

This section draws heavily from SCCS, as described by Marc Rochkind in "The Source Code Control System" (*IEEE Transactions on Software Engineering*, Dec. 1975, pp. 364–370,) and from the Revision Control System, as described by Walter Tichy in "RCS—a system for version control" (*Software— Practice and Experience*, July 1985, pp. 637–654).

3.3.1 Basic Version Control Facilities

Version control systems typically support the following fundamental operations.

1. Display a Table of Contents.   Attribute lists can be extracted from the version file to get a summary of the working file's development. The command

```
info mkupd.c
```

or (if appending ''.*v*'' to the working file's name gives the version file's name)

```
info mkupd.c.v
```

might produce

```
Version 3 of mkupd.c
Date: 10/15/86
Time: 11:21:58
Author: wcm
Comment: Added -w option to suppress warning messages.

Version 2 of mkupd.c
Date: 8/21/86
Time: 09:47:11
Author: wcm
Comment: Fixed bug caused by subscript overflow in examin().

Version 1 of mkupd.c
Date: 6/4/86
Time: 15:02:36
Author: wcm
Comment: Initial version of a program to build UPDATE files.
```

Command flags may request certain attributes. For example,

```
info -a mkupd.c
```

might report just the author of each version.

2. Extract a Version.   A version of the working file can be recreated by specifying either a version number or a cutoff date and time. The command

```
extract -v 2 mkupd.c
```

might extract version 2 of *mkupd.c* from *mkupd.c.v*. Similarly, the command

```
extract -d 6/10/86 mkupd.c
```

might extract the version of *mkupd.c* that was current as of June 10, 1986; in the above example that would be Version 1. (The missing time fields might default to 00:00:00 o'clock.) *Extract* might allow other selection criteria, such as author's name or the appearance of given keywords in the comment.

Execution of the *extract* command proceeds as follows (at least conceptually, though the actual implementation might be different). First, retrieve the master version of the working file from the version file. If that version is not the desired one, then fetch and apply the appropriate edit scripts.

3. Install a Version.   Another version of the working file can be added to the version file. Typing

```
install mkupd.c
```

might add the contents of *mkupd.c* to *mkupd.c.v* as a new version. *Install* can automatically fill in the version number (which would be 4 in the above example), date, time, and author, and can prompt the user to supply the comment.

In effect, *install* extracts the last version existing in the version file, computes an edit script for the working file and the extracted version, and places the edit script in the version file. If the implementation stores the most recent version and uses edit scripts to reconstruct earlier ones, then the new version is installed as the version file's new master version.

3.3.2 Embellishments

4. A Tree of Versions.   Arranging versions in a serial list as Version 1, Version 2, Version 3, . . . may not adequately reflect the file's development. Pictorially, it may be natural to generalize the linear arrangement of versions

to a version tree

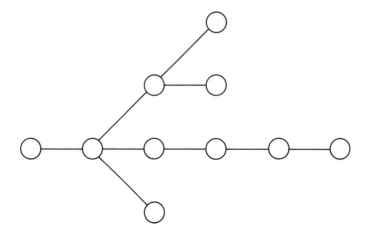

A version tree is appropriate whenever a file version has more than one immediate descendent, e.g., when a version has variants that run under different operating systems.

However, automatic numbering schemes for the versions in a tree may be somewhat unsatisfactory. For example, numbering the immediate descendents of version x as $x.1$, $x.2$, $x.3$, . . . is completely unwieldy because, e.g., the last version in a linear arrangement of six versions would be called Version 1.1.1.1.1.1 instead of Version 6.

The Revision Control System (RCS) numbers versions on the main trunk of the version tree as

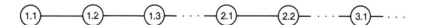

The two fields of a version number are the *release number* and the *level number*. Presumably, the release number is raised only for a major change. For example, suppose that the last installed version is 1.3, that is, Revision 1, Level 3. A command

```
install filename
```

after a minor file revision automatically numbers the new version 1.4. On the other hand, if a major change is made, then the command

```
install -v 2 filename
```

or

```
install -v 2.1 filename
```

will raise the release number, creating Version 2.1.

RCS branches leaving, say, Version 1.2 are numbered 1.2.1, 1.2.2, 1.2.3, etc. Versions along branch 1.2.x are numbered 1.2.x.1, 1.2.x.2, 1.2.x.3, etc. Thus, an RCS version tree might appear as

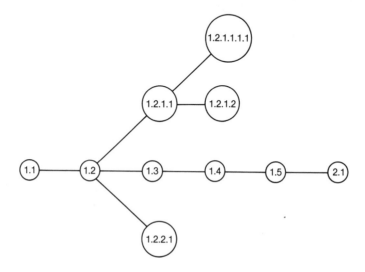

Exercise 1 points out a minor inconsistency in this numbering scheme.

Another approach is to let users label the versions. Whereas an automatic numbering scheme for versions may be necessary to avert chaos on a multiperson project, individual users may prefer to name versions themselves, just as with ordinary files. Indeed, the installation times and explanatory comments uniquely identify each version, so an additional label may be superfluous.

5. Locking and Access Control.   When used for a multiperson project, the version control system can prevent two project members from installing conflicting revisions. For example, suppose programmers A and B extract the latest version, modify it independently, and install their revisions as new versions, with A's version installed before B's. Then A's revisions are undone by B's installation. A's changes are not lost since all revisions are saved, but the changes do not appear in later versions.

One prevention mechanism "locks" an extracted version if the user intends to modify it and install the revised version. Versions can be extracted freely for other uses (e.g., to be read or compiled), but only a user who has locked a version may install revisions to it. For example,

```
extract -l mkupd.c
```

might lock the extracted version by recording the user's name in the version file. When the user subsequently installs a new version, the lock is removed.

Access to the version file can be further restricted by supplying it with a list of user names and corresponding access privileges. The programs that access the file can check whether the person running them has the appropriate rights. This approach offers flexibility beyond that provided by typical file system protection facilities. For example, a user might be granted the right to read versions below 3.4 and to update versions in Release 1.

6. Display the Differences Between Successive Versions.   Users of a version control system occasionally want to know what changes were introduced with a particular version. A simple utility program can format the edit scripts for readability (just as the *info* command displays attribute lists). For example,

```
vdiff -v 2 mkupd.c
```

might produce the following list of differences between Versions 1 and 2 of *mkupd.c*.

```
Line 14 changed from:
      int i;
to:
      int i, lim;

Line 94 changed from:
        for (j = 0; j < i; ++j) {
to:
        lim = min(i, MAXLINE);
        for (j = 0; j < lim; ++j) {
```

7. Automatic Identification.   The version control program can expand certain keywords. For example, suppose that *mkupd.c* contains the string

```
$Date$
```

The command

```
extract -v 2 mkupd.c
```

might replace the string with

```
$Date: 8/21/86$
```

If the extracted version is modified, installed back in the version file, and extracted again, then the *Date* stamp can be automatically updated.

Similarly, there might be meaningful strings

```
$Version$
$Time$
$Author$
$Comment$
etc.
```

to automatically stamp an extracted version with its attributes. The keyword *$Info$* might be expanded to give a complete history of a version as produced by the *info* command. Moreover, information not in a version's attribute list, such as the time the version was extracted from the version file, might also be provided.

To see the value of this facility, imagine the problems faced by a software distributor whose customers hold various releases of the distributor's products. If the customer wants to register a complaint, how can the customer know which versions of the product's modules she is using, especially if she has only object code for the program? Identifying keywords embedded in program declarations, such as the C declaration

```
static char version_id[] = "$Version$ $Date$";
```

provide an easy solution. When the program is extracted from the version file, the built-in macros will be expanded to give a line like

```
static char version_id[] = "$Version: 2$ $Date: 8/21/86$";
```

This allows both the source and compiled programs to be identified, since the string

```
$Version: 2$ $Date: 8/21/86$
```

exists, in some form, in the compiled program. In fact, on UNIX it is possible to use the *find* program of Section 1.1 in a command like

```
find Version: file1.o
```

provided that the source program contains a statement like

```
static char version_id[] = "\n$Version$\n";
```

The additional newline characters are needed so that the desired pattern appears on a short "line" in the object file. (With other operating systems, *find* may not work in this application, and a special-purpose program may be needed to scan object code for embedded character strings.)

8. Handling a Family of Related Files.   Some basic operations on families of version files are straightforward. For example, the command

```
extract *.v
```

might extract the latest version from every version file in the current directory. Similarly,

```
extract -d 6/10/86 *.v
```

might restore the contents of all working files as of June 10, 1986.

RCS provides further assistance for dealing with collections of files by permitting the user to assign arbitrary symbolic names to paths or versions in a version tree. Suppose a program has two version files, say, *file1.c.v* and *file2.c.v*. Let the UNIX version of *file1.c* be Version 1.3.1.2, and let the UNIX version of *file2.c* be Version 2.2.1.3. RCS allows the user to assign the symbolic name *UNIX* to the string ''1.3.1.2'' in *file1.c.v*, and to the string ''2.2.1.3'' in *file2.c.v*. A command like

```
extract -v UNIX *.v
```

can then be used to restore the UNIX versions of the two working files.

To account for changing source file names during program development, the *UPDATE* file (Chapter 2) can be maintained by the version control system. Exercises 2–6 and Programming Assignment 2 investigate interactions between the version control system and *update*.

9. Safety Precautions.   The contents of version files are often precious enough to justify extra protection. As a simple precaution, *install* can report the size of the change before modifying the version file, as in

```
  3 lines deleted
  5 lines inserted
261 lines unchanged
OK?
```

If the user makes a mistake and gets the prompt

```
261 lines deleted
263 lines inserted
  3 lines unchanged
OK?
```

then the installation can be called off. In any case, *install* can request confirmation if the new version is identical to the old one.

Further steps may be warranted to guarantee that version files are not accidently corrupted. What happens if a user running the *install* command hits the interrupt key? What happens if one user tries to extract a version while another user is running the *install* program? To lessen the likelihood of losing a version file because *install* is interrupted, the new version file can be created in a temporary file, then given its proper name. (However, this strategy may mean that other users cannot keep links to the version file.) Foolproof techniques for averting disaster depend heavily on the operating system. Methods for catching interrupts on UNIX are explained on pages 225–229 of *The UNIX Programming Environment* by Brian Kernighan and Rob Pike (Prentice-Hall, 1983). The prevention of simultaneous access is discussed in courses on operating systems, often under the title ''critical sections'' or ''semaphores.''

3.3.3 Implementation

In designing the format of the version file, consideration must be given to such administrative information as:

1. The file's name.
2. The list of locks currently in place. A lock might consist of a user's login name and a version number.
3. A list of users and their access rights.
4. A list of symbolic names and corresponding branches or version numbers. (See Embellishment 8.)

This information might appear at the beginning of the version file, followed by the versions themselves.

The versions might be recorded in the following format:

```
Version: 2.3
Date: 10/15/86
Time: 11:21:58
Author: wcm
Comment: Fixed bug caused by subscript overflow in examin()
Predecessor: 2.2
Script:
14d1
14i1
    int i, lim;
94d1
94i2
        lim = min(i, MAXLINE);
        for (j = 0; j < lim; ++j) {
```

In this example, editor instructions consist of a line number, an operation, and a count of the lines affected. Thus "94i2" means "insert the following two lines after line 94".

Insert/delete scripts are not the only option; the append/copy scripts discussed in Section 3.1 provide a viable alternative. In fact, the append/copy script is sometimes far smaller than the insert/delete script for the same two files, and it is occasionally much more economical to compute. (At least, this is true compared to *fcomp*, which does poorly when the files are quite different.)

Moreover, there is a choice for the "direction" of the edit script. If most accesses request recent versions, then it is desirable for the last installed version be the "master" version, with edit scripts used to construct earlier versions. For example, a version is extracted from an RCS version file by the following steps: begin at the most recent version on the main trunk of the version tree, apply "backward" edit scripts to get to the proper branch leaving the main trunk, then apply "forward" edit scripts to reach the desired version. The paper by Tichy discusses a data structure, call a *piece table*, for efficient implementation of this process.

SCCS uses a completely different implementation. Edit scripts are not stored separately, but instead are interleaved with the original file. If the working file initially contains

```
Line 1
Line 2
Line 3
Line 4
```

then the corresponding version file appears as

```
I1.1      (insert at Version 1.1)
Line 1
Line 2
Line 3
Line 4
E1.1      (end of operation for Version 1.1)
```

Suppose that at Version 1.2, line 2 is deleted and the lines

```
a new line
another new line
```

are inserted after line 3. The resulting SCCS version file looks like

```
I1.1
Line 1
D1.2
Line 2
E1.2
```

```
line 3
I1.2
a new line
another new line
E1.2
line 4
E1.1
```

A version can be extracted in a single scan of the version file, and the extraction time is the same for all versions.

EXERCISES

1. Show that the RCS numbering scheme for version trees does not allow the third field of a version number to be incremented in a manner analogous to raising the release number (e.g., creating Version 2.1 as an offspring of Version 1.3). Devise a numbering scheme that avoids this inconsistency.

Instructions for Exercises 2–6. Exercises 2–6 explore potential interactions between version control systems and the *update* program of Chapter 2. *Update* easily solves the problem of automatically extracting nonexistent working files (Exercises 2 and 3). For the general problem of automatically updating version files, it is sometimes (but not always) adequate to compare modification times of version and working files (Exercise 4). A more effective approach is for *update* to record the time of the last *install* or *extract* operation, instead of relying on time stamps automatically provided by the file system (Exercise 5). However, certain unnecessary *install* or *extract* operations are easiest to avoid if the version control system itself checks file modification times (Exercise 6).

For Exercises 2–6 consider a version control system where versions in a version file are identified by installation time. The version file for the working file *foo* is named *foo.v*. The command

```
extract -d 6/10/86 foo
```

extracts the newest version installed before 6/10/86; *extract foo* extracts the most recent version. Unless *extract* is given a cutoff date predating the version file's creation, it always overwrites the working file. (This rule is not in effect for Exercise 6.) The dynamic macro *TARGET* equals the name of the file being updated (Section 2.1); *tweak* changes a file's modification time to the current time (Section 1.1).

2. Suppose the entries

```
sources -> PRIMARIES

PRIMARIES ->
        extract TARGET
```

were added to the third sample *UPDATE* file of Section 2.1. Describe the effect of the command

```
update sources
```

3. Consider the *UPDATE* entries

```
#define SOURCES header.h file1.c file2.c file3.c
#define OBJECTS file1.o file2.o file3.o
prog -> SOURCES OBJECTS
      cc -o prog OBJECTS

SOURCES ->
      extract TARGET
```

Suppose that *prog*, the object files and *file1.c* do not exist, but *file1.c* is archived in *file1.c.v*. (*Header.h*, *file2.c*, and *file3.c* exist.)

(a) What commands would be generated by an *update prog* command?

(b) What would be the answer to part (a) if *SOURCES* were removed from the precursor list of *prog*? Explain.

(c) Give the commands generated off line by

```
update -n prog
```

Explain.

(d) If off-line updating does not perform properly in this situation, explain how *update* can be modified to correct the problem. (*Hint:* Consider the conditions for adding a ".c" file to the precursor list for a ".o" file.)

4. Consider the *UPDATE* file:

```
#define DATE 1/1/99
#define VERSION_FILES header.h.v file1.c.v file2.c.v file3.c.v
#define SOURCES header.h file1.c file2.c file3.c
#define OBJECTS file1.o file2.o file3.o

prog -> OBJECTS
      cc -o prog OBJECTS

install_all -> VERSION_FILES

extract_current ->
      extract SOURCES
      tweak VERSION_FILES

extract_old ->
      extract -d DATE SOURCES

%.v -> %
      install %
```

The final ''generic'' entry (Programming Assignment 1 of Section 2.3) says that for any file *foo* such that *foo* and *foo.v* exist:

```
foo.v -> foo
      install foo
```

Suppose the *DATE* macro can be defined on the command line, as in

```
update extract_old DATE=6/10/86
```

(Programming Assignment 4 of Section 2.3). If *DATE* is not specified, the future date *1/1/99* given in *UPDATE* selects the most recent version. Answer (a)–(d). Assume that *install* leaves the version file younger than the working file, while *extract* leaves it older.

(a) Suppose a program version is frozen with

```
update install_all
```

Editing continues; some source files are changed and some aren't. Tell which working files are installed in their version files by a second command

```
update install_all
```

(b) Suppose program development is suspended and source files are removed. Later, a new version is begun with

```
update extract_current
```

Some source files are edited. Tell which working files are installed in their version files by the command

```
update install_all
```

(c) Suppose program development is suspended and source files are removed. Later, a new version is begun with

```
update extract_old DATE=6/10/86
```

Some source files are edited. Tell which working files are installed in their version files by the command

```
update install_all
```

Why is it wise for *extract_old* to omit the *tweak* command used by *extract_current*?

(d) Discuss the effects on the answers to parts (a)–(c) of having version control commands that modify version files without installing a new version. For instance, *install* might associate a second version name with a version that was installed earlier.

Also, discuss the effects on the answers to parts (a)–(c) of using the version control system on a multiperson project. Assume that several programmers share the version files, but each programmer keeps personal copies of working and derived files. Let the versions be organized as a tree, where two programmers can simultaneously update different branches, and suppose that the project manager can change the permission status of a programmer by appropriately modifying version files.

5. Consider the *UPDATE* file:

```
#define DATE 1/1/99
#define SOURCES header.h file1.c file2.c file3.c
#define OBJECTS file1.o file2.o file3.o

prog -> OBJECTS
        cc -o prog OBJECTS

install_all -> vcs.time

vcs.time -> SOURCES
        install YOUNGER
        tweak vcs.time

extract_current ->
        extract SOURCES
        tweak vcs.time

extract_old ->
        extract -d DATE SOURCES
```

The zero-length file *vcs.time* is kept for its modification time. Answer parts (a)–(d) of Exercise 4 for this *UPDATE* file. In addition, complete part (e).

(e) The *extract_current* and *extract_old* entries do not economize extractions. For example, let the command sequence be

```
update extract_old DATE=5/1/86
(some files are edited; file1.c is not modified)
update install_all
update extract_old DATE=6/10/86
```

and suppose that *file1.c* did not change between 5/1/86 and 6/10/86. The above *UPDATE* file leads to an unnecessary second extraction of *file1.c*. Is there a way to modify *UPDATE* (perhaps using *YOUNGER*) to avoid this unnecessary operation? Either show how to modify *UPDATE* or argue informally why it can't be done.

6. Suppose each version file records (i) the installation time or version number of the version accessed by the most recent *install* or *extract* command and (ii) the working file's modification time at the end of the most recent *install* or *extract* command.

(a) Explain how *install* and *extract* can use this information to avoid unnecessary operations.

(b) Is your approach guaranteed to work correctly? Either give a set of circumstances in which the approach erroneously skips an *install* or *extract* operation, or explain why it is foolproof.

(c) Can the approach be made to work on a project where several programmers share the version files? Explain.

PROGRAMMING PROJECTS

1. Design and implement a version control system.

2. (Assumes knowledge of Chapter 2.) Write a version control system that is integrated with *update* to support development of a program with several source files. Instead of just "one-file" version control commands like

　　　　　　　extract the June 10, 1986, version of *foo.c*

your system should allow

　　　　　extract and compile the June 10, 1986, UNIX program version

Each version file can contain several parallel versions (the standard UNIX version, the expanded UNIX version, a version for another operating system, etc.) and each parallel version can be occasionally revised (to fix a bug, add enhancements, etc.). Cutoff dates may be more useful than version numbers since *file1.c* may be at version 1.6 when *file2.c* is at version 3.2.

Reasons for integrating the version control system with *update* include:

- It is natural to have an "extract and compile" command that uses *update*'s ability to recompile economically. A single command should restore all program files, both source and object.
- *UPDATE* should include all major command sequences for program development and should display all important relationships among the program's files (including version files). Programmers will read the program's *UPDATE* file to learn how the program is maintained.
- *UPDATE* contains information that is useful for version control. For example, the number of source files in a program can depend on the particular version and can change with time, and *UPDATE* lists the source files constituting a particular program version. (This produces a version control problem for *UPDATE*.)

However, *update*, as presented in Chapter 2, must be augmented. In particular, there must be a way to pass information like "June 10, 1986" from the *update* command line to the version control programs.

Version control should be efficient, just as *update* recompiles economically. Reconstructing an earlier program version should not involve unnecessary extractions from version files. Overwriting a working file with an identical version would both waste the extraction time and provoke an unnecessary recompile by *update*. *Update*'s ability to compare modification times of a source and a version file is inadequate for efficient version control (Exercises 4 and 5), in part because a version file has a single modification time but holds several versions.

The following hypothetical scenario illustrates the desired capabilities. You have just completed work on the HOS (hypothetical operating system) version of *prog*. Program source consists of the system-independent files *header.h*, *file1.c*, and *file2.c*, and the system-dependent files *system1.c* and *system2.c*. A single command like

```
update install_all
```

should install every *changed* working file in its version file; if the just-completed work involved changing *file2.c* and *system1.c*, then *file2.c* could be installed without a version name (with name '''' to reflect its system-independence) and *system1.c* could be installed as a new HOS version. Then a command like

```
update extract_and_compile version=UNIX date=6/10/86
```

(in some appropriate syntax) should restore the UNIX version of *prog* dated June 10, 1986. Suppose that the UNIX program source of that date consists of the same three system-independent files (*header.h*, *file1.c*, and *file2.c*) and the single system-dependent file *system.c*. Moreover, suppose *header.h* and *file1.c* have not changed since 6/10/86 (the most recently installed versions are the current working versions), but *file2.c* was recently modified. The above *update* command could extract and compile an unnamed version of *file2.c* and a UNIX version of *system.c* (both versions current as of 6/10/86); it should not extract *header.h* or *file1.c* or compile *file1.c*. It may be desirable to automatically remove the unnecessary files *system1.c*, *system2.c*, *system1.o*, and *system2.o*.

One possible approach to these problems is outlined below. Parts (a) and (b) extend *update*'s macro capability to allow passing command arguments to version control programs. Part (c) generalizes the use of modification times to provide efficient version control.

(a) Modify *macout()* of *macmod.c* (Section 1.2) to allow "escaped" macro names. In particular, if the character '[' appears in the input string, then the '[' and corresponding ']' are removed and intervening characters are copied to the output string without scanning for embedded macro names. For example, expansion of the two input lines

```
#define NAME defn
NAME [NAME] [x[NAME]y]
```

should produce

```
defn NAME x[NAME]y
```

It should be easy for the user to change the quoting characters. The reserved macro name *NEWQUOTES* in the line

```
#define NEWQUOTES {}
```

could change the quoting characters from '[' and ']' to left and right curly brackets. Thus, the input lines

```
#define NAME defn
#define NEWQUOTES {}
NAME {NAME}
```

would produce

```
                    defn NAME
```

(b) Complete Programming Assignment 4 of Section 2.3.

(c) Implement *install* and *extract* so that versions are specified by giving both a *version name* and an installation time. The command

```
        install -v UNIX foo
```

should install the contents of *foo* in *foo.v* as a new *UNIX* version and record the installation time. The command

```
            install foo
```

should install *foo* as a *standard version*. Thus, each version in the version file is either a standard (unnamed) version or has an associated version name.

The *extract* command can have the forms

```
1) extract foo
2) extract -d 6/10/86 foo
3) extract -d 1/1/99 foo
4) extract -v UNIX foo
5) extract -v UNIX -d 6/10/86 foo
```

If the version is unspecified (forms 1–3), then a standard version is extracted. If the cutoff date is unspecified (forms 1 and 4), or if a future date is given (form 3), then the most recent version with the appropriate name is extracted.

With each version, store a *signature*, that is, some value (or values) that will change if the file's contents change. Values returned by *modtime()* on UNIX may not be adequate; the commands

```
tweak file1 file2 (Section 1.1)
print modtime(file1)
move (rename) file2 to file1
print modtime(file1)
```

can produce identical times. (On the other hand, modification times provide an ordering of files that is unnecessary for this application.) On many UNIX systems, the following procedure returns an adequate two-word signature.

```
#include <sys/types.h>
#include <sys/stat.h>

/* signature - one or both returned values change if file's contents change */
signature(file, sig1_ptr, sig2_ptr)
char *file;
int *sig1_ptr, *sig2_ptr;
{
    struct stat buf;

    if (stat(file, &buf) < 0)
        *sig1_ptr = *sig2_ptr = 0;                      /* file does not exist */
    else {
        *sig1_ptr = buf.st_mtime;                       /* modification time */
        *sig2_ptr = 1000*buf.st_ino + buf.st_dev;       /* inode and device */
    }
}
```

(Even this implementation of *signature()* is not completely safe. For example, it is possible to change a file then set the file's modification time back to its previous value with the UNIX system call *utime()*. The interested reader can think about such possibilities and their countermeasures.)

In the following pseudocode, signatures provide a quick method for spotting unnecessary *install* and *extract* operations. Whenever the version file is synchronized with the working file by *install* or *extract*, the version control system records:

(i) *working_vers* — tells which version currently exists in the working file and

(ii) *working_sig* — the working file's signature.

(In a multiprogrammer environment, values *working_vers* and *working_sig* might be saved for each programmer.) Until the working file's signature changes, requests to install or extract that version can be ignored as follows:

```
install(file, version_name)
{
    determine the predecessor of the new version, i.e., the most
    recent version with version_name
    if working_vers ≠ predecessor or working_sig ≠ signature(file) {
        install the new version in the version file
        name[new version] = version_name
        install_time[new version] = current_time()
        working_vers = new version
        working_sig = signature(file)
    }
}

extract(file, version_name, cutoff_time)
{
    vers = version with version_name that was current at cutoff_time
    if working_vers ≠ vers or working_sig ≠ signature(file) {
        extract version; store in file
        working_vers = vers
        working_sig = signature(file)
    }
}
```

The following *UPDATE* file illustrates the use of *install* and *extract* with *update*. The file describes the UNIX version of the program in the hypothetical scenario discussed on page 137.

```
#define VERSION UNIX
#define DATE 1/1/99
#define STD_SOURCES header.h file1.c file2.c
#define SYS_SOURCES system.c
#define OBJECTS file1.o file2.o system.o

prog -> OBJECTS
      cc -o prog OBJECTS

OBJECTS -> header.h

install_all ->
      install STD_SOURCES -v VERSION UPDATE SYS_SOURCES

restore ->
      extract -v VERSION -d DATE UPDATE
      update regenerate [DATE]=DATE

regenerate -> extract_all prog
      keeponly STD_SOURCES SYS_SOURCES          /* remove unwanted files */

extract_all ->
      extract -d DATE STD_SOURCES -v VERSION SYS_SOURCES
```

Suppose that work has just been completed on a new HOS version of *prog* and let the current HOS version of *UPDATE* differ from the above UNIX version in the macro definitions:

```
#define VERSION HOS
#define DATE 1/1/99
#define STD_SOURCES header.h file1.c file2.c
#define SYS_SOURCES system1.c system2.c
#define OBJECTS file1.o file2.o system1.o system2.o
```

(It might also differ by having a *prog* entry like

```
prog -> ship_to_HOS

ship_to_HOS -> STD_SOURCES SYS_SOURCES
      to_HOS YOUNGER
      tweak ship_to_HOS
```

where *ship__to__HOS* is a zero-length file and *to__HOS* is a command that sends files to a machine running the HOS operating system.)

Now it is time to fix a bug in the UNIX version of 6/10/86. The command

```
update install_all
```

archives source files with the command

```
install header.h file1.c file2.c -v HOS UPDATE system1.c system2.c
```

Only the altered working files are added to their version files; *install* detects unchanged files by checking signatures. Then the command

```
update restore VERSION=UNIX DATE=6/10/86
```

executes the commands

```
extract -v UNIX -d 6/10/86 UPDATE
update regenerate DATE=6/10/86
```

The *extract* command overwrites *UPDATE* with the appropriate version (the one given above) and *update* is reinitiated to extract all source files and generate *prog*. *Keeponly*, a hypothetical program that removes from the current directory all source (and associated object) files not in its argument list, discards the unnecessary files *system1.c*, *system1.o*, *system2.c*, and *system2.o*.

Suppose the system-independent files *header.h* and *file1.c* have not changed since 6/10/86. That is, the current working versions of *header.h* and *file1.c* for the HOS program are valid for the UNIX program version of 6/10/86. Because signatures are used, *header.h* and *file1.c* will not be touched by *extract*, so *update* will not recompile *file1.c*.

(d) Make it possible to automatically stamp an extracted version with the cutoff date from the *extract* command. How is this useful?

4

PATTERN MATCHING

This chapter considers the problem of searching through a file for lines that contain a segment matching a specified pattern. The simplest patterns are *keywords*, i.e., specific character strings. The *find* program of Section 1.1 searches for keywords. Section 4.1 takes a closer look at the problem of searching for keywords and gives a very efficient implementation of *find*.

One often wants patterns that are more expressive than keywords. Instead of seeing all lines containing the variable *foo*, one might want only those lines where *foo* occurs on the left-hand side of an assignment statement, or all lines containing a subscripted variable that begins with the letter *f*. To achieve such expressiveness in patterns, certain characters are designated *meta-characters*, endowed with special significance. Sections 4.2–4.4 deal with *regular expressions*, which include such patterns.

Consider the problem of locating the definition of "regular expression" in a text file. The pattern *regular* would match lines containing such words as *irregular* and *regularly*, so it would be better to use a pattern that does not allow *regular* to be embedded in a longer word. Perhaps more important, the pattern *regular* will miss sentences that begin "Regular . . .". We need a pattern that matches just the words *regular* and *Regular*.

The problem of capital *R* is solved by the regular expression

```
[rR]egular
```

which picks out lines containing either *r* or *R*, immediately followed by *egular*. Cases where the pattern occurs as part of a longer word are eliminated by

$$[\Box\backslash n][rR]egular[\Box\backslash n]$$

($\Box$ indicates a position where a blank should be typed) which matches lines where *regular* or *Regular* immediately follows either a blank or the beginning of the line, and is immediately followed by either a blank or the end of the line. (Every line, even the first line of a file, is thought of as having newline characters at each end.)

For another illustration of the expressiveness of regular expressions, consider the problem of sifting through a large number of C source files for the definition of the function *macin()*. Although many lines may contain the substring *macin(*, the regular expression

$$[!a-z]macin[!a-z][!;]*\backslash n$$

is a good bet to single out the desired line. This regular expression specifies that *macin* appears immediately after a character other than a lower case letter; this condition allows the function name to follow a newline, a blank, a tab character, or a type declaration like "*char * *". Moreover, the character just after *macin* is required to be something other than a lower case letter, and the remainder of the line must match *[!;]* *, meaning zero or more nonsemicolons. This precludes lines in which *macin()* is invoked.

Many pattern-matching programs, including the two given in this chapter, work in two phases. The first phase "compiles" the pattern into an internal representation. The second, and more time-consuming, phase uses the compiled pattern to scan text lines. Figure 4.1 is a pictorial representation of the two phases. Following the conventions used in Fig. 2.1, rectangles designate processing modules and ellipses depict data modules. Data flow is indicated by dashed lines, control flow by solid lines.

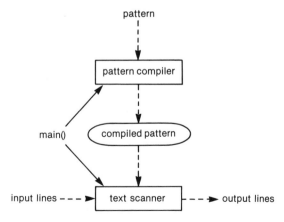

Figure 4.1 Typical structure of pattern-matching programs.

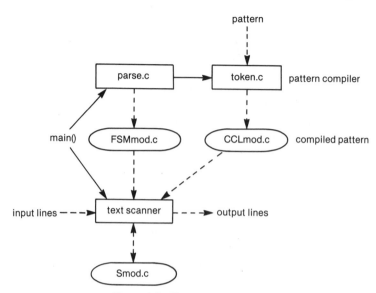

Figure 4.2 The structure of *match*.

With *match*, the pattern-matcher given in Sections 4.2–4.4, the internals of the two phases can be pictured as Fig. 4.2. The "compiled pattern" consists of two data structures:

1. The "finite-state machine" (file *FSMmod.c*), which encodes a process for matching the regular expression.
2. Character class lists (file *CCLmod.c*), a data structure that facilitates deciding if a given character is contained in a given character class (the characters permitted by pattern elements like *[rR]* and *[!a–z]*).

There are three conceptually distinct computations corresponding closely to the respective Sections 4.2, 4.3, and 4.4, and to the order in which *match* was written.

1. The parser (file *parse.c*) implicitly produces the expression tree of the regular expression. It, in turn, calls the lexical analyzer (file *token.c*) to dissect the regular expression into its constituent parts. As a side effect, the lexical analyzer generates the character class lists.
2. Procedures that could build the expression tree are instead implemented to construct the finite-state machine. This simple construction is performed inside *FSMmod.c*.
3. Using the finite-state machine, the character class lists, and an auxiliary data structure (file *Smod.c*), input lines are scanned for those matching the regular expression.

The top-to-bottom order of writing *match* simplified the testing process. For example, *FSMmod.c* could be tested with the help of *token.c* and *parse.c*. Thus, data could be given as a regular expression; it was not necessary to manually construct parse trees for data. Indeed, you will see the two test drivers used for building *match*.

Regular expressions have been studied in great depth, though much of what is known about them is irrelevant to practical pattern matching. For an excellent discussion of "applied" regular expressions, see Chapter 3 of *Compilers: Principles, Techniques and Tools* by Alfred V. Aho, Ravi Sethi and Jeffrey D. Ullman (Addison-Wesley, 1986).

4.1 EFFICIENT SCANNING FOR KEYWORDS

The main computations performed by *find* (Section 1.1) are:

1. Reading text lines from external files to a character array.
2. Scanning the array for positions where an occurrence of *pat* might begin.
3. Checking character by character to confirm a match with *pat*.
4. Printing matched lines.

Detailed checks (step 3) are required to verify a complete match with *pat*. Similarly, step 4 is unavoidable. However, with typical input, step 3 occurs infrequently and step 4 is even less common. In one set of measurements (cited in detail later in this section), step 1 cost 65% of the execution time and step 2 accounted for most of the remaining 35%. To achieve a striking gain in efficiency, both steps 1 and 2 must be accelerated. This section discusses a keyword-matching program that combines faster input procedures with an efficient scanning algorithm to achieve a dramatic reduction in computing time. For a systematic approach to program efficiency see the book *Writing Efficient Programs* by Jon Louis Bentley (Prentice-Hall, 1982).

Consider text scanning (step 2). The crucial insight is to ask if an occurrence of *pat* can possibly *end* at a given position in *text*. For example, suppose we want to know if a copy of *abcac* occurs at a particular position in *text*:

$$\textit{pat:}\qquad \text{a}\quad \text{b}\quad \text{c}\quad \text{a}\quad \text{c}$$

$$\textit{text:}\quad .\quad .\quad .\quad .\quad .\quad ?\quad .$$

$$\uparrow$$

The rules are:

- If the character in question is *a*, then *pat* cannot occur at this position. The next candidate for a match is one position to the right.

- If the character is b, then *pat* cannot occur at this position. The next candidate for a match is three positions to the right. A match cannot occur one position to the right because of the rightmost a in *pat*. Two positions to the right won't work because of the c in the middle of *pat*.

- If the character is c, then *pat* might occur in this position. A character-by-character check should be performed.

- If the character is not a, b, or c, then *pat* cannot occur in this position. The next candidate for a match is five positions to the right, since any earlier position aligns this character with a character in *pat*.

In brief, these rules define a table that tells how far to shift the candidate position: *shift['a']* = 1, *shift['b']* = 3, *shift['c']* = 0, and *shift[x]* = 5 whenever x is different from a, b, and c.

If this pattern-matching strategy is applied to the text line *ababcababcac*, initial alignment gives

$$
\begin{array}{lllllllllll}
\textit{pat:} & \text{a} & \text{b} & \text{c} & \text{a} & \text{c} \\
\textit{text:} & \text{a} & \text{b} & \text{a} & \text{b} & \text{c} & \text{a} & \text{b} & \text{a} & \text{b} & \text{c} & \text{a} & \text{c} \\
& & & & & \uparrow
\end{array}
$$

Since *shift['c']* = 0, the character-by-character check is applied. After it is determined that *pat* does not appear in its entirety at this position, *pat* is moved right one position:

$$
\begin{array}{lllllllllll}
\textit{pat:} & & \text{a} & \text{b} & \text{c} & \text{a} & \text{c} \\
\textit{text:} & \text{a} & \text{b} & \text{a} & \text{b} & \text{c} & \text{a} & \text{b} & \text{a} & \text{b} & \text{c} & \text{a} & \text{c} \\
& & & & & \uparrow
\end{array}
$$

The shifting process is applied. *Pat* is shifted by *shift['a']* = 1

$$
\begin{array}{lllllllllll}
\textit{pat:} & & & \text{a} & \text{b} & \text{c} & \text{a} & \text{c} \\
\textit{text:} & \text{a} & \text{b} & \text{a} & \text{b} & \text{c} & \text{a} & \text{b} & \text{a} & \text{b} & \text{c} & \text{a} & \text{c} \\
& & & & & & \uparrow
\end{array}
$$

then by *shift['b']* = 3:

$$
\begin{array}{lllllllllll}
\textit{pat:} & & & & & & \text{a} & \text{b} & \text{c} & \text{a} & \text{c} \\
\textit{text:} & \text{a} & \text{b} & \text{a} & \text{b} & \text{c} & \text{a} & \text{b} & \text{a} & \text{b} & \text{c} & \text{a} & \text{c} \\
& & & & & & & & & \uparrow
\end{array}
$$

Since *shift['c']* = 0, the character-by-character check is invoked. The complete match fails and *pat* is moved right one position:

$$
\begin{array}{lllllllllll}
\textit{pat:} & & & & & & & \text{a} & \text{b} & \text{c} & \text{a} & \text{c} \\
\textit{text:} & \text{a} & \text{b} & \text{a} & \text{b} & \text{c} & \text{a} & \text{b} & \text{a} & \text{b} & \text{c} & \text{a} & \text{c} \\
& & & & & & & & & & \uparrow
\end{array}
$$

The shifting process is resumed with *shift['a'] = 1*:

$$pat: \qquad\qquad\qquad\quad \text{a} \quad \text{b} \quad \text{c} \quad \text{a} \quad \text{c}$$

$$text: \text{a} \quad \text{b} \quad \text{a} \quad \text{b} \quad \text{c} \quad \text{a} \quad \text{b} \quad \text{a} \quad \text{b} \quad \text{c} \quad \text{a} \quad \text{c}$$

$$\uparrow$$

Since *shift['c'] = 0*, the character-by-character check is applied and a match is confirmed.

In reality, the pointer to *text* is a character pointer *pos*, and the algorithm assumes the form

```
/* compile the pattern */
m = pattern length
for every permissible text character x
    shift[x] = m
for j = 1, 2, . . . , m
    shift[pⱼ] = m − j, where pat is p₁p₂ . . . pₘ

/* scan the text */
point pos to text[m]
repeat {
    /* skim text to find the next candidate position */
    while pos points to a character of text and shift[*pos] > 0
        pos += shift[*pos]
    if all text characters have been scanned
        return no match
    if a character-by-character check matches pat
        return match
    ++pos

}
```

Figure 4.1.1   An improved keyword-scanning algorithm.

The *shift[]* array is initially filled with *m*'s (the pattern length) then adjusted for characters in *pat* by

```
for j = 1, 2, . . . , m
    shift[pⱼ] = m − j, where pat is p₁p₂ . . . pₘ
```

If *x* occurs in *pat*, then the final value of *shift[x]* is the distance from the right end of *pat* to the right-most occurrence of *x*. For example, if *pat* is *abcac*, then *shift['a']* is initialized to 5, set to 4, and reset to 1.

Comments on Fastfind.c.   *Fastfind.c* implements the improved keyword-scanning algorithm using UNIX-specific input functions. The *shift[]* array is filled in by the lines

```
length = strlen(pat);
for (i = 0; i < 128; ++i)
     shift[i] = length;
for (p = pat; *p != '\0'; ++p)
     shift[*p & 0177] = --length;
```

The expression

$$*p \ \& \ 0177$$

copes with potential ''sign-extension''; if the left-most bit of a *char* is 1, then some machines will convert the *char* to a negative *int*. The problem is solved by taking the ''logical and'' with the bit string 00 . . . 01111111 (seven 1's).

Use of the UNIX input routine *read()* instead of procedures from the standard I/O library complicates the program. Files are read in fixed-size blocks of *BUFSIZ* characters, where *BUFSIZ* is a constant defined in *stdio.h.* (For example, one version of UNIX has a *BUFSIZ* of 1024.) As a file is read, successive calls to *read()* will read a series of zero or more blocks of size *BUFSIZ*, then (usually) a partial block of fewer than *BUFSIZ* bytes. Thereafter, *read()* returns the byte count 0.

As a file is read, *fastfind* must keep both the current input block and the previous one. If a matching line is spread across two blocks, with the keyword appearing in the second block, then *fastfind* needs the earlier block to print the full matching line. Moreover, the instance of the keyword in the text line may be broken by a block boundary. To correctly handle these cases, *fastfind* uses two buffers that can be pictured as forming a circle, around which *pat* is shifted:

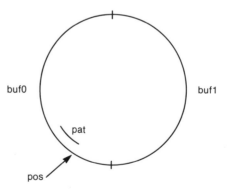

The *while* loop that shifts *pos* is implemented in *scan()* by

```
while (pos < lim && (increment = shift[*pos & 0177]) > 0)
     pos += increment;
```

The condition *pos* < *lim* tests for the end of the text buffer or of the file. When a shift sends *pos* across the boundary to the other buffer, *read()* is called to fill that buffer before scanning continues.

Efficiency Measurements.   The following table summarizes execution times from one experiment. Table entries give average execution times for each program divided by the time required to merely read the same text files with the UNIX input routines *open()*, *read()*, and *close()* that are used in *fastfind*.

		3-Character Keywords	10-Character Keywords
1	reading files with UNIX input	1.0	1.0
2	*fastfind*	2.1	1.5
3	optimized *find* with UNIX input	2.6	3.7
4	reading files with *fgets()*	5.6	5.6
5	*find*	8.5	8.7
6	*match*	11.6	12.1

Fastfind is the program listed at the end of this section. For short keywords, *fastfind* appears to spend about half its time reading text files. For long patterns, this I/O time dominates the computation.

Row 3 gives times for a keyword-matching program derived from *find* by two changes. First, input is done with the UNIX-specific procedures used in *fastfind*. Second, the efficient loop

```
while (*++pos != first_char)
    ;
```

is used to scan past positions where the match fails on the first character of *pat*. (The end-of-buffer test is accomplished by putting a copy of *first_char* just after the legitimate text characters in the buffer.) Thus, rows 2 and 3 of the table reflect inherent differences between pattern-matching algorithms, rather than differences in I/O procedures or programming practices. The superiority of *fastfind* is slight for short patterns and substantial for long ones.

Row 4 indicates the time needed just to read the input files with the standard I/O library procedure *fgets()*. The entries in the line are identical because the time is independent of the pattern. Under the conditions of this experiment, any program that reads text with *fgets()* must be several times slower than *fastfind*, even if it just tosses the lines away.

The *find* program timed in line 5 was taken directly from Section 1.1, while *match* is the general pattern-matching program developed in Sections 4.2–4.4. *Find* spends about 65 percent of its time making calls to *fgets()*, while *match* spends just under half. Overall, *find* is roughly 35–40 percent more efficient than *match*.

Further Reading.   The subject of scanning for keywords has received considerable attention in the literature and a number of efficient algorithms have been developed. The following papers are especially interesting and enjoyable.

- "Efficient string matching: an aid to bibliographic search" by Alfred V. Aho and Margaret J. Corasick (*Communications of ACM*, June 1975, pp. 333–340).
- "A fast string searching algorithm" by Robert S. Boyer and J. Strother Moore (*Communications of ACM*, Oct. 1977, pp. 762–772).
- "Fast pattern matching in strings" by D. E. Knuth, J. H. Morris and V. R. Pratt (*SIAM J. Computing*, June 1977, pp. 323–350).

The Boyer-Moore paper explains several embellishments to the algorithm used in *fastfind*.

EXERCISES

1. Suppose that *find* and *fastfind* are applied to a pattern of length m and a text line of length n.
   (i) For *find*, show that the number of comparisons between a pattern character and a text character could be nearly $m \times n$.
   (ii) For *find*, argue informally that the number of comparisons is unlikely to exceed n by much.
   (iii) For *fastfind*, argue informally that the expected number of comparisons is bounded by roughly n/m.
2. Why doesn't *fastfind* have a "$-n$" option to report line numbers?
3. Let *gap* denote the space between the right-most character in *pat* and the second-from-the-right occurrence of that character. Show that the shift after the failure of a potential match can be changed from

```
++pos;
```

to

```
pos += gap;
```

PROGRAMMING ASSIGNMENTS

1. Implement *fastfind* on your computer system and compare its efficiency with *find*'s.
2. Modify *fastfind* to make it even more efficient and measure the improvement. *Hints:* If appropriate changes are made elsewhere in the program, then the central loop

```
while (pos < lim && (increment = shift[*pos & 0177]) > 0)
    pos += increment;
```

can be simplified to

```
while ((increment = shift[*pos & 0177]) > 0)
        pos += increment;
```

At the cost of further degrading program portability, it may be possible to omit the operation

```
& 0177
```

You might also experiment with

```
while (increment = shift[*pos])
        pos += increment;
```

and

```
while (*pos != last_char)
        pos += shift[*pos];
```

where *last__char* is the last character in *pat*.

How much is gained by using *register* declarations or compiling with an "optimization" option?

3. What happens if *fastfind* is applied to a nontext file, such as an object file or a directory? Could *print__line()* get stuck in an infinite loop because newline bytes are very scarce? What should *fastfind* do about such files? Modify *fastfind* accordingly.

```
/*
 * fastfind - print lines containing a given pattern string.
 *
 *
 * Program description:
 *
 *     A command line has the form
 *         fastfind pat [file1] [file2] ...
 *     where pat is any sequence of characters.  A character pair "\n" at the
 *     beginning or end of pat matches the beginning or end of a text line.
 *     If no file is named, then standard input is read. If more than one file
 *     is named, then each printed line is preceded by its file's name.
 *
 *
 * Source files:
 *
 *     fastfind.c     - this file
 *     lib.c          - library of C procedures
 *
 *
 * Portability:
 *
 *     Files are read with the UNIX routines:
 *
```

```
*           close(fd)
*           int fd;
*                Close the file with descriptor fd.
*
*           int open(file, mode)
*           char *file;
*           int mode;
*                Open the named file in the indicated mode.  (Mode = 0
*                means read-only.)  The returned value is a "file
*                descriptor" that is used for subsequent references to
*                the file.  A negative value is returned if the file
*                could not be opened.
*
*           int read(fd, buffer, max_chars)
*           int fd, max_chars;
*           char buffer[];
*                Read at most max_chars characters from the file with
*                file descriptor fd to the buffer.  The returned value
*                is the actual number of characters read.
*
*      File lines should be separated by '\n'. (Some systems use the pair "\r\n".)
*/

#include <stdio.h>

/*
* Two buffers of length BUFSIZ (defined in stdio.h) are arranged as a circle;
* the location just left of the current buffer is the end of the other buffer.
*/
#define TO_LEFT              buf[1-curbuf] + BUFSIZ - 1
#define DECREMENT(x)         if (x == buf[curbuf]) x = TO_LEFT; else --x    DECREMENT
#define INCREMENT(x)         if (x == TO_LEFT) x = buf[curbuf]; else ++x    INCREMENT
#define PROG_NAME            "fastfind"

int     curbuf,              /* current buffer */
        fd,                  /* file descriptor */
        nfile,               /* number of files */
        shift[128];          /* shift table */

char    buf[2][BUFSIZ],      /* text buffers */
        *end_pat,            /* last position in the pattern */
        *file,               /* name of the file */
        *lim,                /* limit for search */
        *pat,                /* pattern */
        *pos;                /* search pointer to the text */

main(argc, argv)                                                           main
int argc;
char *argv[];
{
    int i, length;
    char *p;
    savename(PROG_NAME);     /* for error messages */
    if (argc == 1)
        fatal("No pattern was given.");
    pat = argv[1];

    /* handle newline characters in the pattern */
    if (pat[0] == '\\' && pat[1] == 'n')
        *++pat = '\n';
```

```
    if ((length = strlen(pat)) == 0)
        fatal("Pattern length is zero.");
    if (length > 1 && pat[length-2] == '\\' && pat[length-1] == 'n') {
        pat[length-2] = '\n';
        pat[length-1] = '\0';
        --length;
    }
    end_pat = pat + length - 1;
    for (i = 0; i < 128; ++i)
        shift[i] = length;
    for (p = pat; *p != '\0'; ++p)
        shift[*p & 0177] = --length;
    if ((nfile = argc - 2) == 0) {
        fd = 0;                 /* standard input */
        scan();
    } else
        /* for each specified file */
        for (i = 2; i < argc; ++i) {
            file = argv[i];
            if ((fd = open(file, 0)) < 0)
                fprintf(stderr, "%s: Cannot open %s.\n",
                    PROG_NAME, file);
            else {
                scan();
                close(fd);
            }
        }
    exit(0);
}

/* scan - find lines in file that contain the pattern string */
scan()                                                                       scan
{
    int increment;

    buf[1][BUFSIZ-1] = '\n'; /* in case the first line matches */
    curbuf = 1;
    lim = pos = buf[1];         /* force an immediate call to fill_buffer() */

    for ( ; ; ) {
        /*
         * Pos points to a text position that might end an occurrence of
         * pat. If that character differs from the last character of pat,
         * then pos is shifted to the next position that might yield a
         * match.  The shifting stops when pos reaches the end of the
         * buffer or an instance of the last pattern character.
         */
        while (pos < lim && (increment = shift[*pos & 0177]) > 0)
            pos += increment;
        if (pos < lim) {        /* shifting ended with pos in buffer */
            if (is_match())
                print_line();
            ++pos;
        }
        /* else past end of buffer; fill the other buffer */
        else if (fill_buffer() == EOF)
            break;
    }
}
```

```
/*
 * fill_buffer - fill other buffer; point pos to first char read; point lim just
 * beyond the last character read; return EOF at end of file.
 */
int fill_buffer()                                                           fill_buffer
{
    curbuf = 1 - curbuf;
    pos = buf[curbuf];
    if ((lim = pos + read(fd, pos, BUFSIZ)) == pos)
        return(EOF);
    return(!EOF);
}

/* is_match - tell if a copy of the pattern ends at pos */
int is_match()                                                              is_match
{
    char *t = pos, *p = end_pat;  /* already know that *t == *p */

    while (--p >= pat) {
        DECREMENT(t);
        if (*p != *t)
            return(0);
    }
    return(1);
}

/* print_line - print the line pointed to by pos; move pos to the end of line */
print_line()                                                               print_line
{
    char *t;

    if (nfile > 1)
        printf("%s:", file);

    /* find the start of the line */
    if (*pos == '\n')
        DECREMENT(pos);
    for (t = pos; *t != '\n'; )
        DECREMENT(t);

    /* print the portion of the line before the match */
    while (t != pos) {
        INCREMENT(t);
        putchar(*t);
    }

    /* print the portion of the line after the match */
    while (*pos != '\n') {
        if (++pos >= lim && fill_buffer() == EOF)
            break;
        putchar(*pos);
    }
}
```

4.2 REGULAR EXPRESSIONS AND EXPRESSION TREES

The structural properties and computer representation of regular expressions are easy to understand if you keep in mind the analogy with arithmetic expressions. This section begins with a quick review of arithmetic expressions, then discusses regular expressions by exploiting the analogy. The rest of the section considers the problem of parsing a regular expression and a simple ''recursive descent'' parser is developed.

4.2.1 Arithmetic Expressions

We can think of arithmetic expressions as constructed from two kinds of basic building blocks, namely constants and variables, by applying the binary operators

$$+ \; - \; * \; /$$

and the unary operator $-$. Unary minus has the highest precedence. (Thus, the minus in $-a*b$ applies to a, not to the product $a*b$.) Following unary minus in precedence are $*$ and $/$, which are grouped left to right ($a/b*c$ means $(a/b)*c$). Binary $-$ and $+$ have the lowest precedence and are grouped left to right. Parentheses can be used to specify order of evaluation.

The *expression tree* of an arithmetic expression has the expression's basic building blocks as its leaves, operators at its interior nodes, and makes explicit the operands of every operation. Constructing the expression tree, in essence just determining the operands of each operation, is called *parsing* the expression. Figures 4.3(a) and 4.3(b) give examples of expression trees.

4.2.2 Regular Expressions

As with arithmetic expressions, regular expressions are constructed from certain basic building blocks by applying unary and binary operators. Again, precedence rules and use of parentheses order the operations, and the order can be displayed with an expression tree.

Literals: The Basic Building Blocks.   Regular expressions are constructed from the following three kinds of atomic expressions for specifying single characters. An occurrence of any of these atomic expressions within a regular expression is called a *literal* of the expression. Thus, a literal of a regular expression is analogous to a constant or variable in an arithmetic expression.

1. *Character constants.* A character other than one of the special characters

$$\backslash \; . \; [\;] \; ! \; - \; | \; + \; * \; (\;)$$

specifies itself. If preceded by the escape character $\backslash$, a character from this list specifies itself. The newline character is denoted ''$\backslash n$'', and specifies the beginning or end of a text line. (Notice that this use of backslash alters the meaning of the ordinary character n; its other uses turn special characters into ordinary characters, as in ''$\backslash\backslash$''.)

2. *The wild card.* The special character '.' matches any character. Thus, the set of strings specified by the regular expression *a.e* includes *axe*, *ape*, *a3e*, and *a#e*.

3. *Character classes.* The pair *[ ]* can be used to specify a class of characters. For instance, the expression *[abc]* matches a single character, which may be *a*, *b*, or *c*. A *]* character can be included in a character class by listing it first or by escaping it. The only characters that have special meaning in character classes are

$$\setminus \ - \ !$$

Newline characters, again denoted ''*n*'', can be included in a character class.

Within a character class specification an occurrence of the − character between two digits, between two lower case letters, or between two upper case letters indicates a range of characters. For instance,

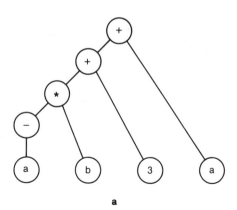

a

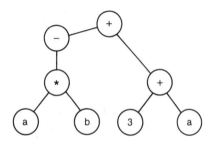

b

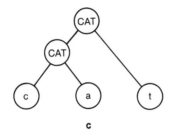

c

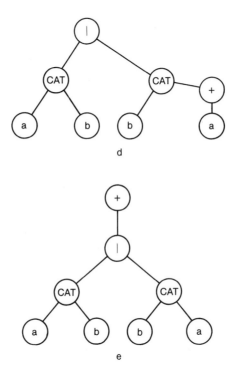

d

e

Figure 4.3   (a) Expression tree for −a*b+3+a. (b) Expression tree for −(a*b)+(3+a). (c) Expression tree for cat. (d) Expression tree for ab|ba+. (e) Expression tree for (ab|ba)+.

$$[a-z0-9+]$$

specifies a character that can be a lower case letter, a digit or a plus sign (operator characters and parentheses become ordinary characters inside character classes designators). In other contexts, such as *[−az]*, *[az−]* or *[a−Z]*, the − represents a minus character.

   If the first character after *[* is *!*, then the class consists of all characters *not* listed, and the class is called a *negated* character class. Thus, *[!a−z]* specifies a character other than a lower case letter. A *!* character that does not appear first in the class, or one preceded by \, has no special meaning.

UNIX users should note the differences between the above interpretation of newline characters and the UNIX view. In particular, the patterns

$$[!a-z]$$

and

$$\cdot \cdot$$

match every line, since every line has two newline characters.

Operators.   Regular expressions are constructed using two binary operators and two unary operators.

Alternation.   The | operator indicates alternation. For example,

$$dog|cat$$

specifies a three-letter string that can be either *dog* or *cat*.

Concatenation.   Concatenating two regular expressions (placing one immediately after the other) specifies the set of strings consisting of a string matching the first expression followed by a string matching the second expression.

Repeated Expressions.   The unary operator + indicates repetition one or more times, while the unary operator * indicates repetition zero or more times. For example, *[0–9]+* specifies the unsigned integer constants, while *[0–9]** specifies the set consisting of these constants plus the character string of length zero. Notice that the expression *[0–9]+* is equivalent to *[0–9][0–9]**, since both specify the set of strings consisting of a digit concatenated with zero or more digits.

Precedence, Parentheses, and Expression Trees.   Parentheses are used for grouping, just as in arithmetic expressions. The following precedence rules sometimes allow them to be omitted. The unary operators * and + have the highest precedence; concatenation is next; | has the lowest precedence. All operators group left to right. Figures 4.3(c) to (e) give examples of expression trees for regular expressions. As with expression trees for arithmetic expressions, these trees have the expression's basic building blocks (in this case literals) as the leaves, and the expression's operators at interior nodes.

Choice of Meta-Characters.   It is common for some of the characters

$$\backslash \, . \, [\,] \, ! \, - \, | \, + \, * \, (\,)$$

to have special significance for a command interpreter. First-time users of *match* invariably type a command like

```
match ab.*c file1
```

which gets the message

```
No match.
```

from one popular UNIX command interpreter. The message is not from *match*. Instead, the command interpreter has failed to find any file name of the form

```
ab<period><0 or more characters>c
```

For this command interpreter, the special character * matches any string; thus, it works like a character pair ''.*'' for *match*.

A temporary solution is to ''quote'' the string so that the command interpreter will consider all characters in the pattern as ordinary characters. On UNIX, the command then has the form

```
match "ab.*c" file1
```

where the quotation marks are stripped off by the command interpreter before the pattern is passed to *match* as *argv[1]*. With the ''Berkeley C shell'' it is particularly difficult to turn off the special meaning of *!*; each occurrence must be preceded by a backslash.

A more permanent solution is to replace meta-characters by symbols that have no special significance for the command interpreter. This can be done by changing the line

```
#define STAR '*'
```

in *match.h* to

```
#define STAR '#'
```

The command then becomes

```
match ab.#c file1
```

Breaking a Regular Expression Into Tokens.   The first step in constructing an expression tree is to break the regular expression into its constituent parts, called *tokens*. The symbolic names *CHAR*, *CCL*, and *NCCL* are used for literals, and '.' represents itself. Tokens of type *CHAR, CCL,* and *NCCL* have an associated value giving the specifics about the token. With *CHAR*'s, this value is the actual character. With *CCL*'s and *NCCL*'s, the value is a "character class ID," which is a unique identifying integer that has been assigned to the class. For tokens other than *CHAR, CCL,* or *NCCL* the associated value is unused.

The tokens for the operators and parentheses are

$$| + * ( )$$

Concatenation has no token because there is no symbol for it in the regular expression; the parser has the task of inserting concatenation nodes (labeled *CAT*) in the expression tree. A null character terminates the token stream for a regular expression.

The regular expression

$$[!]\backslash na]a.*(bc|[d-g])+\backslash n$$

is used by a test driver (given below) to exercise much of the code for the "front end" of *match*. The associated token stream is shown in the table.

Token Stream for [!]\na]a.*(bc|[d – g]) + \n

Original	Token	Value
[!]\na]	NCCL	ID for the class determined by *]*, newline and *a*
a	CHAR	a
.	.	
*	*	
(	(	
b	CHAR	b
c	CHAR	c
|	|	
[d–g]	CCL	ID for the class determined by *d, e, f,* and *g*
)	)	
+	+	
\n	CHAR	the newline character
\0	\0	

Parsing Algorithm for Regular Expressions.   Given the token stream for a regular expression, how is its expression tree constructed? Since alternation (i.e., |) has the lowest precedence of all operators, it is done last. This suggests breaking the regular expression into simpler expressions that are separated by | operators, constructing expression trees for the simpler expressions, then joining the smaller trees together with | nodes. These simpler expressions, called "terms," contain no | operators except inside parentheses. For example *ab|d(b|c)* decomposes into the terms *ab* and *d(b|c)*, so expression trees for those two subexpressions can be constructed, then made the operands of a | node.

Suppose *token* is an *extern* variable that initially contains the first token of a regular expression. Assume we have at our disposal a procedure *term()* that will construct an expression tree for a term, then return a "pointer" to the tree; in doing so, *term()* calls *get_token()* to get new tokens and leaves the variable *token* containing the token just beyond the term. Then, the following procedure constructs an expression tree for an arbitrary regular expression and leaves *token* pointing just beyond the end of the expression.

```
expression()
{
    subtree = term()
    while (token == '|') {
        token = get_token()
        create a tree with a | root and operands subtree
            and term(), and point subtree to that tree
    }
    return(subtree)
}
```

For an example of how *expression()* works, consider the regular expression *ab|d(b|c)*. Initially, we have

$$a \quad b \quad | \quad d \quad (\quad b \quad | \quad c \quad)$$
$$\uparrow$$

where ↑ indicates the value of *token*. The line

$$subtree = term()$$

constructs the expression tree for the first term and repositions *token*:

$$a \quad b \quad | \quad d \quad (\quad b \quad | \quad c \quad)$$
$$\uparrow$$

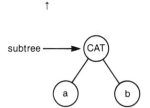

Since *token* is |, *expression()* gets the next token

$$a \quad b \quad | \quad d \quad (\quad b \quad | \quad c \quad)$$
$$\uparrow$$

then calls *term()* again and joins the resulting subtree to the first one with a | node:

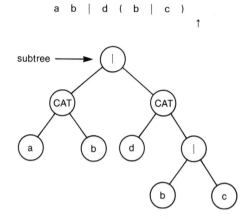

a b | d (b | c)

Now the problem is reduced to designing *term()*, i.e., to parsing regular expressions consisting of a concatenation of "factors" that contain no | or concatenation operations except within parentheses. Thus, a factor must be either a literal or a parenthesized regular expression, followed by any number of * and + operators. For example, the term $xy + (ab|c)$ has the three factors x, $y+$, and $(ab|c)$.

Assume we have a procedure *factor()* that constructs the expression tree for the factor beginning at *token* and leaves *token* pointing just past the end of the factor. Then, the following algorithm parses terms.

```
term()
{
      subtree = factor()
      while (token == '(' || token is a literal)
            create a tree with a CAT root and operands subtree
                  and factor(), and point subtree to that tree
      return(subtree)
}
```

Let us trace the behavior of *term()* on the term $xy + (ab|c)$. Given the initial setting of *token*,

x y + (a b | c)

term() calls *factor()* to parse the leading factor, producing

x y + (a b | c)

Since *token* is a literal, *factor()* is called again, and the subtrees are concatenated to give

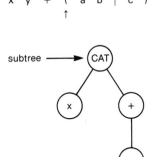

A third call to *factor()* then finishes the job of parsing the term:

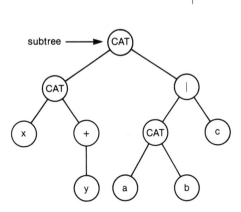

This leaves only the problem of parsing factors, which is accomplished by the following algorithm:

```
factor()
{
    /* get subtree for parenthesized expression or literal */
    if (token == '(') {
        token = get_token()
        subtree = expression()
```

```
    } else {
        create a one-node tree for the token, which must be a literal
        point subtree to that tree
    }
    token = get__token()
    /* add nodes for subsequent unary operators */
    while (token == '*' || token == '+') {
        create a tree with a * or + root and operand subtree,
        point subtree to that tree
        token = get__token()
    }
    return(subtree)
}
```

When applied to the factor $(a|b)+$, *factor()* inspects *token*

```
(   a   |   b   )   +
↑
```

and discovers that it is dealing with a parenthesized expression (as opposed to a literal). It increments *token*

```
(   a   |   b   )   +
    ↑
```

and calls *expression()*, which produces

```
(   a   |   b   )   +
            ↑
```

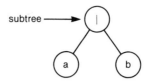

Then *get__token()* is called to scan past the ')':

```
(   a   |   b   )   +
                ↑
```

The *while* loop is executed once, which completes the parsing of the factor:

```
(   a   |   b   )   +
                    ↑
```

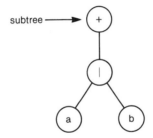

A recursive chain of calls from *expression()* to *term()* to *factor()* to *expression()* to . . . must eventually terminate because *factor()* reduces the length of the pattern (by stripping off a left parenthesis) before calling *expression()*.

Comments on Token.c and Parse.c.   The "front end" of *match* is responsible for parsing the regular expression. It is divided into two files: *token.c*, which breaks the regular expression into tokens, and *parse.c*, which does the parsing per se.

The main entry point for *token.c* is *get__token()*, which returns the type and value of the next token of the regular expression. Most of the complexity comes from the special cases that arise with character classes. For example, a − character signifies a range of values only when certain conditions are met; otherwise, it is a character constant.

The file *parse.c* implements the parsing algorithm described in this section. The parser does not create an explicit data structure to hold the expression tree, but rather performs a sequence of calls to functions *treelit()* and *treeop()* that could easily build the tree. In the next section, those functions are implemented to create a data structure that is more useful than the expression tree.

Along with *token.c* and *parse.c* comes *test.parse.c*, a test harness for checking that they work properly. The harness provides stubs for the routines that record character classes and tree nodes; the stubs do little more than print their arguments in a reasonable format.

EXERCISES

1. Find a regular expression matching the lines of a C program that reference a subscripted variable beginning with the letter *f*.

2. Find a regular expression matching the lines of a C program where *foo* occurs on the left-hand side of an assignment statement. (*Hint:* You do not want lines like

```
foo == thud;
```

which might occur if a *for* statement were spread across several lines.) What can happen if assignment statements span more than one line? What if they have embedded comments?

3. What are the literals of the regular expression *[a[b*c]]*?

4. Does the character pair ''\n'' always mean the same thing to *fastfind* and *match*?

5. How does *token.c* interpret the character class *[g–a]*? What about *[a–c–g]*? Is this reasonable?

6. Trace the complete sequence of procedure calls and the history of *token* when *expression()* is begun as follows:

$$a \quad b \quad | \quad d \quad (\quad b \quad | \quad c \quad)$$
$$\uparrow$$

7. Discuss the problems that would arise in designing a regular-expression pattern-matching program that can match across line boundaries. With this extended capability, the pattern

```
regular[□\n]expression
```

could be matched where one line ends with . . . *regular* and the next begins with *expression . . . .*

```
/*
 * match.h - macros for the match program
 */

#include <stdio.h>

#define PROG_NAME "match"      /* name of this program */

/*
 * To alter the meta-characters for regular expressions (perhaps because the
 * current ones have special meaning for your command interpreter) you can
 * change the following macro definitions.
 */
#define ANY          '.'
#define CCL          '['
#define CCL_END      ']'
#define ESCAPE       '\\'
#define L_GROUP      '('
#define NCCL         '!'
#define OR           '|'
#define PLUS         '+'
#define R_GROUP      ')'
#define RANGE        '-'
#define STAR         '*'

/* symbolic token for characters */
#define CHAR         'a'

/* label for concatenation nodes in the expression tree */
#define CAT          'x'

#define LITERAL(x)   (x == CHAR || x == '.' || x == CCL || x == NCCL)       LITERAL

/* maximum size for the regular expression */
#define EXPRMAX      200
```

```
/* nil value for the finite-state machine */
#define NIL -1

/*
 * token.c - break a regular expression into tokens
 *
 *
 * Entry points:
 *
 *     int get_token(val_ptr)
 *     int *val_ptr;
 *         Return the next token, where the regular expression is divided
 *         into the tokens:
 *               CHAR  CCL  NCCL  .  |  +  *  (  )  '\0'
 *         For tokens CHAR, CCL and NCCL, get_token()'s argument is used
 *         to return an additional value, namely the specific character
 *         for CHAR, or the character class ID for CCL or NCCL.
 *
 *     tokinit(pattern)
 *     char *pattern;
 *         Prepare to break the given regular expression into tokens.
 *
 *
 * External procedure calls:
 *
 *     cclin(c)                          .. file CCLmod.c
 *     char c;
 *         Store c in the current character class.  Character classes
 *         (and negated character classes) are saved by calling cclnew()
 *         to get a character class ID, then storing the characters one
 *         at a time by calling cclin(char).
 *
 *     int cclnew()                      .. file CCLmod.c
 *         Return a character class ID, which is a small integer used
 *         for later identification of the character class.
 */

#include "match.h"

static char *pscan;      /* scans pattern */

/* tokinit - initialize for producing tokens */
tokinit(pattern)
char *pattern;
{
    pscan = pattern;
}

/* get_token - return token (and perhaps value) */
int get_token(val_ptr)
int *val_ptr;
{
    int c;

    /* Replace symbolic meta-characters by the standard ones. */
    switch(c = *pscan++) {
        case ANY:
            c = '.';
            return(c);
        case CCL:
            return(bldccl(val_ptr));
```

tokinit

get_token

```
            case L_GROUP:
                c = '(';
                return(c);
            case OR:
                c = '|';
                return(c);
            case PLUS:
                c = '+';
                return(c);
            case R_GROUP:
                c = ')';
                return(c);
            case STAR:
                c = '*';
                return(c);
            case '\0':
                return (c);
            case ESCAPE:
                if ((c = *pscan++) == '\0')
                    return(c);
                if (c == 'n')
                    c = '\n';
                /* a \ has been stripped from the front of a token --
                 *  fall through to the code for character constants */
            default:
                *val_ptr = c;
                return(CHAR);
        }
    }


/*
 * bldccl - build a character class or negated character class
 *
 * The character class ID is returned through the argument; the function's value
 * is CCL or NCCL.
 */
static int bldccl(id)
int *id;                                                                            bldccl
{
    int token;
    static char digits[] = "0123456789";
    static char lowers[] = "abcdefghijklmnopqrstuvwxyz";
    static char uppers[] = "ABCDEFGHIJKLMNOPQRSTUVWXYZ";
    char ch, *index();

    /* assign an ID to the character class */
    *id = cclnew();
    /* distinguish between a CCL and a NCCL */
    if (*pscan == NCCL) {
        token = NCCL;
        pscan++;
    } else
        token = CCL;
    /* a leading ] should be treated as a character constant */
    if (*pscan == CCL_END)
        cclin(*pscan++);
    /* scan the list of characters */
    for ( ; *pscan != CCL_END && *pscan != '\0'; ++pscan)
        /* look for a newline character, specified as "\n" */
```

```
        if (pscan[0] == ESCAPE && pscan[1] != '\0')
            if ((ch = *++pscan) == 'n')
                cclin('\n');
            else
                cclin(ch);
        else if (pscan[1] != RANGE || pscan[2] == CCL_END)
            cclin(*pscan);
        /* remaining cases handle a - between other characters */
        else if (index(digits,*pscan) > 0 && index(digits,pscan[2]) > 0)
            expand(digits);
        else if (index(lowers,*pscan) > 0 && index(lowers,pscan[2]) > 0)
            expand(lowers);
        else if (index(uppers,*pscan) > 0 && index(uppers,pscan[2]) > 0)
            expand(uppers);
        else
        /* characters around '-' were incomparable; its a plain '-' */
            cclin(*pscan);
    if (*pscan++ != CCL_END)
        fatal("Character class not properly terminated.");
    return(token);
}


/* expand - expand the range of characters pscan[0]-pscan[2] */
static expand(chars)                                                        expand
char *chars;
{
    char *from, *index(), *k, *to;

    from = index(chars, *pscan++);
    to = index(chars, *++pscan);
    for (k = from; k <= to; ++k)
        cclin(*k);
}


/*
* parse.c - parse a regular expression
*
*
* Entry point:
*
*     parse(pattern)
*     char *pattern;
*         Parse the given regular expression.
*
*
* External procedure calls:
*
*     get_token(val_ptr)                      .. file token.c
*     int *val_ptr;
*         Return the next token, where the regular expression is divided
*         into the tokens:
*             CHAR   CCL   NCCL   .   |   +   *   (   )   '\0'
*         For tokens CHAR, CCL and NCCL, get_token()'s argument is used
*         to return an additional value, namely the specific character
*         for CHAR, or the character class ID for CCL or NCCL.
*
*     tokinit(pattern)                        .. file token.c
*     char *pattern;
*         Prepare to break the given regular expression into tokens.
```

```
 *
 *
 *     int treelit(type, value)            .. file FSMmod.c
 *     int type, value;
 *         Create a one-node expression tree for a literal with the given
 *         type and value.  Return a number that uniquely identifies the tree.
 *
 *     int treeop(type, lson, rson)        .. file FSMmod.c
 *     int type, lson, rson;
 *         Create an expression tree with root node of the given type
 *         and whose left and right subtrees have the given identifying
 *         numbers.  Return a number that uniquely identifies the tree.
 */

#include "match.h"

static int token;    /* the current token */
static int value;    /* the value associated with the current token */

/* parse - entry point to build an expression tree */
parse(pattern)
char *pattern;
{
    tokinit(pattern);
    token = get_token(&value);
    expression();
    if (token != '\0')
        fatal("Syntax error in pattern.");
}


/*
 * expression - build the expression tree for the expression beginning at token;
 *         raise token just past the expression.
 */
static int expression()
{
    int subtree;

    /* break expression into terms; get expression trees; join with | nodes */
    subtree = term();
    while (token == '|') {
        token = get_token(&value);
        subtree = treeop((int)'|', subtree, term());
    }
    return(subtree);
}


/*
 * term - build the expression tree for the term beginning at token;
 *         raise token just past the term.
 */
static int term()
{
    int subtree;

    /* break term into factors; get expression trees; join with CAT nodes */
    subtree = factor();
    while (token == '(' || LITERAL(token))
        subtree = treeop(CAT, subtree, factor());
    return(subtree);
}
```

parse

expression

term

```
/*
 * factor - build the expression tree for the factor beginning at token;
 *          raise token just past the factor.
 */
static int factor()                                                             factor
{
    int subtree;

    /* get subtree for parenthesized expression or literal */
    if (token == '(') {
        token = get_token(&value);
        subtree = expression();
        if (token != ')')
            fatal ("Unbalanced parentheses in regular expression.");
    } else if LITERAL(token)
        subtree = treelit(token, value);
    else
        fatal("Syntax error in the regular expression.");
    token = get_token(&value);

    /* add nodes for subsequent unary operators */
    while (token == '*' || token == '+') {
        subtree = treeop(token, subtree, 0);
        token = get_token(&value);
    }
    return(subtree);
}


/*
 * test.parse.c - test harness for the regular expression parser
 *
 * Link it with the object files for token.c, parse.c and lib.c.
 * With the regular expression
 *     [!]\na]a*.(bc|[d-g])+\n
 * it produces:
 *
 *     new ccl given ID 1; its members are:
 *         ] newline a
 *     1:    NCCL      1
 *     2:    CHAR      a
 *     3:    2         *
 *     4:    1         CAT       3
 *     5:    .
 *     6:    4         CAT       5
 *     7:    CHAR      b
 *     8:    CHAR      c
 *     9:    7         CAT       8
 *     new ccl given ID 2; its members are:
 *         d   e   f   g
 *     10:   CCL       2
 *     11:   9         |         10
 *     12:   11        +
 *     13:   6         CAT       12
 *     14:   CHAR      newline
 *     15:   13        CAT       14
 */

#include "match.h"

static int nodes = 0;           /* number of nodes currently in the parse tree */
static int list_ccl = 0;        /* tells if currently listing CCL or NCCL */
```

```
main(argc, argv)                                                             main
int argc;
char *argv[];
{
    if (argc != 2)
        fatal("Needs exactly one argument, the regular expression.");
    parse(argv[1]);
}

/* cclin - stub for the procedure that inserts a character in a character class */
cclin(c)                                                                      cclin
char c;
{
    if (c == '\n')
        printf("newline  ");
    else
        printf("%c  ", c);
}

/* cclnew - stub for the procedure that begins a new character class */
int cclnew()                                                                  cclnew
{
    static int next_ccl = 0;

    printf("new ccl given ID %d; its members are:\n\t", ++next_ccl);
    list_ccl = 1;
    return(next_ccl);
}

/* treelit - stub for the procedure that installs literals in the parse tree */
int treelit(type, value)                                                      treelit
int type, value;
{
    if (list_ccl == 1) {
        list_ccl = 0;
        putchar('\n');
    }
    printf("%d:\t", ++nodes);
    switch(type) {
        case (CHAR):
            printf("CHAR\t");
            if (value == '\n')
                printf("newline\n");
            else
                printf("%c\n", value);
            break;
        case('.'):
            printf(".\n");
            break;
        case(CCL):
            printf("CCL\t%d\n", value);
            break;
        case(NCCL):
            printf("NCCL\t%d\n", value);
            break;
        default:
            fatal("treelit(): Illegal node type.");
    }
    return(nodes);
}
```

```
/* treeop - stub for the procedure that installs operators in the parse tree */
int treeop(type, lson, rson)                                              treeop
int type, lson, rson;
{
    if (list_ccl == 1) {
        list_ccl = 0;
        putchar('\n');
    }
    printf("%d:\t", ++nodes);
    switch(type) {
        case('|'):
            printf("%d\t%c\t%d\n", lson, type, rson);
            break;
        case(CAT):
            printf("%d\tCAT\t%d\n", lson, rson);
            break;
        case('+'):
        case('*'):
            printf("%d\t%c\n", lson, type);
            break;
        default:
            fatal("treeop(): Illegal node type.");
    }
    return(nodes);
}
```

4.3 FINITE-STATE MACHINES

A *finite-state machine* is a highly idealized model of a simple computing device that is closely related to a regular expression. As you will see, the relationship is so intimate that the finite-state machine can be constructed "on the fly" as the expression is parsed; it is unnecessary to explicitly build the expression tree.

Formally, a finite-state machine is a directed graph whose nodes are called *states*. Each state has at most two edges leaving it, and each state is either a *labeled state* that is labeled with a literal, or a *NIL state* that has no label. In addition, each finite-state machine has one state that is designated the *start state*, and one *final state*, which is the only state with no edges leaving it. (In technical terms, these are "nondeterministic" machines with labeled states, as opposed to labeled edges. Several variants of these definitions would have worked about as well.)

A finite-state machine *matches* a string of characters if there is a path from the start state to the final state such that the sequence of labels on states along the path matches the sequence of characters. For example, the strings matched by the finite-state machine

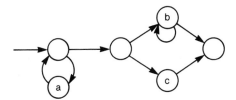

(the tail-less arrow indicates the start state) are the strings consisting of zero or more a's followed by either (i) one or more b's or (ii) a single c. Thus, the machine is *equivalent* to the regular expression $a*(b+|c)$ in the sense of matching the same strings.

Any regular expression is equivalent to a finite-state machine. Indeed, the following systematic process constructs an equivalent machine from an arbitrary regular expression.

Any literal x is equivalent to the finite-state machine:

Moreover, finite-state machines can be constructed from simpler machines by a process that exactly parallels the construction of regular expressions from simpler expressions. In other words, for each of the four ways of building up large regular expressions from small ones, namely concatenation, |, +, and *, there is a parallel method for building up large finite-state machines from small ones. In order to describe the constructions, let the machine M

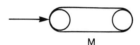

be equivalent to the regular expression R, and let N

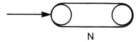

be equivalent to S.

First consider concatenation. A machine equivalent to RS is constructed by merely adding an edge from the final state of M to the start state of N. The start state of the new machine is the start state of M, while the final state of the new machine is the final state of N. The construction can be pictured:

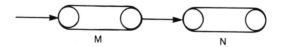

Take a moment to convince yourself that this machine is equivalent to the regular expression obtained by concatenating R and S. First, verify that the constructed graph satisfies the definition of a finite-state machine. (How do you know that no state of the resulting graph has more than two edges leaving it? Is there exactly one dead-end state in the new graph?) Then, verify that a string matches *RS* if and only if it matches the sequence of labels along some start-to-finish path through the new graph. Similar reasoning validates the following constructions for |, +, and * operations.

A machine equivalent to *R|S* can be built from *M* and *N* by adding two NIL states, as follows:

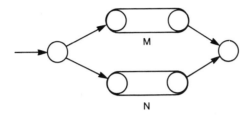

The first NIL state points to the start states of *M* and *N*; it becomes the start state for the new machine. The final states of *M* and *N* are modified to point to the second new NIL state, which becomes the final state for the new machine.

For *R+*, add two NIL states to *M*, as follows.

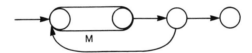

R∗ is the same except for the start state of the new machine:

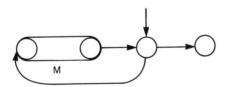

For example, applying this construction to the regular expression *a*∗(b+|c)* produces the following sequence of machines:

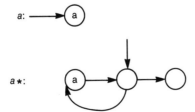

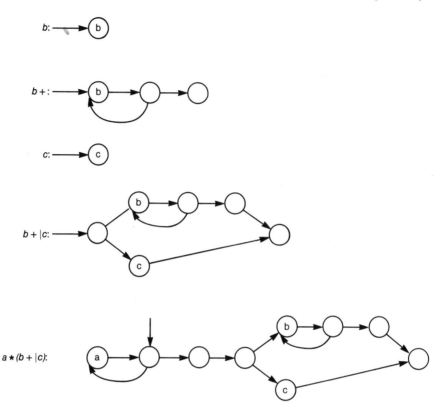

The machines are listed in the same order that *parse.c* calls *treelit()* and *treeop()* while parsing $a*(b+|c)$. *FSMmod.c* follows the above approach and implements *treelit()* and *treeop()* so they construct finite-state machines instead of expression trees. A test driver named *test.fsm.c* is given for testing *FSMmod.c*.

Notice that the finite-state machine constructed by this process bears at least a slight similarity to the expression tree: both are graphs that have one node for each of the expression's literals, plus some other nodes. The similarity ends there, however, since the expression's operators do not label machine states. Instead, the operators are mirrored by the way that the machine's states are connected with edges.

EXERCISES

1. Show that the process described above produces a finite-state machine with no more than twice as many states as there are symbols in the regular expression. How is this fact used in *FSMmod.c*?

2. Modify the process of building a finite-state machine so that fewer NIL states are created. (*Hint:* Compare the first and last machines shown in this section.)

PROGRAMMING ASSIGNMENTS

1. Modify *FSMmod.c* in accordance with your solution to Exercise 2.

```
/*
* FSMmod.c - build and save the finite-state machine
*
*
* Entry points:
*
*     state(i, type_ptr, value_ptr, lson_ptr, rson_ptr)
*     int i, *type_ptr, *value_ptr, *lson_ptr, *rson_ptr;
*         Return the information associated with state i.  For labeled
*         states, the type and value give the literal associated with the
*         state.  For NIL states, the type and value are NIL.  The states
*         adjacent to state i are returned through the last two arguments.
*         The start state is the left son of the pseudo state i = 0.
*
*     int treelit(type, value)
*     int type, value;
*         Create a one-state machine labeled by type and value.  Return
*         the number of the state.
*
*     int treeop(op, left, right)
*     int op, left, right;
*         Apply the construction for op (CAT, |, + or *) to submachines
*         with the given start states.  Return the start state of the new
*         machine.
*
* Implementation:
*
*     States are stored in "parallel" arrays.
*/
#include "match.h"

static int
     last[2*EXPRMAX],      /* final state for machine starting here */
     lson[2*EXPRMAX],      /* first adjacent state or NIL */
     next_state = 0,       /* states are numbered 0, 1, 2, ... */
     rson[2*EXPRMAX],      /* second adjacent state or NIL */
     type[2*EXPRMAX],      /* label (for literals) or NIL */
     value[2*EXPRMAX];     /* literal's value (for a labeled state) */

/* state - return the attributes of a state */
state(i, type_ptr, value_ptr, lson_ptr, rson_ptr)        state
int i, *type_ptr, *value_ptr, *lson_ptr, *rson_ptr;
{
     if (i < 0 || i >= next_state)
          fatal("Impossible state number.");
     *type_ptr = type[i];
     *value_ptr = value[i];
     *lson_ptr = lson[i];
     *rson_ptr = rson[i];
}

/* treelit - build the one-state machine for a literal */
int treelit(typ, val)                                    treelit
int typ, val;
{
```

```
        int start_state;

        if (next_state == 0)      /* initialize the pseudo state */
            make_state(NIL, NIL, NIL, NIL, NIL);
        start_state = next_state;
        make_state(typ, val, NIL, NIL, next_state);
        return(lson[0] = start_state);
}

/* treeop - build the machine for the subtree rooted at an operator node */
int treeop(op, left, right)
int op, left, right;
{
        int start_state;

        switch (op) {
            case CAT:
                /* join the left machine to the right machine */
                start_state = left;
                lson[last[left]] = right;
                last[start_state] = last[right];
                break;
            case '|':
                /* create a state pointing to the two start states */
                start_state = next_state;
                make_state(NIL, NIL, left, right, next_state+1);
                /* point the two final states to a new final state */
                lson[last[left]] = lson[last[right]] = next_state;
                make_state(NIL, NIL, NIL, NIL, NIL);
                break;
            case '+':
            case '*':
                /* create a new state following the old final state */
                start_state = (op == '+') ? left : next_state;
                lson[last[left]] = next_state;
                make_state(NIL, NIL, left, next_state+1, NIL);
                /* create a new final state */
                last[start_state] = next_state;
                make_state(NIL, NIL, NIL, NIL, NIL);
                break;
        }
        return(lson[0] = start_state);
}

/* make_state - create a state with specified attributes */
static make_state(typ, val, left, right, final)
int typ, val, left, right, final;
{
        type[next_state] = typ;
        value[next_state] = val;
        lson[next_state] = left;
        rson[next_state] = right;
        last[next_state++] = final;
}

/*
 * test.fsm.c - test harness for the finite-state machine builder
 *
 * Link it with the object files for parse.c, token.c, FSMmod.c and lib.c .
 * With the regular expression
```

treeop

make__state

```
*    a*.(bc|d)+\n
* it produces:
*
     STATE        TYPE        LEFT        RIGHT
       1:         a           2
       2:         NIL         1           3
       3:         NIL         4
       4:         .           8
       5:         b           6
       6:         c           9
       7:         d           9
       8:         NIL         5           7
       9:         NIL         10
      10:         NIL         8           11
      11:         NIL         12
      12:         newline
     The start state is 2.
     The final state is 12.
*/

#include "match.h"
#define max(x,y)    (x > y) ? x : y                                    max

main(argc, argv)                                                       main
int argc;
char *argv[];
{
    int i, final, lson, max_state, rson, type, value;

    if (argc != 2)
        fatal("Wrong argument count.");
    parse(argv[1]);
    printf("\nSTATE\tTYPE\tLEFT\tRIGHT\n");

    for (i = max_state = 1; i <= max_state; ++i) {
        state(i, &type, &value, &lson, &rson);
        max_state = max(lson, max_state);
        max_state = max(rson, max_state);
        printf("  %d:\t ", i);
        switch (type) {
            case CHAR:
                if (value == '\n')
                    printf("newline");
                else
                    putchar(value);
                break;
            case '.':
                putchar('.');
                break;
            case CCL:
                printf("CCL %d", value);
                break;
            case NCCL:
                printf("NCCL %d", value);
                break;
            case NIL:
                printf("NIL");
                break;
            default:
                fatal("Illegal type of machine state.");
```

```
        }
        if (lson == NIL) {
            putchar('\n');
            final = i;
        } else if (rson == NIL)
            printf("\t    %d\n", lson);
        else
            printf("\t    %d\t    %d\n", lson, rson);
    }
    state(0, &type, &value, &lson, &rson);
    printf("The start state is %d.\n", lson);
    printf("The final state is %d.\n", final);
}

/* cclin - stub for the procedure that inserts a character in a character class */
cclin(c)
char c;
{
    if (c == '\n')
        printf("newline  ");
    else
        printf("%c  ",c);
}

/* cclnew - stub for the procedure that begins a new character class */
int cclnew()
{
    static int next_ccl = 0;

    printf("\nnew ccl given ID %d; its members are:\n\t", ++next_ccl);
    return(next_ccl);
}
```

cclin

cclnew

4.4 MATCHING A REGULAR EXPRESSION

The finite-state machine described in the previous section is the main component of the "compiled pattern" for *match*. This section considers the problem of using the finite-state machine to match text lines.

Given a finite-state machine and a text string, how can we check for a match in a single scan of the string? That is, how do we determine if there is a path from the start state to the final state whose labels "spell out" the string? The best place to start is with an example. The discussion uses the following finite-state machine, which is equivalent to the regular expression

.*ab*a

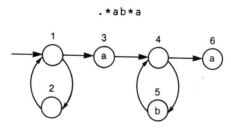

States have been numbered to simplify the discussion.

As the text string is scanned, there will generally be several paths from the start state that match what has been seen so far (i.e., such that the sequence of literals that label states along the path matches the known portion of the string). For example, the following paths match the scanned characters *aa*:

$$1 \rightarrow 3 \rightarrow 4 \rightarrow 6 \text{ (labels } a, a)$$
$$1 \rightarrow 2 \rightarrow 1 \rightarrow 3 \text{ (labels } '.', a)$$
$$1 \rightarrow 2 \rightarrow 1 \rightarrow 2 \text{ (labels } '.', '.')$$

After seeing *aa*, we must retain information about all three paths. If it turns out that *aa* is the complete input string, then the first path is needed to verify that the machine matches the string. On the other hand, if the input string is *aaba*, then the second path is the one that extends to a matching path (by adding the segment $\rightarrow 4 \rightarrow 5 \rightarrow 4 \rightarrow 6$). Detection of the match with *aacaa* requires extension of the third path.

It is not necessary to retain entire matching paths; only their last state must be remembered. In other words, as a text string is scanned, we will remember the set S consisting of all labeled states lying at the end of a path that matches the known portion of the text string. In our example, the state set $S = \{2, 3, 6\}$ is retained after scanning *aa*.

When the next input character is seen, S can be updated as follows. First, find the set T of all labeled states that can be reached from a state in S along a path (with at least one edge) that does not cross any labeled states. Then, S is replaced by the set of states in T whose labels match the new character. In our example with $S = \{2, 3, 6\}$, the set T contains the following states:

2, because of the path $2 \rightarrow 1 \rightarrow 2$,

3, because of the path $2 \rightarrow 1 \rightarrow 3$,

5, because of the path $3 \rightarrow 4 \rightarrow 5$,

6, because of the path $3 \rightarrow 4 \rightarrow 6$.

If the next input character is c, then S would be updated to $\{2\}$, since state 2 is the only member of T whose label matches c.

The following helps formulate the general algorithm. Suppose that a "pseudostate" numbered 0 is added to the finite-state machine, with a single edge leading from state 0 to the machine's start state. (*FSMmod.c* is implemented this way.) The *initial state set* equals $\{0\}$. Every other *state set* is a collection of labeled states. A state is *reachable* from a state set if there is a (nonvoid) path from a state in the set to the state in question, where the path does not cross any labeled states. A state set is *final* if either (i) it contains the final state of the finite-state machine or (ii) the final state is unlabeled and is reachable from the set. While finite-state machines, as defined in Section 4.3, can have only one final state, there are generally several final state sets. In the diagram at the start of this section, the final state sets are just the sets containing state 6.

With these definitions, the pattern-matching algorithm can be stated:

```
S = {0}
for each input character c {
    T = set of labeled states that are reachable from S
    S = set of states in T whose labels match c
}
if S is final
    the string matches
else
    the string does not match
```

Figure 4.4.1 Regular-expression matching algorithm.

The following table traces the algorithm for the above finite-state machine and input string *aacaa*.

Character	T	S
		{0}
a	{2, 3}	{2, 3}
a	{2, 3, 5, 6}	{2, 3, 6}
c	{2, 3, 5, 6}	{2}
a	{2, 3}	{2, 3}
a	{2, 3, 5, 6}	{2, 3, 6}

Gaining Efficiency.   The pattern matching algorithm given above is rather slow; each input character causes S to be laboriously recomputed. A straightforward implementation might run twenty times slower than *find* (Section 1.1) when matching keywords. (This claim is based on an experiment.)

Faster construction of the finite-state machine would not improve efficiency significantly. In a typical use, the regular expression is unlikely to exceed, say, 50 characters in length, so only an amazingly slow way of building the machine would take an appreciable amount of time. Any gains in efficiency must come from the text-scanning phase, where it is not unusual to scan 100,000 characters.

The above algorithm performs a tremendous amount of redundant computation. This redundancy is apparent even in the above table that traces the scanning of *aacaa*. Twice in that computation, S equals {2, 3} and the scanned text character is a. The redundant computation occurs when the algorithm recomputes $T = \{2, 3, 5, 6\}$ and $S = \{2, 3, 6\}$.

The following simple idea eliminates the redundant computation and makes pattern matching much more efficient. Each time the algorithm computes a new set S' from a given set S and input character c the result is saved. The next time the algorithm faces the same combination of a set S and input character, it merely looks up the value S' in a table. To make this process efficient, a number is assigned to each set S that arises during the computation. S_0 (the set numbered 0) is always $\{0\}$, and the other sets S are assigned the numbers 1, 2, 3, . . . in order of their first appearance. The number assigned to a set S is its S_number. Information about how to update S for a given input character c is saved in a two-dimensional array $new\_S[][]$ that is indexed by S_number and input character; the array entry contains the S_number of the resulting set S.

At a typical point in the computation, the current state set is S_{nbr_S} (where nbr_S is a variable that holds the S_number of the current state set); let the scanned text character be a. If $new\_S[nbr\_S]['a']$ is defined, then nbr_S is updated to $new\_S[nbr\_S]['a']$ and the next input character is considered. If $new\_S[nbr\_S]['a']$ is not defined (this is the first encounter with this combination of state set and scanned character), then the program computes the next state set "by hand." First, the states in T_{nbr_S} are retrieved (they will have been computed when S_{nbr_S} was first encountered). The states in T_{nbr_S} whose labels match a are collected to form the new state set S. The S_number of S is determined and saved as $new\_S[nbr\_S]['a']$, then nbr_S is set to that number and the next input character is considered.

The following process determines the S_number of the new set S when S is "computed by hand." First, S is compared with the state sets that have already been assigned S_numbers. If S equals one of those sets, then the old S_number is used. Otherwise, the next available number is assigned to S and the algorithm computes and saves (i) the corresponding set T (of labeled states that are reachable from S) and (ii) a bit telling whether or not S is final.

In summary, the improved algorithm is

```
record that S₀ = {0}; compute T₀ and whether S₀ is final
nbr__S = 0
for each input character c
    if new__S[nbr__S][c] is defined
        nbr__S = new__S[nbr__S][c]
    else {
        /* this is a new combination of S and c */
        S = set of states in T_nbr_s whose labels match c
        /* save the results of all this work */
        nbr__S = new__S[nbr__S][c] = the S__number assigned to S
        ( if S has not been assigned an S__number this involves:
            1. assigning S the next available number
            2. computing the corresponding set T
            3. computing whether S is final
        )
    }
if nbr__S is the S__number of a final state set
    the string matches
else
    the string does not match
```

Figure 4.4.2 Improved pattern-matching algorithm.

For an example, return to the finite-state machine pictured at the start of this section and the input string *aacaa*. Before any text is scanned, the following information about the initial state set is recorded:

$$S_0 = \{0\}$$
$$T_0 = \{2, 3\}$$
S_0 is not final.

When the first input character is scanned:

        state set: S_0;   input: a   a   c   a   a
                                    ↑

new_S[0]['a'] is undefined, and hence is computed. This involves determining which states in T_0 have labels that match *a*. Since both labels match, the new S is $\{2, 3\}$. This is the first appearance of a set S containing just these states, so S is assigned the next available S_number, and the following information is recorded.

$$S_1 = \{2, 3\}$$
$$T_1 = \{2, 3, 5, 6\}$$
S_1 is not final.
new_ S[0]['a'] = 1

This gives the first known entry for the *transition function new_S[][]*. In informal terms, the entry says that if you are in state set 0 and reading the character '*a*', then go to state set 1. The same rule can be pictured as the *transition diagram*:

When the next character is inspected

        state set: S_1;   input: a   a   c   a   a
                                ↑

and *new_S[1]['a']* is seen to be undefined, the following information is computed and saved:

$$S_2 = \{2, 3, 6\}$$
$$T_2 = \{2, 3, 5, 6\}$$
S_2 is final.
new_ S[1]['a'] = 2

This adds to the transition diagram:

Double circles signify a final state set.

The next input character

state set: S_2; input: a   a   c   a   a
↑

leads to the following discoveries.

$S_3 = \{2\}$
$T_3 = \{2, 3\}$
S_3 is not final.
new__S[2]['c'] = 3

This adds a new node and an edge to the growing transition diagram:

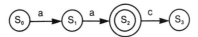

The payoff for our efforts begins with the next input character:

state set: S_3; input: a   a   c   a   a
↑

Since *new__S[3]['a']* is undefined, the next set S is computed and found to equal $\{2, 3\}$. But $S = S_1$, so the only new information that needs to be recorded is

new__S[3]['a'] = 1

In terms of the transition diagram, the new information gives an additional edge:

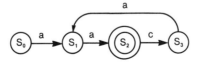

With the input character

state set: S_1; input: a   a   c   a   a
↑

the algorithm finds that *new__S[1]['a']* = 2, so this one array reference completes the processing of the input character. Finally, with

state set: S_2; input: a   a   c   a   a
↑

the algorithm sees that S_2 was earlier found to be final, and reports a match.

On typical pattern matching problems, with a modest-sized regular expression and thousands (or even hundreds of thousands) of input characters, the vast majority of input characters are processed with just a reference to *new__S[][]*. For typical keywords searches, *match* takes only 35–40% more execution time than the simple *find* program of Section 1.1.

Comments on Match.c, CCLmod.c, and Smod.c.   The improved pattern matching algorithm is implemented in *match.c*. Space is saved by declaring *new__S[][]* to be an array of type *char*. Of course, this drastically limits the legal S__numbers; the limit 127 is hardwired into *Smod.c*.

Match does not require that the entire line match the pattern, but only that a portion match. For example,

```
match abc
```

will print the line *xabcy* which does not, itself, match the pattern. To do this, *match* adds the three characters *.*(* to the front of the original pattern and adds *).** to the rear. The augmented pattern matches the entire line if and only if the original pattern matches a portion of the line.

The procedure specifications listed under "External procedure calls:" in the leading comments of *token.c* and *match.c* define the requirements for the two remaining data structures:

1. the module to handle character classes (file *CCLmod.c*)
2. the module to convert between sets *S* and S__numbers (file *Smod.c*)

CCLmod.c needs the access functions:

cclin()   store a character in a character class
cclmem() tell if a character is in a character class
cclnew()   prepare to record a character class; return the class ID

A large *char* array is used to implement these functions. The ID of a class is the first subscript of consecutive array entries holding the characters in the class.

Suppose there are two character classes, *[abc]* and *[!de]*. The classes would be recorded by the calls

```
cclnew();
cclin('a');
cclin('b');
cclin('c');
cclnew();
cclin('d');
cclin('e');
```

As a result of these calls, the array would contain

$$subscript: \quad 1 \quad 2 \quad 3 \quad 4 \quad 5 \quad 6 \quad 7$$

$$entry: \qquad a \quad b \quad c \quad \backslash 0 \quad d \quad e \quad \backslash 0$$

and the class ID's would be 1 and 5.

The required access functions for *Smod.c* are

final()	tell if a set S is final
S_number()	return the S_number of a set of states
T_first()	return a pointer to the list of states in a set T

The implementation is similar to *CCLmod.c*. Again, a long array holds lists of entries. This time, however, the entries have type *int* and lists are separated by −1.

In the example considered above, the information

$$S_0 = \{0\}$$
$$T_0 = \{2, 3\}$$
$$S_1 = \{2, 3\}$$
$$T_1 = \{2, 3, 5, 6\}$$

would be recorded by:

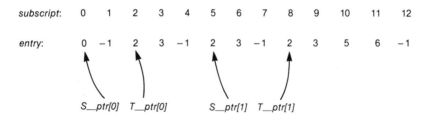

The recursive procedure *reachable()* in *Smod.c* determines T by performing a depth-first search (Section 2.2) of the finite-state machine from each state in S. To avoid redundant computation (including infinite looping caused by cycles in the graph), states are "marked" (see Modification 2 in Section 2.2) by placing them in a list of reached states.

EXERCISES

1. Construct the sequence of state sets S and T that arise from the pattern

$$.*(c|ab)+a$$

and input line *abcdabca*.

2. Can a finite-state machine have two final state sets that are disjoint (don't share a state)?

3. Show that a finite-state machine constructed as in Section 4.3 can have a cycle (nonvoid path that starts and ends at the same state) containing only unlabeled states. Explain in detail how *Smod.c* avoids becoming stuck in an infinite loop.

4. Is there any point in checking whether the set *S* has become empty? Explain.

PROGRAMMING ASSIGNMENTS

1. Add the *?* operator, denoting 0 or 1 occurrence. Thus *ab?c* is matched by *ac* and *abc*, but not by *abbc*.

2. The given version of *match* quits if the number of sets *S* exceeds 128, or if twice that number plus the total number of states in the sets *S* and *T* exceeds *LIMIT*. (The tests are performed by procedures *S_number()* and *save_state()* in *Smod.c*.) Modify *match* so that it can keep going even if it cannot allocate an S_number. (*Hint:* Compute *S* by hand as long as necessary. When an *S* that has already been assigned an S_number is encountered, or when the end of the input line is reached, go back to the table-lookup approach.)

3. Instrument *match* with code to determine
   (a) the number of state sets *S* that are generated,
   (b) the number of entries that are computed for the array *new_S[][]*, and
   (c) the average number of states in a state set *S*.
   Gather statistics for a variety of regular expressions and bodies of text. Do the results suggest that bubble sort (*sort_states()* in *Smod.c*) should be replaced by a more efficient procedure? Is it worthwhile to avoid saving a separate copy of *T* if it equals an earlier *S* or *T*?

4. The classical theory of regular expressions suggests the alternative of computing all potentially relevant entries of *new_S[][]*, then scanning the text without interruption. Modify *match.c* to implement this approach and gather statistics giving
   (a) the number of state sets *S* that are generated, and
   (b) the number of entries that are computed for the array *new_S[][]*.
   Compare the results with the statistics gathered for Programming Assignment 3, and compare execution times of the two approaches.

   The new approach begins by parsing the regular expression and determining the entries *new_S[0][x]* for all possible values *x*. This process will generate new state sets

$$S_1, S_2, \ldots, S_{S\_max}$$

and the procedure can be applied to compute *new_S[i][x]* for $i = 1, 2, \ldots$ and for all possible values *x*. Eventually, *i* will catch up with *S_max*.

   In the vocabulary of regular expression theory, *new_S[][]* gives the *transition function* for a *deterministic finite automaton* that is equivalent to the *nondeterministic finite automaton* implemented by *FSMmod.c*. For a thorough discussion of these ideas, see Chapter 3 of *Compilers: Principles, Techniques and Tools* by Alfred V. Aho, Ravi Sethi and Jeffrey D. Ullman (Addison-Wesley, 1986).

```
/*
 * match - print lines that match a regular expression
 *
 *
 * Program description:
 *
 *     A command line has the form
 *         match [-m] [-n] pat [file1] [file2] ...
 *     where pat is any regular expression.  If no file is named, then standard
 *     input is read.  If more than one file is named, then each printed line
 *     is preceded by its file's name.  The -m flag asks for lines that don't
 *     match the pattern.  The -n flag asks that line numbers be printed.
 *
 *
 * Source files:
 *
 *     CCLmod.c        - store expanded character classes
 *     FSMmod.c        - build and save the finite-state machine
 *     lib.c           - a library of C procedures
 *     match.c         - this file; main program and scanning procedure
 *     match.h         - macros for the match program
 *     parse.c         - parse a regular expression
 *     Smod.c          - convert between sets S and S_numbers
 *     token.c         - break the regular expression into tokens
 *
 *
 * Portability:
 *
 *     If the command interpreter attaches a special meaning to any of the
 *     regular expression meta-characters
 *         \ . [ ] !--| + * ( )
 *     then it may be desirable to employ other characters.  The appropriate
 *     macros in match.h can be redefined.
 *
 *
 * External procedure calls:
 *
 *     cclmem(c, class_id)                          .. file CCLmod.c
 *     char c;
 *     int class_id;
 *         Tell if c is in the identified character class.
 *
 *     int final(S_nbr)                             .. file Smod.c
 *     int S_nbr;
 *         Tell if the set S with the indicated S_number is final.
 *
 *     parse(pattern)                               .. file parse.c
 *     char *pattern;
 *         Parse the given regular expression and build an equivalent
 *         finite-state machine.
 *
 *
 *     int S_number(S)                              .. file Smod.c
 *     int S[];
 *         Return the S_number of the given list of states.  The list
 *         must be ended with -1.  If this is the first encounter with S,
 *         then (i) S is stored and a new S_number is allocated for it,
 *         (ii) the set T of labeled states that are reachable from S is
 *         found and stored, and (iii) it is determined whether S is final.
```

```
*
*      state(i, type_ptr, val_ptr, lson_ptr, rson_ptr)      .. file FSMmod.c
*      int i, *type_ptr, *val_ptr, *lson_ptr, *rson_ptr;
*          Return the information associated with state i.  For labeled
*          states, the type and value give the literal associated with the
*          state.  For NIL states, the type and value are NIL.  The states
*          adjacent to state i are returned through the last two arguments.
*          The start state is the left son of the pseudo state i = 0.
*
*      int *T_first(S_nbr)                                  .. file Smod.c
*      int S_nbr;
*          Return a pointer to array of labeled states that are reachable
*          from the designated S. The list is ended with -1.
*/

#include "match.h"
#define MAXTEXT    200
#define YES        1
#define NO         0

static int mflag = NO, nfiles, nflag = NO;

main(argc, argv)                                                        main
int argc;
char *argv[];
{
     static int S[] = {0, -1};
     int i, j;
     char pattern[EXPRMAX];

     savename(PROG_NAME);     /* for error messages */

     for (i = 1; i < argc && argv[i][0] == '-'; ++i)
          for (j = 1; argv[i][j] != '\0'; ++j)
               switch (argv[i][j]) {
                    case 'm':
                         mflag = YES;
                         break;
                    case 'n':
                         nflag = YES;
                         break;
                    default:
                         fatal("Permissible flags are m and n.");
               }
     if (i == argc)
          fatal("No pattern was specified.");
     /* augment pattern so it matches entire lines */
     if (strlen(argv[i]) > EXPRMAX-7)
          fatal("The regular expression is too long.");
     sprintf(pattern,"%c%c%c%s%c%c%c", ANY, STAR, L_GROUP, argv[i],
          R_GROUP, ANY, STAR);
     /* parse the pattern; build the finite-state machine */
     parse(pattern);
     /* record the initial state set */
     S_number(S);
     if ((nfiles = argc - i - 1) == 0)
          scan("");
     else
          while (++i < argc)
               scan(argv[i]);
     exit(0);
}
```

```
/* scan - find lines in file that match the pattern */
static scan(file)                                                          scan
char *file;
{
    FILE *fp, *ckopen();
    int c, i, line_number = 0, nbr_S, S[EXPRMAX], *T_first(), *T_ptr, try;
    char *fgets(), text[MAXTEXT+1], *p;

    /* static variables are guaranteed to start off as 0 */
    static char new_S[128][128];

    if (nfiles == 0)
        fp = stdin;
    else
        fp = ckopen(file, "r");

    text[0] = '\n';      /* implicit newline at the start of each input line */

    while (fgets(text+1, MAXTEXT, fp) != NULL) {
        ++line_number;
        /* begin scanning in the initial state set */
        nbr_S = 0;
        /* loop over the input characters c */
        for (p = text; *p != '\0'; ++p) {
            c = *p & 0177;        /* thwart sign-extension */
            if ((try = new_S[nbr_S][c]) > 0)
                nbr_S = try;
            else {
                /*
                 * This is a new combination of S and c.
                 * For T = set of states that follow a state in S,
                 * compute S = set of states in T that match c.
                 */
                for (i = 0, T_ptr = T_first(nbr_S); *T_ptr != -1; ++T_ptr)
                    if (matches(c, *T_ptr))
                        S[i++] = *T_ptr;
                S[i] = -1;
                /* save the results of all this work */
                nbr_S = new_S[nbr_S][c] = S_number(S);
            }
        }

        if (final(nbr_S) != mflag) {
            if (nfiles > 1)
                printf("%s: ",file);
            if (nflag == YES)
                printf("%d: ", line_number);
            fputs(text+1, stdout);
        }
    }
    if (fp != stdin)
        fclose(fp);
}

/* matches - tell if character c matches the label on state s */
static matches(c, s)                                                       matches
int c, s;
{
    int junk1, junk2, type, value;

    state(s, &type, &value, &junk1, &junk2);
    switch (type) {
```

```
            case '.':
                return (1);
            case CHAR:
                return (c == value);
            case CCL:
                return ( cclmem((char)c, value) );
            case NCCL:
                return ( !cclmem((char)c, value) );
            default:
                fatal("matches(): Cannot happen.");
    }
}


/*
 * CCLmod.c - store expanded character classes
 *
 *
 * Entry points:
 *
 *     cclin(c)
 *     char c;
 *         Store c in the current character class.  Character classes
 *         (and negated character classes) are saved by calling cclnew()
 *         to get a character class ID, then storing the characters one
 *         at a time by calling cclin(char).
 *
 *     int cclmem(c, class_id)
 *     char c;
 *     int class_id;
 *         Tell if c is in the identified character class.
 *
 *     int cclnew()
 *         Prepare to record a character class; return the class ID.
 *
 *
 * Implementation:
 *
 *     Characters are stored in a single array.  Each class is terminated by
 *     the null character.
 */

#define CCLMAX 500              /* limits total sizes of character classes */

static int ccl_next = 0;       /* subscript of next free location */
static char chars[CCLMAX];     /* holds the stored characters */

/* cclin - record a member of the current character class */
cclin(c)
char c;
{
    if (ccl_next >= CCLMAX - 1)       /* -1 for final null character */
        fatal("Too many characters in character classes.");
    chars[ccl_next++] = c;
}


/* cclmem - tell if a character is in the identified character class */
cclmem(c, id)
char c;
int id;
{
```
cclin

cclmem

```
        while (chars[id] != '\0')
            if (chars[id++] == c)
                return(1);
        return(0);
}


/* cclnew - return the subscript of the next free location (= ID of class) */
cclnew()                                                                            cclnew
{
        return(++ccl_next);        /* skip null character */
}


/*
 * Smod.c - convert between sets S and S_numbers
 *
 *
 * Entry points:
 *
 *      int final(S_nbr)
 *      int S_nbr;
 *          Tell if the set S with the indicated S_number is final.
 *
 *      int S_number(S)
 *      int S[];
 *          Return the S_number of the given list of states.  The list must
 *          be ended with -1.  If this is the first encounter with S, then
 *          (i) S is stored and a new S_number is allocated for it, (ii) the
 *          set T of labeled states that are reachable from S is found and
 *          stored, and (iii) it is determined whether S is final.
 *
 *      int *T_first(S_nbr)
 *      int S_nbr;
 *          Return a pointer to array of labeled states that are reachable
 *          from the designated S. The list is ended with -1.
 *
 *
 * Implementation:
 *
 *      The members of sets S and T are stored in the array entry[]. Each list
 *      of states is ended with -1.
 */

#include "match.h"
#define LIMIT 2000                 /* limits total sizes of sets S and T */

static int entry[LIMIT];           /* entries of sets S and T; -1 = end */
static int is_final[128];          /* tell if the i-th S is final */
static int *next_loc = entry;      /* next free location for storing a set S or T */
static int next_S = 0;             /* next free S_number */
static int R[2*EXPRMAX];           /* holds states reachable from the current S */
static int *R_next;                /* points to next free position in R */
static int *S_start[128];          /* points to the first state in the i-th S */
static int *T_start[128];          /* points to the first state in the i-th T */

/* final - tell whether S contains a final state */
int final(S_nbr)                                                                    final
int S_nbr;
{
        return(is_final[S_nbr]);
}
```

```
/* S_number - convert a list of states into an S_number */
int S_number(S)                                                          S_number
int *S;
{
    int nbr, *S_copy;

    /* make a copy of S */
    S_copy = next_loc;
    do
        save_state(*S);
    while (*S++ != -1);

    /* sort the states to simplify checking sets for equality */
    sort_states(S_copy);

    /* search sequentially through the allocated S_numbers */
    for (nbr = 0; nbr < next_S; ++nbr)
        if (same_states(S_copy, S_start[nbr])) {
            /* found S; reset next_loc to discard the copy */
            next_loc = S_copy;
            return(nbr);
        }

    /* search failed; assign a new S_number, compute T and is_final[] */
    if (next_S >= 128)
        fatal("Too many sets of states.");
    S_start[next_S] = S_copy;
    T_start[next_S] = next_loc;
    make_T(S_start[next_S]);
    return(next_S++);
}

/* T_first - convert an S_number into the associated set T */
int *T_first(S_nbr)                                                      T_first
int S_nbr;
{
    return (T_start[S_nbr]);
}

/*
 * make_T - compute T and is_final[] for the state set S
 *
 * T is the set of labeled states that are reachable from S (that is, the
 * states that can be reached from a state in S by a non-void path that
 * crosses only NIL nodes).  S is final if either (i) S contains a state that
 * has only NIL edges out of it or (ii) there is a NIL state that is reachable
 * from S and which has only NIL edges out of it.
 */
static make_T(S)                                                         make_T
int S[];
{
    int lson, rson, type, value;

    R_next = R;     /* empty the list of reached states */

    for ( ; *S != -1; ++S) {
        state(*S, &type, &value, &lson, &rson);
        if (lson == NIL && rson == NIL)
            /* condition (i) for S to be final */
            is_final[next_S] = 1;
```

```
                reachable(lson);
                reachable(rson);
        }
        save_state(-1);
}

/* reachable - process a state that is reachable from S */
static reachable(sta)
int sta;
{
        int lson, *r, rson, type, value;

        if (sta == NIL)
                return;
        /* avoid redundant computation; check if state was reached earlier */
        for (r = R; r < R_next; ++r)
                if (*r == sta)
                        return;

        /* mark state as reached and process it */
        *R_next++ = sta;
        state(sta, &type, &value, &lson, &rson);

        /* if the state is a NIL state ... */
        if (type == NIL) {
                if (lson == NIL && rson == NIL)
                        /* condition (ii) for S to be final */
                        is_final[next_S] = 1;
                /* ... then its offspring are reachable */
                reachable(lson);
                reachable(rson);
        } else    /* its a labeled state, so its in T */
                save_state(sta);
}

/* sort_states - bubble sort the states in S */
static sort_states(S)
int S[];
{
        int i, j, temp;

        for (i = 0; S[i] != -1; ++i)
                for (j = i+1; S[j] != -1; ++j)
                        if (S[i] > S[j]) {
                                temp = S[i];
                                S[i] = S[j];
                                S[j] = temp;
                        }
}

/* same_states - check for identity of two lists of states */
static int same_states(s, t)
int *s, *t;
{
        for ( ; *s == *t; ++s, ++t)
                if (*s == -1)
                        return(1);
        return(0);
}
```

reachable

sort_states

same_states

```
/* save_state - save a state; die if no room is left */
static save_state(state)
int state;
{
    if (next_loc - entry >= LIMIT)
        fatal("Too many states.");
    *next_loc++ = state;
}
```

save__state

5

A SCREEN EDITOR

Interactive text editors may be the most popular software tools. Many users spend most of their computing time editing either documents or program source files.

This chapter describes a "screen editor," one type of interactive text editor. An explanation of the chapter's (and editor's) overall structure requires an introduction to the editor's "screen module."

Types of Editors. Several generations of text editors have appeared in response to changing technology for computer terminals. The earliest interactive editors, often called *line editors*, were designed for hard-copy, typewriter-like terminals operating at transmission rates near 10 characters per second. Inability to replace a printed character and slow transmissions meant that modified lines of text might not be automatically displayed. Line editors are still appropriate for many editing tasks where extensive visual feedback is undesirable, such as making widespread changes with a packaged script of editor commands.

The introduction of video terminals prompted a new breed of editors, often called *screen editors*, *visual editors*, or *display editors*, which automatically present a full screen of text. The user presses keys to move the cursor to a position where, for example, characters are deleted using other keys. At all times, the screen accurately pictures the displayed portion of the file.

Some recent editing systems are operated with only intermittent use of the keyboard. Instead, a mouse, joystick, or even a touch-sensitive screen is used to select an operation from a menu and to indicate where text should be modified.

Structure of Screen Editors. Many screen editors, including the one described in this chapter, have the general structure shown in Fig. 5.1.

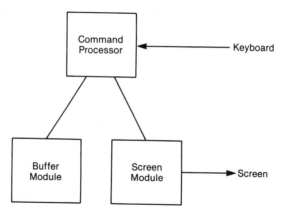

Figure 5.1 Common architecture for screen editors.

The file being edited is copied to the editor's *buffer*, a work area where the copy can be modified without disturbing the original file. The *command processor* then reads edit commands from the keyboard and modifies the buffer's contents accordingly. On command, the editor can copy the buffer's contents to the file.

The *buffer module* supports such operations as inserting, retrieving, and deleting buffer lines. Use of abstract data types can hide such details as whether text lines are stored in main memory or in a temporary file.

The *screen module* maintains the correspondence between the screen image and the edited text. Even when typed characters are being inserted in the buffer, the editor must explicitly print the characters on the screen. (Normally, the operating system echoes each typed character on the screen, but the echoing is turned off during editing so that the text of edit commands does not garble the displayed image of the buffer.)

Independence of the Screen Module.   One natural design for the command processor can be summarized:

```
repeat {
        read a command from the keyboard
        modify the buffer according to the command
        update the screen according to the command
    }
```

The command processor can access the buffer through functions that insert lines, delete lines, etc., and can access the screen through functions that directly alter the displayed characters. Indeed, many screen editors have been built this way.

The design used for *s*, the editor described in this chapter, detaches the screen module from the command processor. Code in the command processor simply makes the appropriate buffer modifications, then calls the screen module:

```
repeat {
    read a command from the keyboard
    modify the buffer according to the command
    call the screen module
}
```

Acting without guidance from the command processor, the screen module compares its record of the current screen contents with the contents of the buffer, determines the difference, and computes a near-optimal set of screen-modification commands.

Use of an autonomous screen module greatly simplifies the command processor. Detailed code to update the screen according to a command is often substantially longer and more complex than the buffer-modifying code. With this design, the command processor's screen-updating code is merely a procedure call, so the complexity is quarantined to the screen module.

Consider the code that inserts a character. Handling the buffer is trivial: fetch the indicated line, insert the new character, and replace the old buffer line by the new one. But, what is involved in updating the screen? In particular:

- Suppose the line contains a tab character after the point of insertion. The character after the tab is displayed at the first "tab stop" (typically columns 9, 17, 25, . . . in increments of 8) that separates it by at least one space from the character before the tab. Thus, the seven-character string

$$12345<tab>x$$

  is displayed with the x in column 9:

$$12345<space><space><space>x$$

  If the first tab after the insertion point is represented by more than one $<space>$ character on the screen, then it absorbs the shift, i.e., characters following the tab do not move. For example, when y is inserted after 3 in

$$12345<tab>x$$

  the x remains in column 9:

$$123y45<space><space>x$$

  On the other hand, if the tab is originally represented by a single $<space>$, then insertion shifts characters after the tab one "tab width" (usually eight columns).

- Suppose the modified line no longer fits in one screen row and the editor folds long lines onto several screen rows to make the entire line visible. (This chapter systematically distinguishes between a buffer *line* and screen *row* because s performs line folding.) Rows below the current row are shifted down and the last character of the current line is placed at the start of the next row.

Clearly, it is desirable if new edit commands can be added (or old ones modified) without considering such details. This is accomplished by having an autonomous screen module. Code to process commands is substantially shorter and simpler than if it depended on how text is displayed.

Detaching the screen module also benefits program development by allowing useful pieces of the command processor to be tested early. Simple throw-away buffer and screen modules can be used to test the command processor. (If nothing else, the throw-away screen module can replace all characters on the screen after every command.) Edit commands can be tested on files not containing tab characters or long lines. If the command processor does not implicitly assume that lines are tab free and short, then it is easily integrated with the "production" buffer and screen modules.

Though an independent screen module seems quite natural in hindsight, it was my third approach. The first attempt constructed a line editor like those appropriate for hard-copy terminals. The screen editor was built as a front end to the line editor. In other words, the screen editor translated the user's commands into line editor commands and managed the screen. This design is discussed by Christopher Fraser in "A compact, portable CRT-based text editor" (*Software—Practice and Experience*, Feb. 1979, pp. 121–125).

The second attempt built more and more powerful "virtual terminals" on top of the physical terminal. The first layer of procedures hid terminal idiosyncrasies and provided a reasonable set of access functions like *clear_row()*, *delete_char()*, etc. The next layer remembered what characters were on the screen. The next worked with buffer lines instead of screen rows; a "delete line" call with a long line might remove several screen rows. And so on.

As you can see, a number of different editor designs are possible. The one used for s leads to relatively clean and understandable code.

Screen-Updating Algorithms.   The screen module's independence from the command processor isolates almost all details about screen updating to one place. ("Almost" is needed in this statement because it proved advantageous to make the buffer module do a little of the work.) Screen updating is complicated; the above observations about inserting before a tab character or in a long line hint at the complexity. A complete discussion involves issues not encountered elsewhere in the book, and some background material is needed to expose the depth of the problems. There are two classes of concerns: high-level, algorithmic issues and low-level, terminal-specific problems.

At an algorithmic level, screen updating is reminiscent of file comparison (Chapter 3). The current screen contents must be converted to the desired screen, rather than converting one text file to another. As illustrated by Sections 3.1 and 3.2, the approach depends strongly on the repertoire of instructions that can be applied.

With modern video terminals, the screen-updating algorithm can generally utilize the following screen instructions. Each screen operation is performed by sending a particular short byte sequence to the terminal.

- *Clear a row.* The characters under and to the right of the cursor are deleted from the screen. Characters to the left and in other rows are unaffected.
- *Delete a character.* The character under the cursor is deleted. Characters to the right are shifted left, creating a blank character at the right end of the row.
- *Delete a row.* The current row is deleted from the screen. Later rows are shifted up, creating a blank row at the bottom of the screen.
- *Insert a character.* A character is inserted at the cursor's location. To make room for the new character, characters are shifted right one position. The character shifted past the right margin of the screen disappears from view.
- *Insert a row.* A blank row is inserted at the cursor's location. Rows previously at and below that position are shifted down, and the bottom row disappears from view.
- *Move the cursor.* The cursor can be moved to an arbitrary row and column of the screen.
- *Overwrite a character.* A given character is displayed at the cursor's location, replacing the character previously at that location.

Speed of data transmission dictates that these capabilities be used wisely. Normally, data travels from the editor to the screen at between 100 and 1000 characters per second (e.g., 1200 or 9600 baud), which is orders of magnitude slower than the editor's computing speed. Thus, it is worthwhile for the screen module to compute a minimal, or near minimal, set of screen-update commands, even if a complex algorithm is required.

However, the screen-update algorithm must be reasonably efficient (in terms of its execution speed, not just the number of bytes it sends to the screen). The desirable properties of an independent screen module are achieved at a cost in execution efficiency. The screen manager operates without knowledge of the user's edit command, so it cannot take shortcuts tailored to particular commands. For example, when characters are being inserted in the buffer, an autonomous screen module applies the updating algorithm for every keystroke, and a character-by-character comparison of two 24 × 80 character arrays (the current screen contents and the desired screen contents) may be too slow.

Terminal Idiosyncrasies.   Beside algorithmic issues, problems arise because the precise set of terminal capabilities varies widely. For example, some terminals have an "automatic wrap" feature that folds a long output line onto several screen rows.

Even when two different terminals provide equivalent capabilities, the required byte sequences may differ. The three-byte command $<escape>[P$ might be needed to delete a character with one terminal, while another might use the two-byte sequence $<escape>Q$. Similarly, terminals vary widely on the command that moves the cursor to a given row and column of the screen. With some, the row is specified before the column; others expect the opposite order. For some, row 6 is specified with a byte having value 6; for others, a value like 32 is added to row and column numbers. For some, the upper left corner of the screen is row 1, column 1; for others, it is row 0, column 0. Moreover, some terminals require that padding characters be sent after a cursor motion command, and the amount of padding may depend on both the transmission speed and the distance that the cursor moved.

Such details should be isolated to a small and easily identified portion of the screen module. Furthermore, it is extremely useful if the editor can be moved among terminals without being recompiled, and this mechanism should not affect other parts of the editor.

The S Editor.   The beginning portions of Sections 5.1–5.3 constitute a user's manual for *s*. Detailed command descriptions are unexciting or even tedious, but necessary.

S is modeled after the UNIX editor *vi*. I opted to mimic an editor of proven popularity and practicality instead of trying to write a novel and elegant editor.

Figure 5.2 and the following two tables help to navigate through the chapter.

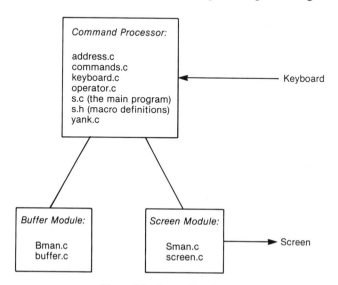

Figure 5.2   Source files for *s*.

Distribution of Code Listings

Contents of Chapter 5

Section 5.1 discusses the editor's repertoire of *addresses*, which specify buffer locations. For example, the address *w* refers to the start of the next word. *Address.c* holds the high-level implementations of all address computations (it reduces them to simple buffer-module calls), including pattern matching.

Section 5.2 covers the *change*, *delete*, and *yank* operators used with addresses. For example, combining the delete operator *d* with the address *w* yields the command *dw*, which deletes a word. Much of the high-level implementation, including the code to insert typed characters into the buffer, is in *operator.c*. *Yank.c* hides details of the "yank buffer" in an abstract data type.

Section 5.3 defines the remaining editor commands, which either lack the operator/address format or abbreviate a common operator/address command. *Commands.c* completes most of the high-level implementation of the editor's commands, leaving only the *redo* and *undo* commands. *S.c* holds the main program and the main loop, which iterates over commands.

Section 5.4 covers the command processor's interaction with the keyboard. The file *keyboard.c* suspends input echoing and implements the *redo* command.

Section 5.5 describes the buffer module. The "buffer manager," *Bman.c*, performs all buffer-module operations except for the actual storage of text lines. Additionally, it implements the *undo* command. The precise method of storing buffer lines is hidden in *buffer.c*, which also keeps a little extra information to assist screen updating. This information permits comparison of the current screen contents and the desired screen contents without an exhaustive character-by-character check.

Section 5.6 explains the editor's *screen manager*, which applies the screen-updating algorithm. Although screen updating is reminiscent of file comparison with insert/delete instructions, the editor's algorithm is unrelated to the approach developed in Section 3.2. This is probably the most interesting section of the chapter, and the related source file, *Sman.c*, is the longest of the book. Folding long lines onto several screen rows, instead of letting them fall off the right margin of the screen, adds substantially to the complexity.

Section 5.7 covers low-level, terminal-specific details. The file *screen.c* hides terminal idiosyncrasies from the rest of *s*. To accommodate a different terminal, it is necessary to edit and recompile *screen.c*; a programming assignment of Section 5.8 allows *s* to be moved among terminals without recompilation.

Section 5.8 outlines a number of possible enhancements to *s*.

5.1 ADDRESSES

A good way to start learning *s* is to edit a familiar file. The command

```
s foo.c
```

copies *foo.c* to the editor's buffer and displays the beginning of the file on the screen. At first, experiment with a few commands that merely move the cursor. When finished, type *q* to quit the editor. If some buffer text has been changed, the editor will ask, "Discard?" Just respond with *y*; the editor will quit without changing the file *foo.c*.

Roughly half of the edit commands simply move the cursor. However, these commands can also be embedded as addresses in more complex commands. Coupled with operators that act on the text traversed as the cursor moves, addresses provide a flexible set of capabilities. For example, the command *fx* moves the cursor to the next occurrence of *x* in the current line (*x* can be replaced by any character). When used with the delete operator *d*, the move command *fx* gives the command *dfx*. This moves the cursor as before, but deletes all characters from the original cursor position up to, but not including, the addressed *x*. In other words, the cursor remains fixed on the screen and the addressed *x* moves over to it, dragging along the remainder of the line. Repetition counts add further flexibility to cursor motion commands. For instance, *3fx* moves to the third subsequent occurrence of *x*.

The Need for Complex Rules. The rules for addresses are complicated. I initially intended to adopt simpler and more consistent rules; however, experience convinced me that ad hoc, but intuitively natural, rules are preferable. Addresses are divided into two categories and many special cases arise, as illustrated by the following example.

From the initial configuration

```
a line
another line
the last line
```

(the underscore indicates the cursor location) each of the three cursor-movement commands *w*, *<return>*, and */a<return>* produces

```
a line
another line
the last line
```

(In general,

$$/ <string> <return>$$

moves the cursor to the next occurrence of the specified character string.) However, they diverge when used as addresses with the *delete* operator. The command
dw gives

```
        a_
        another line
        the last line
```

The command *d<return>* gives

```
        the last line
```

The command *d/a<return>* gives

```
        a another line
        the last line
```

The second case differs from the first because *w* is a "character address," while
<return> is a "line address." Although both *w* and */a<return>* are character
addresses, the third case differs from the first because an ad hoc rule applies when
w is used with the *d* operator.

Line Addresses vs. Character Addresses.   Some movement commands
address specific characters within a line, while others address entire lines. For
example, *fx* addresses a character, whereas *17g* addresses the 17th buffer line. The
interpretation of line and character addresses depends on whether the address is
used with one of the editor's four operators: *c* = change, *d* = delete, *y* = yank,
and :*w* (i.e., *<colon>w*) = write. There are four cases to consider.

A Line Address Used without an Operator.   The cursor is moved to the
first "nonwhite" character of the line. That is, initial blanks and tab characters
are skipped.

A Line Address Used with an Operator.   The block of lines from the current line to the addressed line, inclusive, is affected. For example, if the cursor is
positioned anywhere on line 10, then the command

```
        d17g
```

(or, for that matter, *17dg*) deletes lines 10–17.

A Character Address Used without an Operator.   As you would expect,
the cursor is moved to the addressed character.

A Character Address Used with an Operator.   There is no concise rule,
only the following principle: unless an ad hoc rule is given below, the address's
meaning is not affected by the operator.

The desire for a clean, uniform approach conflicts with users' intuitions about what commands should mean. The *w* command moves to the start of the next word, e.g., from

```
The simple example
```

to

```
The simple example
```

The command *dw* deletes ''simple <*space*>'', producing

```
The example
```

However, what should *cw* mean? (After typing *cw*, type any number of replacement characters ended by <*esc*>.) Typically, users do not want the blank between *simple* and *example* affected, and, accordingly, *cw* deletes one less character in this case than does *dw*.

A similar ad hoc rule arises with the *$* command. Used without an operator, it moves the cursor to the last character in the current line. However, it is natural that the command *d$* delete all characters from the current position through the end of the line. Thus, in effect, a *$* address used with an operator should refer to the position just past the last character in the current line.

The Editor's Line Addresses.   Commands for addressing lines are listed below. Except where noted, the count *n* defaults to 1.

<*n*>*g*	Move to the nth buffer line, where *n* defaults to the number of lines in the buffer.
<*n*>*H*	Move down *n* lines from the top of the screen. (The ''top of the screen'' is interpreted as lying between the first line that is visible on the screen and the preceding buffer line.)
<*n*>*L*	Move up *n* lines from the bottom of the screen.
M	Move to the middle line on the screen. If a count is given, it is ignored.
<*n*> <*return*>	Move down *n* lines from the current line.
<*n*> −	Move up *n* lines from the current line.
<*n*> <*control-D*>	Move down *n* lines from the bottom of the screen. Typically, a sequence of *control-D*'s is used to scroll through a file. The count *n* has a special use for *control-D* and *control-U* commands. Initially, these commands move through the file in half screens (usually

12 lines). Preceding one of them by a count changes the scroll size to *n*. Once changed, it retains the new value until a later *control-D* or *control-U* is used with a count.

<n> <control-U>   Move up *n* lines from the top of the screen. *Control-U* is used like *control-D*, except that it scrolls up in the file.

<n>c   Move down $n - 1$ lines from the current line. The *c* address is used only with the *c* operator. The command *3cc* changes three lines, namely the current line and the two that follow it. The *3* and the second *c* are the address; the first *c* is the *change* operator.

<n>d   Move down $n - 1$ lines from the current line. The *d* address is used only with the *d* operator; for example, *3dd* deletes three lines.

<n>y   Move down $n - 1$ lines from the current line. The *y* address is used only with the *y* operator; for example, *3yy* copies three lines to the yank buffer (Section 5.2).

The Editor's Character Addresses.   Commands for addressing individual characters are listed below, along with the ad hoc rules applied when an operator is present. The count *n* defaults to 1.

<n>b   Move back *n* words to the start of a word, stopping at the beginning of the file. To make this more precise, define an *identifier character* as a letter, digit, or underscore (_) character, and define a *special character* as a character that is neither an identifier character nor a white character. A character in a line is the *start of a word* if either (i) it is an identifier character that is not immediately preceded by an identifier character, or (ii) it is a special character that is not immediately preceded by a special character. That is, a line is partitioned into ''words'' of identifier characters and ''words'' of special characters, perhaps separated by whitespace. A line's first character is the start of a word unless it is a white character. For example, in the two lines of C

```
if (sp2 > 0)
    ++sp2;
```

the characters that start words are indicated below.

```
      ↓    ↓↓          ↓    ↓↓
      i f  ( s p 2  >  0 )
           + + s p 2 ;
             ↑    ↑        ↑
```

Ad hoc rule: When used with an operator, the new address is constrained to lie in the current line. For example, the command *d1000b* deletes the characters to the left of the cursor.

<n>f<char>   Move right *n* occurrences of the given character, staying in the current line. For example, the command *1000fx* moves the cursor to the last *x* in the current line.

<n>F<char>   Move left *n* occurrences of the given character, staying in the current line.

<n>h   Move left *n* characters, staying in the current line. Identical to *<n><backspace>*.

<n>j   Move down *n* lines in the same column.

<n>k   Move up *n* lines in the same column.

<n>l   Move right *n* characters, staying in the current line. Identical to *<n><space>*.

<n>n   Perform *n* repetitions of the previous / or \ command.

<n>w   Move forward *n* words to the start of a word, stopping at the end of the file. The start of a word is defined as for the *b* command.

Ad hoc rule: When used with an operator, the new address is constrained to lie in, or one position after, the current line. For example, the command *d1000w* deletes the remainder of the line.

Ad hoc rule: If the operator is *c* and the position before the target address holds a white character, then the target address is repeatedly decremented until the preceding character is nonwhite. Thus, the command *cw* does not change the whitespace at the end of the current word.

0 (zero)   Move to the start of the current line. If a count is given, it is ignored.

<n>$ Move to the last character of the $(n - 1)^{\text{th}}$ following line.

Ad hoc rule: When used with an operator, the $ address refers to the position just after the end of the line. Thus, the command *d$* deletes the remainder of the line.

<n> <space>   Move right *n* characters, staying in the current line.

Ad hoc rule: When used with an operator, the forward movement stops at the position just after the end of the line. Thus, the command *d1000<space>* deletes the remainder of the current line.

<n> <backspace> Move left *n* characters, staying in the current line.

' (apostrophe)   Move to the location where the last *m* (mark) command was issued (Section 5.3). If a count is given, it is ignored.

Ad hoc rule: When used with an operator, the address refers to an entire line. Thus the command *d'* deletes lines from the current line through the line containing the marked location.

' (backquote)   Move to the previous cursor position (undefined if the last command modified the buffer's contents). This command is useful when an accidental keystroke moves the cursor to a distant part of the buffer. Another common use is to redraw a garbled screen with the command pair *g'* (which works unless the current line is too near the end of the file). If a count is given, it is ignored.

Ad hoc rule: When used with an operator, the address refers to an entire line.

<n>;   Perform *n* repetitions of the previous *f* or *F* command.

<n>/<string> <return>

Move forward *n* occurrences of the given character string, wrapping around from the last line of the buffer to the first line. The character pair ''\n'' can be used at either end of the pattern string to match the start or end of a line. A ''\n'' pair in the middle of the pattern is not treated as a newline. If no string is given, the string is taken from the previous / or \ command.

<n>\<string> <return>

Move back *n* occurrences of the given character string, wrapping around from the first line of the buffer to the last line. The character pair ''\n'' works as with the / command. If no string is given, the string is taken from the previous / or \ command. For example, if a repeated forward search using the *n* command overruns the desired line, typing

$\backslash < return >$

returns to the previous occurrence of the string.

Comments on Address.c.   *Address.c* computes all addresses. The only
entry point is *address()*, which takes the count *n*, the movement command and the
operator (if there is one) and sets the buffer's record of the cursor location to the
appropriate address.

A large *switch* statement treats the cases described above. The following
algorithm skeleton shows the cases $<n> <return>$ (down *n* lines) and
$<n> <space>$ (right *n* characters):

```
line__addr = 0        /* reset by commands that address lines */
switch (command) {
/* ——— Line Addresses: ——— */
    .

    .

    .

    case <return>:
        line__addr = current line + n
        break;

        .

        .

        .

/* ——— Character Addresses: ——— */
    .

    .

    .

    case <space>:
        get the text of the current line
        limit = strlen(text) − 1
        /*
        *        ad hoc rule:
        * operators affect the line's last character
        */
        if an operator is being applied
            ++limit
        set the cursor to position min(current position + n, limit)
            of the current line
        break;

        .

        .

        .

}

/* set the cursor for line addresses */
if line__addr > 0
```

> **if** there is no operator
>> move to the first nonwhite character of the addressed line
>
> **else**
>> set the cursor to position −1 of the addressed line
>> (−1 signals a line address to code that applies operators)

With line addresses, *line__addr* is set to a positive value and the code after the *switch* statement positions the cursor. The cases for character addresses set the cursor individually and apply the ad hoc rules.

The following commands were sufficiently complex to justify separate procedures:

1. vertical-movement commands, *j* and *k*
2. character-locating commands, *f*, *F*, and ;
3. word-locating commands, *b* and *w*
4. string-locating commands, /, \, and *n*

Groups 2–4 are straightforward. In particular, the function *locate()* is similar to the *find* program of Section 1.1.

The *j* and *k* vertical-movement commands proved somewhat troublesome. Whereas other parts of the command handler are simplified by the screen module's autonomy, code for *j* and *k* (as well as the *H*, *L*, and *M* commands) depends on the screen representation. Suppose the cursor is positioned

```
<tab>cd<tab>xy
tuvw<tab>0123456789
```

(Here <*tab*> denotes a tab character.) Where does a *j* (down) command move the cursor? The *x* is in position 4 of the top line (positions start with 0). Assuming that tab stops occur every eight screen columns and that column numbers begins with 1, the first line is displayed with *c* in column 9, *d* in column 10, and *x* in column 17. In the second line, the character displayed in column 17 is *8*, which lies in position 13 of the line. Thus, the *j* command moves the cursor from position 4 of the top line to position 13 of the next line

```
<tab>cd<tab>xy
tuvw<tab>0123456789
```

This computation involves converting between lines, which count tab characters as one character, and screen columns, where a tab expands to between one and eight columns. The functions *pos__to__col()* and *col__to__pos()* in *address.c* perform these conversions.

An easier problem to handle is an uninterrupted sequence of *j* and/or *k* commands. For example, start with

```
1 2 3 4 5
a b
v w x y z
```

Because the displayed cursor is restricted to valid buffer locations, a *j* command moves it to

```
1 2 3 4 5
a b
v w x y z
```

However, procedure *do__up__down()* in *address.c* keeps trying to place the cursor in column 4, so a second *j* command produces

```
1 2 3 4 5
a b
v w x y z
```

EXERCISES

1. Is it possible to have a negative count *n*?

2. Why does *address()* have the operator as an argument? That is, why not have *address()* determine ''nonoperator'' addresses and let the editor's code for operators apply the ad hoc rules?

3. Suppose the cursor is positioned

```
ababababab
```

How do the commands

```
/ abab
```

and

```
\ abab
```

reset the cursor? What modification to *address.c* removes this inconsistency?

4. Trace the computations performed by *address.c* for the commands *1000fx* and *d1000w*. Show how to modify *address.c* to make these computations more efficient.

```
/*
 * s.h - macro definitions for the screen editor
 */
#include <stdio.h>
#include <ctype.h>
```

```
#define CR                  '\r'                  /* sent by <return> key */
#define ctrl(x)             ('x' & 037)           /* control character 'x' */         ctrl
#define ESCAPE              27                    /* end-of-insertion character */
#define MAXTEXT             200                   /* maximum length of a line */
#define SCROLL_SIZE         12                    /* number of rows to scroll */
#define TAB_WIDTH           8                     /* columns per tab character */

#define abs(x)              ((x > 0) ? x : -(x))                                       abs
#define max(x,y)            (x > y) ? x : y                                            max
#define min(x,y)            (x < y) ? x : y                                            min

/* for an unknown command, ring the bell */
#define UNKNOWN  putc(7, stderr)


/*
 * address.c - process addresses
 *
 *
 * Entry point:
 *
 *     address(n, c, op)
 *     int n;
 *     char c, op;
 *         Reposition the cursor as specified by the count n, the motion
 *         command c and the operator op.  For pure cursor movement,
 *         op = ' ' (the blank character).  For line addresses used with an
 *         operator (op != ' '), the cursor position in the addressed line
 *         is set to -1.  If the addressing operation fails, then the
 *         cursor's location is unchanged.
 *
 *     A list of the addressing commands follows.  The default value of the
 *     count <n> is 1, except for commands g (where it is the number of lines
 *     in the buffer) and ctrl(d) and ctrl(u) (where it is half of a screen).
 *     Commands M, 0 (zero), ' (apostrophe), and ' (backquote) ignore the count.
 *
 *                              Line Addresses:
 *     <n>g                     - line n of the buffer
 *     <n>H                     - down n lines from the top of the screen
 *     <n>L                     - up n lines from the bottom of the screen
 *     M                        - the middle line of the screen
 *     <n><return>              - down n lines from the current line
 *     <n>-                     - up n lines from the current line
 *     <n>ctrl(d)               - down n lines from the bottom of the screen
 *     <n>ctrl(u)               - up n lines from the top of the screen
 *     <n>c                     - down n-1 lines (only with the c operator)
 *     <n>d                     - down n-1 lines (only with the d operator)
 *     <n>y                     - down n-1 lines (only with the y operator)
 *
 *
 *                              Character Addresses:
 *     <n>b                     - back n words
 *     <n>f<char>               - right n occurrences of <char>
 *     <n>F<char>               - left n occurrences of <char>
 *     <n>h                     - left n characters (same as <n><backspace>)
 *     <n>j                     - down n lines in the same column
 *     <n>k                     - up n lines in the same column
 *     <n>l                     - right n characters (same as <n><space>)
 *     <n>n                     - n repetitions of the previous pattern search
 *     <n>w                     - forward n words
 *     0 (zero)                 - the start of the current line
 *     <n>$                     - the end of the (n-1)th following line
```

```
*      <n><space>                       - right n characters
*      <n><backspace>                   - left n characters
*      ' (apostrophe)                   - return to the marked location
*      ' (backquote)                    - return to the previous location
*      <n>;                             - n repetitions of the previous f or F command
*      <n>/<string><return>             - forward n occurrences of string
*      <n>\<string><return>             - back n occurrences of string
*
*
* External procedure calls:
*
*      b_getcur(line_ptr, pos_ptr)    .. file Bman.c
*      int *line_ptr, *pos_ptr;
*          Return the line and position of the cursor.
*
*      b_getmark(line_ptr, pos_ptr)   .. file Bman.c
*      int *line_ptr, *pos_ptr;
*          Return the line and position of the mark.
*
*      b_gets(k, s)                   .. file Bman.c
*      int k;
*      char s[];
*          Copy the k-th buffer line to s.
*
*      b_setcur(line, pos)            .. file Bman.c
*      int line, pos;
*          Set the cursor location.
*
*      b_setline(line)                .. file Bman.c
*      int line;
*          Set the cursor to line's first nonwhite character.
*
*      int b_size()                   .. file Bman.c
*          Return the number of lines in the buffer.
*
*      int k_getch()                  .. file keyboard.c
*          Return the next character from the keyboard.
*
*      char k_lastcmd()               .. file keyboard.c
*          Return the first letter in the last command.
*
*      int s_firstline()              .. file Sman.c
*          Return the number of the first line visible on the screen.
*
*      char *s_getmsg(msg)            .. file Sman.c
*      char *msg;
*          Print msg; return the user's reply.
*
*      int s_lastline()               .. file Sman.c
*          Return the number of the last line visible on the screen.
*/

#include "s.h"

address(n, c, op)                                                            address
int n;
char c, op;
{
     static int prev_line = 0, prev_pos, scroll_size = SCROLL_SIZE;
     int cur_line, cur_pos, direction, limit, line_addr, mark_line, mark_pos,
         new_line, new_pos;
     char ch, text[MAXTEXT-1];
```

```
/* set default count to 1, except for three special cases */
if (n == 0 && c != 'g' && c != ctrl(d) && c != ctrl(u))
      n = 1;
b_getcur(&cur_line, &cur_pos);        /* cursor location */
line_addr = 0;        /* reset by commands that address lines */

switch (c) {

/* ---------- Line Addresses:  ---------- */
     case 'g':
           /* ad hoc default value for the count */
           if (n == 0)
                 n = b_size();
           line_addr = n;
           break;
     case 'H':
           line_addr = s_firstline() + n - 1;
           break;
     case 'L':
           line_addr = max (s_lastline() - n + 1, 1);
           break;
     case 'M':
           line_addr = (s_firstline() + s_lastline())/2;
           break;
     case CR:        /* <return> */
           line_addr = cur_line + n;
           break;
     case '-':
           line_addr = max (cur_line - n, 1);
           break;
     case ctrl(d):
           /* ad hoc interpretation of the count */
           if (n != 0)
                 scroll_size = n;
           line_addr = s_lastline() + scroll_size;
           break;
     case ctrl(u):
           if (n != 0)
                 scroll_size = n;
           line_addr = max (s_firstline() - scroll_size, 1);
           break;
     case 'c':
     case 'd':
     case 'y':
           if (op == c)
                 line_addr = cur_line + n - 1;
           break;

/* ---------- Character Addresses:  ---------- */
     case 'b':
           while (n-- > 0)
                 loc_word(-1);
           /*
            *         ad hoc rule:
            * operators affect only the current line
            */
           if (op != ' ') {
                 b_getcur(&new_line, &new_pos);
                 if (new_line != cur_line)
                       b_setcur(cur_line, 0);
           }
           break;
```

```
case 'f':
case 'F':
    direction = (c == 'f') ? 1 : -1;
    ch = k_getch();
    while (n-- > 0)
        loc_char(ch, direction);
    break;
case 'h':
case '\b':      /* <backspace> */
    b_setcur(cur_line, max(cur_pos - n, 0));
    break;
case 'j':
    do_up_down(n);
    break;
case 'k':
    do_up_down(-n);
    break;
case 'l':
case ' ':
    b_gets(cur_line, text);
    limit = strlen(text) - 1;
    /*
     *          ad hoc rule:
     * operators affect the line's last character
     */
    if (op != ' ')
        ++limit;

    b_setcur(cur_line, min(cur_pos + n, limit));
    break;
case 'n':
    while (n-- > 0)
        loc_string('\0');
    break;
case 'w':
    while (n-- > 0)
        loc_word(1);
    /*
     *          ad hoc rule:
     * operators affect only the current line
     */
    if (op != ' ') {
        b_getcur(&new_line, &new_pos);
        if (new_line != cur_line ||
          new_pos == cur_pos) {     /* last word in buffer */
            /* set cursor past the end of line */
            b_gets(cur_line, text);
            b_setcur(cur_line, strlen(text));
        }
    }
    /*
     *          ad hoc rule:
     * c does not affect the whitespace at the end of a word
     */
    if (op == 'c') {
        b_getcur(&new_line, &new_pos);
        b_gets(new_line, text);
        while (new_pos > 0 && isspace(text[new_pos-1]))
            --new_pos;
        b_setcur(new_line, new_pos);
```

```
            }
            break;
    case '0':        /* zero */
            b_setcur(cur_line, 0);
            break;
    case '$':
            new_line = cur_line + n - 1;
            b_gets(new_line, text);
            new_pos = strlen(text) - 1;
            /*
             *          ad hoc rule:
             * operators affect the line's last character
             */
            if (op != ' ')
                ++new_pos;

            b_setcur(new_line, new_pos);
            break;
    case '\'':        /* apostrophe */
            b_getmark(&mark_line, &mark_pos);
            if (mark_line == 0)
                break;
            b_setcur(mark_line, mark_pos);
            /*
             *          ad hoc rule:
             * operators treat the marked location as a line address
             */
            if (op != ' ')
                line_addr = mark_line;

            break;
    case '`':        /* backquote */
            if (prev_line == 0)
                break;
            b_setcur(prev_line, prev_pos);
            /*
             *          ad hoc rule:
             * operators treat the previous location as a line address
             */
            if (op != ' ')
                line_addr = prev_line;

            break;
    case ';':
            while (n-- > 0)
                loc_char('\0', 0);
            break;
    case '\\':
    case '/':        /* pattern matching */
            loc_string(c);
            while (n-- > 1)
                loc_string('\0');
            break;
    default:
            break;
}

/* set the cursor for line addresses */
if (line_addr > 0 ) {
    line_addr = min (line_addr, b_size());
```

```
            if (op == ' ')        /* no operator */
                /* move to the first nonwhite character of line */
                b_setline(line_addr);
            else
                /* use position -1 to signify a line address */
                b_setcur(line_addr, -1);
        }

    /* handle the previous location for the  ' (backquote) command */
    if (op == ' ') {
        b_getcur(&new_line, &new_pos);
        if (new_line != cur_line || new_pos != cur_pos) {
            prev_line = cur_line;
            prev_pos = cur_pos;
        }
    } else if (op == 'c' || op == 'd')
        /* buffer change; the previous location becomes undefined */
        prev_line = 0;
    /* else op is yank or write; do nothing */
}

/*
------------------- the j and k commands  --------------------
*
* Entry point:
*
*     do_up_down(i)
*     int i;
*         Move the cursor i lines, staying in the same column. Throughout
*         an uninterrupted sequence of j and k commands, the cursor stays
*         in the same column subject to the constraint that it always lie
*         on a buffer character.
*/

static do_up_down(i)                                              do_up_down
int i;
{
    static int col;       /* remembered column */
    int cur_line, cur_pos, new_line, new_pos;
    char k_lastcmd();

    b_getcur(&cur_line, &cur_pos);
    if (i > 0)
        new_line = min (cur_line + i, b_size());
    else
        new_line = max (cur_line + i, 1);
    /* if the last command was neither j nor k, compute a new column */
    if (k_lastcmd() != 'j' && k_lastcmd() != 'k')
        col = pos_to_col(cur_line, cur_pos);
    /* translate the screen column to a position in the new line */
    new_pos = col_to_pos(new_line, col);
    b_setcur(new_line, new_pos);
}

/* col_to_pos - convert a screen column to a line position */
static int col_to_pos(line, col)                                 col_to_pos
int line, col;
{
    int c, p;
    char text[MAXTEXT-1];
```

```
    b_gets(line, text);
    for (c = 1, p = 0; c < col && text[p] != '\0'; ++c, ++p)
        /* keep column c corresponding to position p */
        if (text[p] == '\t')
            while (c%TAB_WIDTH != 0)
                if (++c >= col)
                    return(p);
    if (p > 0 && text[p] == '\0')
        --p;
    return(p);
}

/* pos_to_col - convert a line position to a screen column */
static int pos_to_col(line, pos)                                          pos__to__col
int line, pos;
{
    int c, p;
    char text[MAXTEXT-1];

    b_gets(line, text);
    for (c = 1, p = 0; p < pos && text[p] != '\0'; ++c, ++p)
        /* keep column c corresponding to position p */
        if (text[p] == '\t')
            while (c%TAB_WIDTH != 0)
                ++c;
    return(c);
}

/*
------------------- the f, F, and ; commands  --------------------
*
* Entry point:
*
*     loc_char(ch, way)
*     char ch;
*     int way;
*          Set cursor to the next position of ch in the current line.
*          If way = 1, then search to the right; otherwise, way = -1 and
*          the search moves left. If ch = '\0', then ch and way are taken
*          from the previous call to loc_char.
*/

static loc_char(ch, way)                                                  loc__char
char ch;
int way;
{
    static int w;              /* remembered way */
    int cur_line, cur_pos;
    static char c = 0;         /* remembered ch */
    char *b, buf[MAXTEXT-1];

    if (ch != 0) {
        c = ch;
        w = way;
    } else if (c == 0)
        return; /* no character specified or remembered */
    b_getcur(&cur_line, &cur_pos);
    b_gets(cur_line, buf);
    for (b = buf + cur_pos + w; b >= buf && *b != '\0'; b += w)
        if (*b == c) {
```

```
                b_setcur(cur_line, b - buf);
                break;
        }
}

/*
------------------- the b and w commands --------------------
*
* Entry point:
*
*     loc_word(way)
*     int way;
*         Set cursor to the start of the next word.  If way = 1, then
*         search toward file's end; otherwise, search toward file's
*         beginning. Do not "wrap around" at the ends of the file.
*/

static loc_word(way)                                                      loc__word
int way;
{
    int cur_line, cur_pos;
    char *b, buf[MAXTEXT-1];

    b_getcur(&cur_line, &cur_pos);
    b_gets(cur_line, buf);
    /* try the current line */
    for (b = buf + cur_pos + way; b >= buf && *b != '\0'; b += way)
        if (word_start(b, buf))
            break;
    /* try other lines */
    while (!word_start(b,buf)) {
        cur_line += way;
        if (cur_line > b_size() || cur_line < 1)
            break;
        b_gets(cur_line, buf);
        b = (way == 1) ? buf : buf + strlen(buf) - 1;
        while (b >= buf && *b != '\0' && !word_start(b,buf))
            b += way;
        }
    if (word_start(b, buf))
        b_setcur(cur_line, b - buf);
}

/* define "identifier character" and "special character" */
#define ident_char(x) (isalnum(x) || x == '_')                           ident__char
#define special_char(x) (!ident_char(x) && !isspace(x))                  special__char

/* word_start - tell if s points to the start of a word in text */
static int word_start(s, text)                                           word__start
char *s, *text;
{
    if (s < text || *s == '\0')
        return(0);
    if (s == text)
        return(!isspace(*s));
    if (ident_char(*s) && !ident_char(s[-1])
        || special_char(*s) && !special_char(s[-1]))
            return(1);
    return(0);
}
```

```
/*
------------------ the /, \, and n commands  --------------------
*
* Entry point:
*
*     loc_string(ch)
*     char ch;
*         Set cursor to the next instance of a user-supplied string.
*         (Loc_string prompts the user to provide the string.)
*         If ch = '/', then the search is forward in the file and
*         wraps around from the end of the file to the start.  If
*         ch = '\', then the search is backward (toward the start of
*         the file) and wraps around from the first line to the last line.
*         For commands /<return> and \<return> the string is taken
*         from the previous call to loc_string.  If ch = '\0', then the
*         string and way are taken from the previous call to loc_string.
*/

static loc_string(ch)                                                    loc_string
char ch;
{
    static int way;                 /* remembered direction */
    static char string[MAXTEXT-1];  /* remembered pattern */

    int cur_line, cur_pos, first, last, len, line, pos;
    char cur_text[MAXTEXT+1], out[2], *pat, *s_getmsg(), text[MAXTEXT+1];

    if (ch != '\0') {           /* get new pattern and direction */
        way = (ch == '/') ? 1 : -1;
        out[0] = ch;
        out[1] = '\0';
        pat = s_getmsg(out);
        if (*pat == '\b')
            /* user backspaced off left margin */
            return;
        if (*pat != '\0') {
            if (pat[0] == '\\' && pat[1] == 'n')
                *++pat = '\n';
            len = strlen(pat);
            if (len > 1 && pat[len-2] == '\\' && pat[len-1] == 'n') {
                pat[len-2] = '\n';
                pat[len-1] = '\0';
            }
            strcpy(string, pat);
        }
    }
    if (string[0] == '\0')
        /* want to use the old string, but none exists */
        return;

    b_getcur(&cur_line, &cur_pos);
    line = cur_line;
    text[0] = cur_text[0] = '\n';
    /* split the current line at the current position */
    b_gets(cur_line, cur_text+1);
    len = strlen(cur_text);
    cur_text[len] = '\n';     /* newlines were removed when file was read */
    cur_text[len+1] = '\0';
    cur_text[cur_pos+1] = '\0';    /* +1 for leading '\n' */
    if (way > 0) {
```

```
            first = cur_pos + 2;
            last = 0;
        } else {
            first = 0;
            last = cur_pos + 2;
        }
        /* search the first section of the current line */
        pos = locate(&cur_text[first], string, way);
        if (pos >= 0)
            pos += first;

        /* if that fails, search the other lines */
        while (pos < 0) {
            if (way > 0)
                line = (line < b_size()) ? line + 1 : 1;
            else
                line = (line > 1) ? line - 1 : b_size();
            if (line == cur_line)
                break;
            b_gets(line, text+1);
            len = strlen(text);
            text[len] = '\n';
            text[len+1] = '\0';
            pos = locate(text, string, way);
        }

        /* if that fails, search the other section of the current line */
        if (pos < 0) {
            line = cur_line;
            pos = locate(&cur_text[last], string, way);
            if (pos >= 0)
                pos += last;
        }

        if (pos >= 0) {        /* found a match */
            --pos;            /* compensate for leading '\n' in text buffer */
            pos = max(pos, 0);       /* if leading '\n' in pattern */
            b_gets(line, text);
            pos = min(pos, strlen(text)-1);    /* if matched '\n' after line */
            b_setcur(line, pos);
        }
    }
}

/* locate - return the position of a pattern in a text line */
static int locate(text, pat, way)                                        locate
char *text, *pat;
int way;
{
    int i, lim;
    char *p, *t;

    if (way > 0) {
        i = 0;
        lim = strlen(text);
    } else {
        i = strlen(text) - 1;
        lim = -1;
    }
```

```
for ( ; i != lim; i += way)
    for (p = pat, t = &text[i]; *p == *t; ++p, ++t)
            if (p[1] == '\0')
                    return(i);
return(-1);      /* no match */
}
```

5.2 OPERATORS AND THE YANK BUFFER

This section discusses:

- operators c (change), d (delete), and y (yank)
- commands p and P for copying the yank buffer to the main buffer

The remaining operator, :w (write), is covered in the next section.

The *yank buffer* provides temporary storage for a block of consecutive lines from the main buffer. A c, d, or y operator with a line address (Section 5.1) fills the yank buffer with the indicated lines. The p and P commands insert the yank buffer's contents back into the main buffer, either after (with p) or before (with P) the current line.

"Cut-and-paste" operations can be performed with d, y, p, and P. Consider the problem of moving line 3 to the top of the file when the cursor rests on line 1:

```
line1
line2
line3
line4
```

The command *2dd* copies lines 1 and 2 to the yank buffer, then deletes them from the main buffer:

```
line3
line4
```

A p command then copies the yank buffer to the main buffer:

```
line3
line1
line2
line4
```

An alternative sequence of edit commands for the task is

```
3g    go to line 3
dd    delete one line
1g    go to line 1
P     put the yank buffer's contents before the current line
```

To copy lines from one part of the main buffer to another, use y with either p or P; y copies lines to the yank buffer without deleting them from the main buffer.

Details about commands c, d, p, P, and y are given below. In general, an operator is followed by an address. For c and d, both character addresses and line addresses can be used; y requires a line address. If the address contains a repetition count, then the count can appear before the operator. Thus, both $d17g$ and $17dg$ delete lines from the current line to line 17, inclusive.

$c<addr>$ Change the buffer segment bounded by the cursor location (Location 1) and $<addr>$ (Location 2). In particular, the following steps are performed.

1. If necessary, Locations 1 and 2 are interchanged so that Location 1 precedes Location 2. (The command is invalid if the locations are identical.)

2. If $<addr>$ is a line address, then complete lines from Location 1 to Location 2, inclusive, are copied to the yank buffer (after the yank buffer is emptied).

3. If $<addr>$ is a line address, then the lines from Location 1 to Location 2, inclusive, are replaced on the screen by a single empty row. The cursor is positioned at the left of this row, ready for input. Typed characters are placed in the main buffer. The *change* operation is ended by $<esc>$, and the cursor is left on the last inserted character.

   With both line addresses and character addresses, the $<backspace>$ key backs up over typed characters, but not beyond the place where insertion began or beyond the start of a line. Characters erased this way temporarily remain on the screen; if they are not subsequently overwritten, they are removed from the screen when $<esc>$ is pressed.

4. If $<addr>$ is a character address, then the character just before Location 2 (the last character doomed for deletion) is replaced by the character $\$$, and the cursor is positioned at Location 1. The user then types in characters, terminated by $<esc>$. These characters overwrite displayed characters until the $\$$ is replaced; thereafter, typed characters cause the remainder of the line to be shifted right. If the $\$$ has not been overwritten when $<esc>$ is pressed, then characters from the cursor location to the $\$$ are deleted from the screen.

For example, suppose the cursor rests on x in

abcd
w<u>x</u>yz

and let the command be

c\c<*return*>123<*esc*>

Here <*addr*> is \c<*return*>, which searches backward for c. Step 1 interchanges Location 1 and Location 2, then $\$$ replaces w and the cursor is positioned for input, giving

ab<u>c</u>d
$xyz

Typing *123* produces

ab123<u> </u>
$xyz

and pressing <*esc*> deletes doomed text, giving:

ab12<u>3</u>xyx

d<*addr*>   Delete the buffer segment bounded by the cursor location and <*addr*>. Specifically, steps 1 and 2 in the description of *change* are performed, and the deleted text is as described under steps 3 and 4.

p Copy the yank buffer's contents into the main buffer just after the current line. The cursor is placed at the start of the first inserted line.

P Copy the yank buffer's contents into the main buffer just before the current line. The cursor is placed at the start of the first inserted line.

y<*addr*>   Copy the buffer segment bounded by the cursor location and <*addr*> to the yank buffer, where <*addr*> must be a line address. Specifically, steps 1 and 2 in the description of *change* are performed.

Comments on Operator.c and Yank.c.   The operators c, d, and y are implemented in *operator.c* and *yank.c*. The function *operator()* in *operator.c* performs steps 1–4 as described above. The function *in__chars()* transfers characters from the keyboard to the main buffer. *Operator.c* is provided with an entry point, *do__insert()*, needed by commands discussed in the next section.

The yank buffer is implemented as an abstract data type with access functions *do__put()* and *do__yank()*:

```
/*
 * yank.c - yank buffer
     ...
 * Implementation:
 *
 *    Simple linked list.  Storage is allocated dynamically with malloc()
 *    (not ckalloc()) so execution can continue if storage is exhausted.
 */
     ...
struct y_line {
    char *y_text;
    struct y_line *next;
}
     ...
/* do_yank - copy lines from main buffer to yank buffer; tell if successful */
int do_yank(line1, line2)
int line1, line2;
{
    struct y_line ... *q;
    char *malloc(), *r, ..., text[MAXTEXT-1];

    free_ybuf();

    for ( ; line1 <= line2; ++line1) {
        b_gets(line1, text);
        q = (struct y_line *) malloc(sizeof(struct y_line));
        r = malloc((unsigned)strlen(text)+1);
        if (q == NULL || r == NULL) {
            free_ybuf();
            return(0);
        }
        ... (the line is linked to the end of the yank buffer)
    }
    return(1)
}
```

Do__yank() first calls *free__ybuf()* to empty the yank buffer. For each line being yanked, *malloc()* is asked to find storage for (i) a structure pointing to the line's text and to the next yanked line and (ii) the text itself. If either call fails, *free__ybuf()* liberates storage in the partly finished yank buffer and *do__yank()* returns 0 to signal failure. If *malloc()* never fails, then *do__yank()* eventually reports success by returning 1.

When an operator is used with a line address, *do__yank()* is called. If *do__yank()* fails with a *c* or *d* operator, the user decides whether to complete the operation. The relevant code is in *operator.c*:

```
/*
 * operator.c - operators c, d and y
     ...
/* operator - apply operators */
operator(op, line1, pos1)
```

```
char op;
int line1, pos1;
{
    int keep_going, line_addr, ...;
    ...
    line_addr = (pos2 < 0);
    ...
    if (!line_addr)
        keep_going = 1;
    else if ((keep_going = do_yank(line1, line2)) == 0 && op != 'y') {
        s_putmsg("Cannot yank lines; should operation be completed? ");
        keep_going = (k_getch() == 'y');
    }

    if (op == 'y')
        if (!keep_going)
            s_savemsg("Cannot yank lines.", 0);
        else ...
            ...
    if (op == 'y' || !keep_going)
        /* return the cursor to its initial position */
        ...
    else if (op == 'd') {
        ...
    } else {      /* op == 'c' */
        ...
    }
}
```

PROGRAMMING ASSIGNMENTS

1. Rewrite *yank.c* so that parts of lines can be yanked and put. (*Hint:* The function *s_errmsg()* in *Sman.c* (Section 5.6) is useful for debugging. Calls like

```
s_errmsg("Calling in_chars() with pos2 = %d", pos2);
```

can be used to print interesting program values without distroying the correspondence between the screen contents and the buffer.)

2. Keep a pool of *y_line* structures; avoid all calls to *free()* for these structures (and some of the calls to *malloc()*).

```
/*
 * operator.c - operators c, d and y
 *
 *
 * Entry points:
 *
 *    do_insert()
 *        Read characters from the keyboard and place them in the buffer
 *        at the cursor location.  Characters at and right of the cursor
 *        are shifted right to make room for the new characters.  Input is
 *        ended by <esc>.
 *
 *    operator(op, line1, pos1)
 *    char op;
```

```
*      int line1, pos1;
*          Apply the operator op.  Let the location addressed in the
*          operator command be (line2, pos2), where, pos2 < 0 for a line
*          address.  With a line address, lines from line1 to line2,
*          inclusive, are affected.  With a character address, the affected
*          buffer segment extends from the earlier (in the buffer) location
*          to one position before later location.
*
*      The commands implemented by operator() are:
*
*      c<addr>      - change a buffer segment
*      d<addr>      - delete a buffer segment
*      y<addr>      - copy a buffer segment to the yank buffer
*
*
* External procedure calls:
*
*      b_delete(first, last)          .. file Bman.c
*      int first, last;
*          Delete a range of buffer lines.
*
*      b_getcur(line_ptr, pos_ptr)    .. file Bman.c
*      int *line_ptr, *pos_ptr;
*          Return the location of the cursor.
*
*      b_gets(k, s)                   .. file Bman.c
*      int k;
*      char s[];
*          Copy the k-th buffer line to s.
*
*      int b_insert(k, s)             .. file Bman.c
*      int k;
*      char s[];
*          Insert s into the buffer as line k; tell if successful.
*
*      b_replace(k, s)                .. file Bman.c
*      int k;
*      char s[];
*          Replace the k-th buffer line by s.
*
*      b_setcur(line, pos)            .. file Bman.c
*      int line, pos;
*          Set the cursor location.
*
*      int b_size()                   .. file Bman.c
*          Return the number of lines in the buffer.
*
*      int do_yank(line1, line2)      .. file yank.c
*      int line1, line2;
*          Copy a range of lines to the yank buffer; tell if successful.
*
*      int k_getch()                  .. file keyboard.c
*          Return the next character from the keyboard.
*
*      s_refresh()                    .. file Sman.c
*          Bring the screen up to date after a buffer change.
*
*      s_savemsg(msg, count)          .. file Sman.c
*      char *msg;
*      int count;
*          Format msg and save it for the next screen refreshing.
*/
```

```
#include "s.h"

/* do_insert - insert text */
do_insert()                                                          do_insert
{
    in_chars(0, 0);
}

/* operator - apply operators */
operator(op, line1, pos1)                                            operator
char op;
int line1, pos1;
{
    int keep_going, line_addr, line2, pos2, size, swap, temp;
    char text[MAXTEXT-1];

    b_getcur(&line2, &pos2);
    line_addr = (pos2 < 0);
    swap = (line2 < line1 || line2 == line1 && pos2 < pos1);
    if (swap) {
        /* swap so that Location 1 precedes Location 2 */
        temp = line1;
        line1 = line2;
        line2 = temp;
        temp = pos1;
        pos1 = pos2;
        pos2 = temp;
    }
    size = line2 - line1 + 1;        /* number of affected lines */

    if (!line_addr)
        keep_going = 1;
    else if ((keep_going = do_yank(line1, line2)) == 0 && op != 'y') {
        s_putmsg("Cannot yank lines; should operation be completed? ");
        keep_going = (k_getch() == 'y');
    }

    if (op == 'y')
        if (!keep_going)
            s_savemsg("Cannot yank lines.", 0);
        else if (!line_addr)
            UNKNOWN;
        else if (size >= 5)
            s_savemsg("%d lines yanked", size);

    if (op == 'y' || !keep_going)
        /* return the cursor to its initial location */
        if (swap)
            b_setcur(line2, pos2);
        else
            b_setcur(line1, pos1);
    else if (op == 'd') {
        if (size >= 5)
            s_savemsg("%d lines deleted", size);
        do_delete(line1, pos1, line2, pos2);
    } else {            /* op == 'c' */
        if (size >= 5)
            s_savemsg("%d lines changed", size);
        if (line_addr) {
            if (line1 < line2)
                b_delete(line1, line2-1);      /* replace the lines.. */
            b_replace(line1, "");              /* ..by an empty line */
```

```
            b_setcur(line1, 0);                    /* start on that line */
            s_refresh();                           /* display all this */
            in_chars(0, 0);                        /* accept input */
        } else {
            /* mark the last overwrite location */
            if (--pos2 >= 0)
                b_gets(line2, text);
            else {
                b_gets(--line2, text);
                pos2 = strlen(text) - 1;
            }
            text[pos2] = '$';
            b_replace(line2, text);
            b_setcur(line1, pos1);                 /* start at the left */
            s_refresh();                           /* display all this */
            in_chars(line2, pos2);                 /* accept input */
        }
    }
}


/*
 * do_delete - delete text from the buffer
 *
 * If pos1 < 0 or pos2 < 0, then complete lines from line1 to line2, inclusive,
 * are deleted.  Otherwise, the deleted text starts at the first address and
 * extends up to, but not including, the second address.  The first address must
 * precede the second.
 */
static do_delete(line1, pos1, line2, pos2)
int line1, pos1, line2, pos2;
{
    char text1[MAXTEXT-1], text2[MAXTEXT-1];

    if (pos1 < 0 || pos2 < 0) {    /* line address */
        b_delete(line1, line2);
        if (b_size() == 0) {
            s_savemsg("No lines in buffer.", 0);
            b_insert(1, "");
        }
        b_setline( min(line1, b_size()) );
    } else {
        /* glue the head of line1 to the tail of line2 */
        b_gets(line1, text1);
        b_gets(line2, text2);
        if (pos1 + strlen(text2 + pos2) > MAXTEXT-1) {
            UNKNOWN;
            s_savemsg("Line length exceeds %d.", MAXTEXT);
            return;
        }
        strcpy(text1 + pos1, text2 + pos2);
        if (line1 < line2)
            b_delete(line1, line2-1);
        b_replace(line1, text1);
        if (pos1 > 0 && text1[pos1] == '\0')
            --pos1;
        b_setcur(line1, pos1);
    }
}


/*
 * in_chars - insert characters into the buffer
```

do_delete

```
 *
 * Read characters from the keyboard and place them in the buffer at the cursor
 * location.  Existing buffer characters are overwritten until the cursor passes
 * the location indicated by in_chars()'s arguments.  Thereafter, characters in
 * the current line are shifted right to accommodate the new ones.  If characters
 * marked for overwriting remain when input is ended (with <esc>), then they are
 * deleted from the buffer.
 */
static in_chars(end_line, end_pos)                                          in__chars
int end_line, end_pos;
{
    int c, cur_line, cur_pos, i, length, start_line, start_pos;
    char text[MAXTEXT-1];

    b_getcur(&cur_line, &cur_pos);
    start_line = cur_line;
    start_pos = cur_pos;
    b_gets(cur_line, text);
    length = strlen(text);
    while ((c = k_getch()) != ESCAPE) {
        switch (c) {
            case '\b':
                /* don't back up past beginning of a line ... */
                if (cur_pos == 0 ||
                /* ... or where the insertion started */
                  cur_line == start_line && cur_pos == start_pos) {
                    UNKNOWN;
                    continue;
                }
                --cur_pos;
                /* doom the backed-over character for removal */
                if (end_line == 0) {
                    end_line = cur_line;
                    end_pos = cur_pos;
                }
                break;
            case CR:
                /* break the current line into two lines */
                c = text[cur_pos];
                text[cur_pos] = '\0';
                b_replace(cur_line, text);
                text[cur_pos] = c;
                if (end_line == cur_line) {
                    /* good chance to delete text */
                    cur_pos = end_pos + 1;
                    end_line = 0;
                }
                if (end_line > cur_line) {
                    b_gets(++cur_line, text);
                    length = strlen(text);
                    cur_pos = 0;
                    break;
                }
                /* shift text to create current line (strcpy()
                   is nonportable when its arguments overlap) */
                for (i = 0; (text[i] = text[cur_pos+i]) != '\0'; ++i)
                    ;
                length -= cur_pos;
                if (b_insert(++cur_line, text) == 0)    /* failed */
                    break;
```

```
                            if (end_line > 0)
                                ++end_line;
                            cur_pos = 0;
                            break;
                    default:
                        if (!isprint(c) && c != '\t') {
                            /* unprintable character */
                            UNKNOWN;
                            continue;
                        }
                        /* insert the character */
                        if (end_line == 0) { /* not overwriting */
                            if (length >= MAXTEXT-1) {
                                UNKNOWN;
                                s_savemsg("Line length exceeds %d.",
                                    MAXTEXT);
                                break;
                            }
                            for (i = ++length; i > cur_pos; --i)
                                text[i] = text[i-1];
                        }
                        if (text[cur_pos] == '\0')
                            text[cur_pos+1] = '\0';
                        text[cur_pos] = c;
                        b_replace(cur_line, text);
                        /* if this is the last doomed location */
                        if (end_line == cur_line && end_pos == cur_pos)
                            end_line = 0;
                        ++cur_pos;
                        break;
                }
                b_setcur(cur_line, cur_pos);
                s_refresh();
            }
        if (end_line > 0)
            /* delete the doomed characters */
            do_delete(cur_line, cur_pos, end_line, end_pos + 1);

        /* position the cursor at the last inserted character */
        b_setcur(cur_line, max(cur_pos-1, 0));
}


/*
 * yank.c - yank buffer
 *
 *
 * Entry points:
 *
 *     do_put(way)
 *     int way;
 *         Copy the yank buffer to the main buffer.  If way = 1, the lines
 *         go after the current line; otherwise, they go before it.
 *
 *     int do_yank(line1, line2)
 *     int line1, line2;
 *         Copy the block of lines from line1 to line2, inclusive, to the
 *         yank buffer; tell if successful.  Line1 cannot exceed line2.
 *
 *
 * External procedure calls:
 *
```

```
*     b_getcur(line_ptr, pos_ptr)    .. file Bman.c
*     int *line_ptr, *pos_ptr;
*          Return the line and position of the cursor.
*
*     b_gets(k, s)                    .. file Bman.c
*     int k;
*     char s[];
*          Copy the k-th buffer line to s.
*
*     b_insert(k, s)                  .. file Bman.c
*     int k;
*     char s[];
*          Insert s into the buffer as line k.
*
*     b_setline(line)                 .. file Bman.c
*     int line;
*          Set the cursor to line's first nonwhite character.
*
*     s_savemsg(msg, count)           .. file Sman.c
*     char *msg;
*     int count;
*          Format msg and save it for the next screen refreshing.
*
*
*
* Implementation:
*
*     Simple linked list.  Storage is allocated dynamically with malloc()
*     (not ckalloc()) so execution can continue if storage is exhausted.
*/

#include "s.h"

struct y_line {
    char *y_text;
    struct y_line *next;
};

static struct y_line *start = NULL;

/* do_put - copy the yank buffer to the file buffer */
do_put(way)                                                          do_put
int way;
{
    struct y_line *p;
    int cur_line, cur_pos, line, size;

    if (start == NULL) {
        UNKNOWN;
        return;
    }
    b_getcur(&cur_line, &cur_pos);
    if (way == 1)
        ++cur_line;
    for (line = cur_line, p = start; p != NULL; p = p->next)
        b_insert(line++, p->y_text);

    /* move to first nonwhite character */
    b_setline(cur_line);
    if ((size = line - cur_line) >= 5)
        s_savemsg("%d lines added", size);
}
```

```
/* do_yank - copy lines from main buffer to yank buffer; tell if successful */
int do_yank(line1, line2)                                                        do__yank
int line1, line2;
{
    struct y_line *p, *q;
    char *malloc(), *r, *strcpy(), text[MAXTEXT-1];

    free_ybuf();

    for ( ; line1 <= line2; ++line1) {
        b_gets(line1, text);
        q = (struct y_line *) malloc(sizeof(struct y_line));
        r = malloc((unsigned)strlen(text)+1);
        if (q == NULL || r == NULL) {
            free_ybuf();
            return(0);
        }
        q->y_text = strcpy(r, text);
        q->next = NULL;
        /* link the line in at the end of the list */
        if (start == NULL)
            start = q;
        else
            p->next = q;
        p = q;      /* p points to the end of the list */
    }
    return(1);
}

/* free_ybuf - free the storage for the yank buffer */
static free_ybuf()                                                               free__ybuf
{
    struct y_line *p, *q;

    for (p = start; p != NULL; p = q) {
        free(p->y_text);
        q = p->next;
        free((char *)p);
    }
    start = NULL;
}
```

5.3 REMAINING COMMANDS

The remaining commands are listed below. For the most part, these are just the commands having no address. The only exceptions are the *p* and *P* commands, which contain no address but were explained earlier, and :*w* (write), which is covered below but can involve an address.

a Append characters after the current location. Characters are entered as with the *change* command (no text is deleted). Beginning with

The simple example

and typing the twelve characters

```
a<space>next<return>very<esc>
```

produces

```
The next
very simple example
```

A   Append characters at the end of the current line. Characters are
          entered as with the *a* command.

C   Change the remainder of the current line. The *C* command is
          synonymous with *c$*. Beginning with

```
The simple example
```

and typing the thirteen characters

```
Ceasy<space>sample<esc>
```

produces

```
The easy sample
```

D   Delete the remainder of the current line. The *D* command is syn-
          onymous with *d$*.

i   Insert characters at the current location. Characters are entered
          as with the *a* command.

J   Join the current line to the next line. In effect, the newline char-
          acter at the end of the current line and any white characters at
          the front of the following line are replaced by a single *<space>*
          character. The cursor is positioned at this *<space>* so it is easy
          to change the editor's way of joining the lines. Beginning with

```
The simple example
<tab>is designed to show
```

and typing *J* produces

```
The simple example is designed to show
```

m   Mark the current location so it can be referenced by an ' (apos-
          trophe) address or used by the *star* command (see below). To
          delete a range of lines, say lines 10–17, move the cursor to line

10, issue an *m* command, move the cursor to line 17 and type *d'*.

o   Insert lines below the current line. Characters are entered as with a *change* command. Beginning with

```
The simple example
is designed to show
```

and typing the thirteen characters

```
ogiven<return>above<esc>
```

produces

```
The simple example
given
above
is designed to show
```

O   Insert lines above the current line. Characters are entered as with the *o* command.

q   Quit the edit session without copying the buffer to the external file. If the buffer has been modified since it was last copied from or written to the external file, then the user is asked to confirm that the modifications should be discarded.

r<*char*>   Replace the current character with the given character. Beginning with

```
Tha simple example
```

and typing the two characters *re* produces

```
The simple example
```

s   Replace the current character with a string of characters, which are entered as with the *a* command.

u   Undo the last edit command that changed the buffer. Beginning with

```
The simple example
is designed to show
```

and typing the thirteen characters

```
ogiven<return>above<esc>
```

produces

```
The simple example
given
above
is designed to show
```

The command *2w* would then move the cursor to the start of
designed, where *u* would undo the *o* command, restoring

```
The simple example
is designed to show
```

<n>x   Delete *n* characters beginning at the cursor, where *n* defaults to
1. Beginning with

```
The simple example
```

and typing *xx* or *2x* produces

```
The mple example
```

ZZ   Quit the edit session after copying the buffer to the external file.
         If the buffer has not been modified since being synchronized with
         the external file, then the copy operation is skipped.

. (period) The *redo* command; repeat the last command that changed the
            buffer. Beginning with

```
The simple example
is designed to show
```

and typing the seven characters

```
cweasy<esc>
```

produces

```
The easy example
is designed to show
```

Then a *3w* command moves the cursor to the start of *designed*,
where a *redo* command repeats the *cweasy<esc>* command,
producing

```
The easy example
is easy to show
```

* (star)   The *star* command; iteratively alternate between the last string-search command and the last buffer-change command. The command is equivalent to typing an alternating sequence of *n* and *redo* commands. (The *n* command repeats the previous string-search command and the *redo* repeats the previous buffer-change command.) Beginning with

```
The easy example is easy to show.
It is so easy that it will make you queasy.
```

and typing the command

```
/easy<return>
```

produces

```
The easy example is easy to show.
It is so easy that it will make you queasy.
```

The command

```
cwsimple<esc>
```

changes *easy* to *simple*:

```
The simple example is easy to show.
It is so easy that it will make you queasy.
```

A *star* command then changes the remaining three occurrences of *easy* to *simple*, producing:

```
The simple example is simple to show.
It is so simple that it will make you qusimple.
```

In general, the range of lines affected by a *star* command is bounded by the current line and the marked line. (If no line is marked, then the last buffer line is used.)

A *star* command is considered improper if the last buffer-change command was *undo* or *:e*.

?   Tell the current location in the buffer. The report takes the form

```
commands.c: line 134 of 583
```

or

```
commands.c: [Modified] line 134 of 583
```

depending on whether the buffer has been modified since last synchronized with the external file.

:e<space> <file> <return>

Edit a new file. If the current buffer contents have been modified, then the user is asked to confirm that the modifications should be discarded. If no file is named, then a fresh copy of the file being edited is read.

:r<space> <file> <return>

Copy *file* to the buffer just below the current line. The command is analogous to the *p* command, except that lines are taken from a file instead of the yank buffer. If no file is named, then the file being edited is read.

:R<space> <file> <return>

Copy *file* to the buffer just above the current line. The command is analogous to the *P* command, except that lines are taken from a file instead of the yank buffer. If no file is named, then the file being edited is read.

:w<addr> <space> <file> <return>

Write the block of lines between the current line and the addressed line, inclusive, to *file*. Lines 10–17 of the buffer can be written to the file *foo.c* by

```
10g
:w17g<space>foo.c<return>
```

If the file already exists, then the user is asked to confirm that it should be overwritten.

There are three abbreviated forms of the command. The command *:w<return>* (no address and file are given) overwrites the file being edited with the entire contents of the buffer. The command *:w<addr> <return>* (no file is specified) writes a range of lines to the current file. The command *:w<space> <file> <return>* (no address is given) overwrites the named file with the buffer's contents.

Comments on Commands.c.   The commands discussed above, as well as the *p* and *P* commands of Section 5.2, are recognized by *simp_cmd()* in *commands.c*. The structure of *commands.c* is much like that of *address.c* (Section 5.1): the entry point is a function that consists of a large *switch* statement, and the file's other functions handle difficult cases. (The implementations of *redo* and *undo* are discussed in later sections.)

For several easy cases, the function *k_donext()* implements one command in terms of another. For example, the *D* command is handled by:

```
case 'D':
        k_donext("d$");
        break;
```

The call to *k_donext(''d$'')* causes *s* to execute the synonymous command *d$*. The next section reveals how *k_donext()* works.

Much of *commands.c* consists of procedures for the I/O commands *:e*, *:r*, *:R*, and *:w*. Care is taken to avoid such disasters as:

- accidentally quitting the editor without saving the buffer modifications
- overwriting a precious file by a typographical error in a *:w* command
- trying to edit a nontext file, such as a directory or a compiled program

The editor also guards against copying an unmodified buffer back to the external file with a *ZZ* command. The execution time for the copy operation is not very important, but skipping it avoids unnecessary recompilations by the *update* tool of Chapter 2. When a source file is overwritten, *update* recompiles it, even if the file's contents are unchanged.

Perhaps the most interesting code in *commands.c* is *do_star()*, which handles the *star* command. The underlying algorithm is

```
do_star()
{
    static int doing_star = 0, start_line, start_pos;

    if !doing_star { /* initialize for this star command */
        start_line,start_pos = current buffer location
        doing_star = 1;
    }
    call address() to execute an n string-search command
    if the search failed or the new address is beyond the mark { /* done */
        return cursor to start_line,start_pos
        doing_star = 0
    } else
        k_donext(''.*'')
}
```

Do_star() executes an *n* command directly, by calling *address()*. If the search fails or passes the mark, then the *star* operation is complete. Otherwise, the string ''.*'' is pushed back on the editor's input. The *redo* repeats the previous buffer-change command, and the *star* causes execution to return to *do_star()*.

The actual implementation of *do_star()* addresses the following additional concerns:

- When the *star* command is initiated, the marked line may precede the current line. *Do_star()* exchanges the two locations, then continues as before.

- The string found by the *n* command can appear more than once in the marked line. If the *redo* changes that line then the mark disappears; the above algorithm could not tell if the next *n* went beyond the original mark. In its initialization step, *do_star()* increments the mark to the following line. (Special care is needed if the last buffer line is initially marked.)

- The *redo* command can produce an error condition. (For example, a resulting line might be too long for *s*.) *Do_star()* stops iterating if a message is waiting to be printed.

- As given above, *do_star()* can fall into an infinite loop. The command sequence

```
/y<return>
ix<esc>
*
```

inserts *x* in front of the next *y* (the cursor is left on *x*), finds the same *y*, inserts another *x*, finds the same *y*, ... (For an alternate command sequence that avoids the problem, see Exercise 3. For other examples of potential infinite loops with *do_star()*, see Exercises 7 and 8.) *Do_star()* pauses after 50 successful changes; the user types another *star* to continue the search-and-change cycle.

Comments on S.c.   The editor's main program is contained in *s.c*. In essence, the program consists of the loop

```
for each editor command {
        get the count, if it exists, from the start of the line
        if the command is recognized by simp_cmd()
            continue
        if the next character is 'c', 'd', or 'y' {
                get the count, if it exists, that follows the operator
                if two counts were given
                    multiply them together
        }
        call address()
        if there was an operator 'c', 'd', or 'y'
            call operator()
    }
```

Counts can be given before the operator, after the operator, or in both places. The commands *16dg*, *4d4g*, and *d16g* are equivalent.

EXERCISES

1. Give a command sequence that writes the current line (and no others) to *file*.

2. Explain why *<return>* cannot be used as the address in a *:w* command. Are there any other address that won't work in a *write* command?

3. Which buffer-change command,

$$ix<esc>$$

or

$$sxy<esc>$$

should be used with *star* to insert *x* in front of every *y*? Explain.

4. Show that the command *r<char>* is synonymous with the four-character command

$$c<space><char><esc>$$

Explain why implementing the *r* command by

```
case 'r':
        sprintf(text, "c %c%c", c_getch(), ESCAPE);
        c_next(text);
        break;
```

is superior to:

```
case 'r':
        b_get(cur_line, text);
        text[cur_pos] = c_getch();
        b_replace(cur_line, text);
        break;
```

(*Hint:* Consider *r<return>* and *r<control-G>*.)

5. Is the command *<n>cc* equivalent to *<n−1><return>*? Is it equivalent to *c<k>g* with *k* = *cur_line* + n − 1, where *cur_line* is the current line number? Is there an easy way to implement *<n>cc* in *commands.c* using *k_donext()*? (*Hint:* It must be possible for a subsequent *redo* command to repeat either *3cc* or *3cw*. Understanding the full complexity of implementing *cc*, *dd*, and *yy* in *commands.c* requires knowing how *k_donext()* and *k_redo()* are implemented (Section 5.4).)

6. Explain why it is not desirable to implement the *A* command by

```
case 'A':
        k_donext("$a");
        break;
```

7. Consider the command sequence:

```
/x<return>
i12345<esc>
*
```

How does *do_star()* keep pointers in bounds?

8. Suppose the edited file consists of two lines, each containing a single *x*. Describe the effect of the command sequence:

```
1g
y<return>
/x<return>
p
*
```

How does *do__star()* avoid an infinite loop?

9. Code for the *:e* (edit) command (procedure *do__io()* in *commands.c*) includes the line:

```
b_newcmd();        /* so the :e command cannot be undone */
```

Because of this line, an *undo* command after an *edit* command empties the buffer, rather than return to editing the previous file. Why is this desirable? (*Hint:* Consider the command sequence:

```
s foo
:e thud
u
ZZ
```

The *undo* command restores the buffer's contents, but does not restore such aspects of the editing environment as the remembered file name.)

```
/*
* commands.c - commands without an address
*    ... also handles the  :w  command, which can contain an address
*
*
* Entry point:
*
*    int simp_cmd(n, c)
*    int n;
*    char c;
*        If the count n, character c and, in some cases, characters that
*        follow c constitute one of the commands listed below, then the
*        command is performed and 1 is returned.  Otherwise, 0 is returned.
*
*    The commands recognized by simp_cmd() are:
*
*    a          - append characters after the cursor location
*    A          - append characters at the end of the current line
*    C          - change the remainder of the line (same as c$)
*    D          - delete the remainder of the line (same as d$)
*    i          - insert characters at the cursor location
*    J          - join two lines together
*    m          - mark the current position
*    o          - insert lines below the current line
*    O          - insert lines above the current line
*    p          - put the contents of the yank buffer below the current line
```

```
*     p          - put the contents of the yank buffer above the current line
*     q          - quit; don't save the modifications
*     r<char>    - replace the current character by <char>
*     s          - substitute for the current character (same as c<space>)
*     u          - undo the most recent buffer-change command
*     <n>x       - delete n characters (same as <n>d<space>)
*     ZZ         - save the modifications and quit
*     ?          - tell the current position in the file
*     .          - redo the most recent buffer-change command
*     *          - iterate the last search-change pair
*     :e         - edit another file
*     :r         - read a file; place its contents below the current line
*     :R         - read a file; place its contents above the current line
*     :w         - write a range of lines to a file
*
*
* External procedures calls:
*
*     address(n, c, op)                 .. file address.c
*     int n;
*     char c, op;
*         Set the buffer's cursor according to the count n,
*         the cursor movement command c and the operation op.
*
*     b_delete(first, last)             .. file Bman.c
*     int first, last;
*         Delete a range of buffer lines.
*
*     b_free()                          .. file Bman.c
*         Free all temporary buffer storage.
*
*     b_getcur(line_ptr, pos_ptr)       .. file Bman.c
*     int *line_ptr, *pos_ptr;
*         Return the line and position of the cursor.
*
*     b_getmark(line_ptr, pos_ptr)      .. file Bman.c
*     int *line_ptr, *pos_ptr;
*         Return the line and position of the mark.
*
*     b_gets(k, s)                      .. file Bman.c
*     int k;
*     char s[];
*         Copy the k-th buffer line to s.
*
*     int b_insert(k, s)                .. file Bman.c
*     int k;
*     char s[];
*         Insert s into the buffer as line k; tell if successful.
*
*     int b_modified()                  .. file Bman.c
*         Tell if buffer contents differ from the external file.
*
*     b_setcur(line, pos)               .. file Bman.c
*     int line, pos;
*         Set the cursor to the indicated location.
*
*     b_setline(line)                   .. file Bman.c
*     int line;
*         Set the cursor to line's first nonwhite character.
*
```

```
*       b_setmark(line, pos)                .. file Bman.c
*       int line, pos;
*           Mark the indicated location.
*
*       int b_size()                        .. file Bman.c
*           Return the number of lines currently in the buffer.
*
*       b_unmod()                           .. file Bman.c
*           Record that buffer contents match the external file.
*
*       do_insert()                         .. file operator.c
*           Read characters from keyboard; insert them in buffer.
*
*       do_put(way)                         .. file operator.c
*       int way;
*           Put the yank buffer on the indicated side of the current line.
*
*       k_donext(command)                   .. file keyboard.c
*       char *command;
*           Arrange for the given editor command to be executed next.
*
*       k_finish()                          .. file keyboard.c
*           Close down the keyboard manager.
*
*       int k_getch()                       .. file keyboard.c
*           Return the next character of the command.
*
*       k_redo()                            .. file keyboard.c
*           Redo the most recent buffer-change command.
*
*       s_finish()                          .. file Sman.c
*           Shut down the display module.
*
*       char *s_getmsg(msg)                 .. file Sman.c
*       char *msg;
*           Print msg; return the user's reply,
*
*       int s_ismsg()                       .. file Sman.c
*           Tell if an error message is pending.
*
*       s_putmsg(msg)                       .. file Sman.c
*       char *msg;
*           Print the message on the last row.
*
*       s_refresh()                         .. file Sman.c
*           Bring the display up to date with the buffer.
*
*       s_savemsg(msg, val)                 .. file Sman.c
*       char *msg;
*       int val;
*           Format msg and save it for the next screen refreshing.
*
*       undo()                              .. file Bman.c
*           Undo the most recent buffer-change command.
*/

#include "s.h"

static char cur_file[MAXTEXT];       /* remembers name of the current file */
```

```
int simp_cmd(n, c)                                                       simp__cmd
int n;
char c;
{
     int cur_line, cur_pos, i;
     char *t, text1[MAXTEXT], text2[MAXTEXT];

     b_getcur(&cur_line, &cur_pos);
     switch (c) {
         case 'a':
             b_gets(cur_line, text1);
             if (text1[0] != '\0') {          /* unless the line is empty */
                 b_setcur(cur_line, cur_pos+1);
                 s_refresh();
             }
             do_insert();
             break;
         case 'A':
             b_gets(cur_line, text1);
             b_setcur(cur_line, strlen(text1));
             s_refresh();
             do_insert();
             break;
         case 'C':
             k_donext("c$");
             break;
         case 'D':
             k_donext("d$");
             break;
         case 'i':
             do_insert();
             break;
         case 'J':
             if (cur_line >= b_size()) {
                 UNKNOWN;
                 break;
             }
             b_gets(cur_line, text1);
             i = strlen(text1);
             /* put a space between the two lines */
             text1[i] = ' ';
             b_gets(cur_line + 1, text2);
             /* strip leading white characters from second line */
             for (t = text2; isspace(*t); ++t)
                 ;
             if (i + 1 + strlen(t) >= MAXTEXT-1) {
                 s_savemsg("Line length exceeds %d.", MAXTEXT);
                 break;
             }
             strcpy(text1 + i + 1, t);
             b_delete(cur_line, cur_line + 1);
             b_insert(cur_line, text1);
             b_setcur(cur_line, i);
             break;
         case 'm':
             b_setmark();
             break;
         case 'o':
             ++cur_line;
             /* no break statement; fall into ... */
```

```c
    case 'O':
        b_insert(cur_line, "");
        b_setcur(cur_line, 0);
        s_refresh();
        do_insert();
        break;
    case 'p':
        do_put(1);
        break;
    case 'P':
        do_put(-1);
        break;
    case 'q':
        if (b_modified()) {
            s_putmsg("Discard? ");
            if (k_getch() != 'y') {
                UNKNOWN;
                break;
            }
        }
        if (s_ismsg())
            s_refresh();
        b_free();
        k_finish();
        s_finish();
        exit(0);
    case 'r':
        sprintf(text1, "c %c%c", k_getch(), ESCAPE);
        k_donext(text1);      /* c<space><char><esc> */
        break;
    case 's':
        k_donext("c ");       /* c<space> */
        break;
    case 'u':
        undo();
        break;
    case 'x':
        if (n == 0)      /* set default */
            n = 1;
        sprintf(text1, "%dd ", n);
        k_donext(text1);      /* <n>d<space> */
        break;
    case 'Z':
        if (k_getch() != 'Z') {
            UNKNOWN;
            break;
        }
        if (b_modified()) {
            sprintf(text1, ":w%cq", CR);
            k_donext(text1);      /* :w<return>q */
        } else
            k_donext("q");
        break;
    case '?':
        sprintf(text1, "%s: %sline %d of %d", cur_file,
            (b_modified()) ? "[Modified] " : "",
            cur_line, b_size());
        s_savemsg(text1, 0);
        break;
```

```
          case '.':
                 k_redo();
                 break;
          case '*':
                 do_star();
                 break;
          case ':':
                 do_io();
                 break;
          default:
                 return(0);
    }
    return(1);
}

/*
-------------------- the star command --------------------
* Entry point:
*
*      do_star()
*          From the minimum of the current and marked lines, alternate
*          between n and redo commands until the maximum of the two lines
*          is reached.  The marked line defaults to the last buffer line.
*/

#define STAR_MAX  50       /* limits the number of n and redo commands */

static do_star()                                                         do_star
{
      static int all_lines, doing_star = 0, iterations, start_line = 0, start_pos;
      int cur_line, cur_pos, done, mark_line, mark_pos, old_line, old_pos;

      if (!b_modified()) {
          UNKNOWN;
          return;
      }
      if (s_ismsg()) {   /* an error message is waiting; don't continue */
          doing_star = 0;
          if (start_line == 0)
                 UNKNOWN;
          else
                 b_setcur(start_line, start_pos);
          return;
      }
      if (!doing_star) {          /* initialize for this star command */
          doing_star = 1;
          iterations = 0;
          b_getcur(&start_line, &start_pos);
          b_getmark(&mark_line, &mark_pos);
          if (mark_line > 0 && mark_line < start_line) {
                 /* guarantee that cursor precedes mark */
                 b_setmark();
                 b_setcur(mark_line, mark_pos);
                 b_getcur(&start_line, &start_pos);
                 b_getmark(&mark_line, &mark_pos);
          }
          if (mark_line == 0 || mark_line == b_size() || start_line == b_size())
                 all_lines = 1;
          else {
                 all_lines = 0;
                 /* move mark to the following line */
```

```
                b_setcur(mark_line+1, 0);
                b_setmark();
                b_setcur(start_line, start_pos);
        }
    }
    /* execute an n command */
    b_getcur(&old_line, &old_pos);
    address(0, 'n', ' ');
    b_getcur(&cur_line, &cur_pos);
    b_getmark(&mark_line, &mark_pos);
    /* done if past mark or if the search fails */
    done = (!all_lines && cur_line >= mark_line ||
        cur_line < old_line ||
        cur_line == old_line && cur_pos <= old_pos);
    if (!done && ++iterations <= STAR_MAX)
        /* execute a redo command then return to this procedure */
        k_donext(".*");
    else {
        if (done)
            if (iterations == 1)
                    s_savemsg("1 change", 0);
            else
                    s_savemsg("%d changes", iterations);
        else
            s_savemsg("%d changes; type '*' to continue.", STAR_MAX);
        doing_star = 0;
        b_setcur(start_line, start_pos);
    }
}


/*
-------------------  I/O commands  --------------------
*
*  Entry point:
*
*    do_io();
*         Read the part of an edit command after ':', then execute it.
*
*/

static do_io()                                                                      do_io
{
    int cur_line, cur_pos, size;
    char *file, *s_getmsg(), msg[80], *reply;

    /* get the remainder of the command */
    reply = s_getmsg(":");
    b_getcur(&cur_line, &cur_pos);

    /* write commands contain an address; treat them as a special case */
    if (*reply == 'w') {
        do_write(reply+1);
        b_setcur(cur_line, cur_pos);
        return;
    }

    /* find the start of the file name */
    for (file = reply+1; *file == ' '; ++file)
        ;
    if (*file == '\0')
        file = cur_file;     /* default: use the current file name */
```

```
        switch (*reply) {
            case 'e':
                if (b_modified()) {
                    s_putmsg("Discard? ");
                    if (k_getch() != 'y')
                        break;
                }
                if (file != cur_file)
                    strcpy(cur_file, file);   /* remember name */
                b_delete(1, b_size());
                b_newcmd();     /* so the :e command cannot be undone */
                if ((size = do_read(file, 1)) > 0) {
                    sprintf(msg, "%s: %d lines", file, size);
                    s_savemsg(msg, 0);
                } else {
                    if (size == -1) {
                        sprintf(msg, "%s is a new file", file);
                        s_savemsg(msg, 0);
                    }
                    b_insert(1, "");
                    b_setcur(1, 0);
                }
                /* record that buffer contents match external file */
                b_unmod();
                break;
            case 'r':
                ++cur_line;
                /* no break statement; fall into ... */
            case 'R':
                if ((size = do_read(file, cur_line)) > 5)
                    s_savemsg("%d lines read", size);
                else if (size == -1) {
                    sprintf(msg, "Cannot read %s.", file);
                    s_savemsg(msg, 0);
                }
                break;
            default:
                UNKNOWN;
                break;
        }
}


/*
 * do_read - read a file to buffer at the indicated line;
 * a returned value >= 0 tells number of lines that were read from the file
 * a returned value -1 means that the file could not be opened for reading
 * a returned value -2 means that the file contains nonprintable characters
 */
static int do_read(file, line)                                        do_read
char *file;
int line;
{
    FILE *fp, *fopen();
    int i, c;
    char text[MAXTEXT];

    if ((fp = fopen(file, "r")) == NULL)
        return(-1);
    /*
     * Read the first ten characters and check that they are printable.
     * Some C I/O packages read '\r' (<return>) characters.  Also,
```

```
      * nonprintable characters in files might be used for, e.g.,
      * printer control characters.
      */
     for (i = 0; (c = getc(fp)) != EOF && i < 10; ++i)
         if (!isprint(c) && c != '\n' && c != '\t' ) {
             sprintf(text, "%s is not a text file", file);
             s_savemsg(text, 0);
             fclose(fp);
             return(-2);
         }
     if (i == 0) {
         sprintf(text, "%s is empty", file);
         s_savemsg(text, 0);
         fclose(fp);
         return(0);
     }

     rewind(fp);
     /* copy the file to the buffer */
     for (i = line; fgets(text, MAXTEXT, fp) != NULL; ++i) {
         text[strlen(text)-1] = '\0';        /* trim off the newline */
         if (b_insert(i, text) == 0)
             break;
     }
     fclose(fp);
     /* move to the first nonwhite character in the first line read */
     b_setline(line);
     return(i - line);
}

/* do_write - write a file according to given specifications */
static do_write(specs)                                                  do_write
char *specs;
{
     int cur_line, cur_pos, n, new_line, new_pos;
     char *addr, *file;

     /* special case: :w<return> writes buffer to current file */
     if (*specs == '\0') {
         write_lines(1, b_size(), cur_file);
         return;
     }
     /* special case: :w<space>file<return> writes buffer to named file */
     if (*specs == ' ') {
         for (file = specs + 1; *file == ' '; ++file)
             ;
         write_lines(1, b_size(), file);
         return;
     }

     /* get the count that follows ":w" */
     n = 0;
     for (addr = specs; isdigit(*addr); ++addr)
         n = 10*n + *addr - '0';
     if (*addr == '\0') {
         UNKNOWN;
         return;
     }

     /* find and mark the end of the address */
     for (file = addr; *file != '\0' && *file != ' '; ++file)
         ;
```

```
        if (*file == ' ')
            *file++ = '\0';

        b_getcur(&cur_line, &cur_pos);
        /* push the address, minus the first character, back on the input */
        k_donext(addr + 1);
        address(n, *addr, ':');
        b_getcur(&new_line, &new_pos);
        if (new_line == cur_line && new_pos == cur_pos) {
            /* the address did not make sense */
            UNKNOWN;
            return;
        }

        /* special case: :w<addr><return> writes to the current file */
        if (*file == '\0')
            file = cur_file;

        if (cur_line <= new_line)
            write_lines(cur_line, new_line, file);
        else
            write_lines(new_line, cur_line, file);
}

/* write_lines - write a range of lines to a file */
static write_lines(from, to, file)                                    write_lines
int from, to;
char *file;
{
        FILE *fopen(), *fp;
        int count = to - from + 1;
        char text[MAXTEXT-1];

        /* be cautious about overwriting files */
        if (!strsame(file, cur_file)) {
            if ((fp = fopen(file, "r")) != NULL) {
                s_putmsg("Overwrite? ");
                if (k_getch() == 'y')
                    fclose(fp);
                else
                    return;
            }
        } else if (from > 1 || to < b_size()) {
            s_putmsg("Write partial buffer to current file? ");
            if (k_getch() != 'y')
                return;
        }

        if ((fp = fopen(file, "w")) == NULL) {
            sprintf(text, "Cannot write %s.", file);
            s_savemsg(text, 0);
            return;
        }
        /* if entire buffer is saved, record that the user is free to quit */
        if (strsame(file, cur_file) && from == 1 && to == b_size())
            b_unmod();
        /* write the lines */
        while (from <= to) {
            b_gets(from++, text);
            fprintf(fp, "%s\n", text);
        }
```

```
        fclose(fp);
        sprintf(text, "%s: %d line%s", file, count, (count == 1) ? "" : "s");
        s_savemsg(text, 0);
}


/*
 * s - a screen editor
 *
 *
 * Source files:
 *
 *          command handler:
 *      address.c       - process addresses
 *      commands.c      - commands without an address
 *      keyboard.c      - read commands
 *      lib.c           - library of C procedures
 *      operator.c      - operators c, d and y
 *      s.c             - this file; contains the main program
 *      s.h             - macro definitions
 *      yank.c          - the yank buffer
 *
 *          buffer module:
 *      Bman.c          - buffer manager
 *      buffer.c        - data structure for the buffer
 *
 *          screen module:
 *      Sman.c          - screen manager
 *      screen.c        - terminal-specific procedures
 *
 *
 * External procedure calls:
 *
 *      address(n, c, op)               .. file address.c
 *      int n;
 *      char c, op;
 *          Set the buffer's cursor according to the count n,
 *          the cursor movement command c and the operation op.
 *
 *      b_getcur(line_ptr, pos_ptr)     .. file Bman.c
 *      int *line_ptr, *pos_ptr;
 *          Return the line and position of the cursor.
 *
 *      b_init()                        .. file Bman.c
 *          Initialize the buffer module.
 *
 *      k_donext(command)               .. file keyboard.c
 *      char *command;
 *          Arrange for the given edit command to be executed next.
 *
 *      int k_getch()                   .. file keyboard.c
 *          Return the next character of the command.
 *
 *      k_init()                        .. file keyboard.c
 *          Initialize the keyboard manager.
 *
 *      k_newcmd()                      .. file keyboard.c
 *          Prepare for reading a new command.
 *
 *      operator(op, line, pos)         .. file operator.c
 *      char op;
 *      int line, pos;
```

```
*          Apply op = 'c', 'd' or 'y' using the indicated buffer
*          location and the cursor location.
*
*    s_init()                            .. file Sman.c
*    Initialize the screen module.
*
*    s_refresh()                         .. file Sman.c
*          Bring the screen up to date with the buffer.
*
*    int simp_cmd(n, c)                  .. file commands.c
*    int n;
*    char c;
*          Apply commands without addresses; tell if successful.
*
*
* System Dependencies:
*
*    To move this editor to a non-UNIX operating system, the function
*    k_flip() in file keyboard.c must be changed.  (This functions flips the
*    terminal driver to and from noecho-raw mode.)
*
*    To operate this editor on a non-ANSI standard video terminal, or one
*    without "autowrap", requires modification of the file screen.c.
*/

#include "s.h"

main(argc, argv)                                                            main
int argc;
char *argv[];
{
     int count, count2, cur_line, cur_pos, new_line, new_pos;
     char c, cmd[MAXTEXT], op;

     if (argc != 2)
          fatal("usage: s file");
     b_init();
     k_init();
     s_init();
     /* do the command:  :e<space><file><return> */
     sprintf(cmd, ":e %s%c", argv[1], CR);
     k_donext(cmd);
     for ( ; ; ) {          /* loop over commands */
          /* prepare to get a new command */
          s_refresh();
          k_newcmd();
          c = k_getch();
          count = get_count(&c);
          /* for simple commands, move on to the next command */
          if (simp_cmd(count, c))
               continue;
          /* for c, d or y operators, get the second count */
          if (c == 'c' || c == 'd' || c == 'y') {
               op = c;
               c = k_getch();
               count2 = get_count(&c);
               if (count > 0 && count2 > 0)
                    count *= count2;
               else
                    count = max(count, count2);
```

```
        } else
            op = ' ';
        /* set the buffer's idea of the cursor to the new address */
        b_getcur(&cur_line, &cur_pos);
        address(count, c, op);
        /* check that cursor actually moved */
        b_getcur(&new_line, &new_pos);
        if (cur_line == new_line && cur_pos == new_pos)
            UNKNOWN;
        else if (op != ' ')
            operator(op, cur_line, cur_pos);
    }
}

/* get_count - determine a count in an edit command */
static int get_count(ch_ptr)                                          get_count
char *ch_ptr;
{
    int ch = *ch_ptr, count;

    if (isdigit(ch) && ch != '0') {      /* a count cannot start with zero */
        count = ch - '0';
        while (isdigit(ch = k_getch()))
            count = 10*count + ch - '0';
    } else
        count = 0;
    *ch_ptr = ch;
    return(count);
}
```

5.4 THE KEYBOARD

The code in *keyboard.c* supports the editor's interaction with the terminal in two main ways. First, it suspends system-dependent interpretations of keyboard data. Second, other parts of the editor can "push a command back on the input stream," so the command is read and executed next.

Suspension of Input Processing.   The operating system normally processes keyboard input in two ways:

- *Echoing.* Typed characters are automatically echoed on the screen.
- *Buffering.* Characters are not made available for program input until the <*return*> key is pressed. This allows corrections to be made as the line is typed (Exercise 1).

A screen editor needs to turn off echoing and buffering of keyboard input. For example, pressing the *w* key should not print *w* on the screen (no echoing), but instead should move the cursor (no buffering). Input without this processing is said to be in *noecho-raw mode*.

The following procedure works on Berkeley 4.2 BSD UNIX systems.

```
/* k_flip - toggle keyboard input to and from noecho-raw mode */
#include <sgtty.h>
k_flip()
{
    struct sgttyb ttyb;

    ioctl(0, TIOCGETP, &ttyb);
    ttyb.sg_flags ^= ECHO | RAW;
    ioctl(0, TIOCSETP, &ttyb);
}
```

Procedure *ioctl()* with option *TIOCGETP* fills the structure *ttyb* with information about the state of the keyboard (the I/O stream with file descriptor 0). The assignment statement uses the bitwise exclusive OR operator ($^$) to toggle the *echo* and *raw* bits. Then *ioctl()* sets the keyboard state to the modified values.

Toggling to noecho-raw mode can have unexpected side effects. With some, but not all, versions of UNIX, *k_flip()* affects the processing of newline characters on input and/or output. The file *s.h* assumes that the <*return*> key sends *s* a '\r' character instead of '\n'. In addition, the procedure *scr_move()* of *screen.c* (Section 5.7) assumes that a "\r\n" pair is needed to move the cursor to the start of the next line.

For a general discussion of UNIX terminal I/O see Chapter 4 of *Advanced UNIX Programming* by Marc J. Rochkind (Prentice-Hall, 1985).

Redoing Commands.   As a command is read from the keyboard by calls to *k_getch()*, copies of the characters are saved. These characters can later be "pushed back" on the input stream to repeat the command. The following pseudocode supplies that capability:

```
static char
    change[],           /* most recent buffer-change command */
    command[],          /* accumulates the current command */
    *cmd_ptr = command, /* next location in command */
    pushed[],           /* pushed-back command */
    *push_ptr = pushed; /* next location in pushed */

/* k_donext—push a command back on the input stream */
k_donext(cmd)
char *cmd;
{
    char *s;

    /* copy cmd to pushed[] in reverse order */
    for (s = cmd + strlen(cmd) - 1; s >= cmd; --s)
        *push_ptr++ = *s;
}
```

```
/* k__getch—get a character of the command */
int k__getch()
{
    int ch;

    /* get pushed character (preferably) or read keyboard */
    ch = (push__ptr > pushed) ? *(−−push__ptr) : getchar();
    /* remember character */
    *cmd__ptr++ = ch;
    return(ch);
}


/* k__newcmd—start a new command */
k__newcmd()
{
    /* if the old command changed the buffer, remember it */
    if (b__changed()) {
        *cmd__ptr = '\0';
        strcpy(change, command);
        b__newcmd();          /* mark buffer "unchanged" */
    }
    cmd__ptr = command;    /* prepare to collect new command */
}


/* k__redo—redo the last buffer−change command */
k__redo()
{
    k__donext(change);
}
```

Suppose *s* is used to change a word to "replacement." As the user types

```
cwreplacement<esc>
```

k__getch() calls *getchar()*, copies the character to the array *command[]*, then passes it back to another procedure in the command processor. (Specifically, *main()* classifies the initial *c* as an operator, *address()* interprets the *w*, and *in__chars()* of *operator.c* reads the remainder.) Before the next command is read, *k__newcmd()* is called and learns from *b__changed()* that the previous command modified the buffer; consequently, *command[]* is copied to *change[]*. Subsequent cursor-movement commands leave *change[]* unaltered. When the cursor reaches the desired word, a *redo* command results in a call to *k__redo()*, which calls *k__donext()* to copy *change[]* to *pushed[]*. (The implementation of *k__getch()* is simplified slightly by copying characters to *pushed[]* in reverse order.) Until *pushed[]* is drained, calls to *k__getch()* return a character from *pushed[]* rather than read the keyboard, so the *c* command is repeated.

The "push back" capability is useful for handling commands that merely abbreviate other commands. *K__donext()* finds several uses in *simp__cmd()* to implement one command in terms of a synonymous command, as discussed in the previous section.

Other Duties. Beyond the tasks just described (and implementation details like avoiding array overflow), *keyboard.c* performs the following duties:

- *Remember a command. K__lastcmd()* supplies the first letter in the previous command. The procedure *do__up__down()* in *address.c* (Section 5.1) needs to know if the last command was *j* or *k*.
- *Share the secret about input source.* Other parts of the command processor cannot distinguish true keyboard input from pushed-back commands. However, the buffer and screen modules need this information, for reasons explained in the next two sections. The calls

```
b_newcmd(push_ptr == pushed);
s_keyboard(push_ptr == pushed);
s_keyboard(0);
```

at various points in *keyboard.c* share the secret. (*Push__ptr* equals *pushed* if and only if input is from the keyboard.)

EXERCISES

1. Write pseudocode for a procedure that accepts a stream of characters from the set

a   #   @   R   \

accumulates them in a character array called a *line buffer*, and occasionally (upon receipt of *R*) writes the line buffer to the output. The characters have the following meanings, which can be escaped:

a ordinary letter: place it in the line buffer.
@ line kill: throw away all characters in the line buffer.
# character kill; throw away the previous character (if any) in the line buffer.
R *<return>*: place *N* (*<newline>*) in the line buffer; if the *R* was not escaped, then output the entire line buffer and empty it.
\ escape: throw away this character and place the following character in the line buffer. (If the following character is *R*, place *N* in the line buffer.)

Your procedure should produce the following transformations of input to output strings.

Input	Output
aa\\#R	aa#N
a\\aa#aRaaa@aa#R	aaaN
	aN
aa\\##aR	aaaN
R#aR	N
	aN
a#\\\\\\#aR	\\#aN
a\\RaaR	aNaaN

Note from the last example that the escaped *R* does not cause an "output buffer" operation. Ignore the possibility of line buffer overflow.

2. Explain why *k_redo()* will never encounter the situation

$$\texttt{change[0] == '\textbackslash 0'}$$

(*Hint:* Study the call to *k_donext()* near the top of *main()* in *s.c.*) Should *k_redo()* nonetheless include code to handle this case? Explain.

3. If you are using a recent Berkeley UNIX system, learn about the difference between *RAW* and *CBREAK* modes. (See *tty* in Section 4 of the manual.) Which would you prefer in *k_flip()*? A factor to consider is that *CBREAK* may permit terminal "handshaking"; see Section 5.7.

PROGRAMMING ASSIGNMENTS

1. Write *keyboard.c* using *malloc()* and *free()* so that only the amount of available memory limits the size of a remembered command. (*Hints:* It must be possible to push commands on top of other commands. For example, the *star* command pushes a ".*" command pair, and the '.' is immediately expanded to another command. The function *s_errmsg()* in *Sman.c* is useful for debugging, as explained in Programming Assignment 1 of Section 5.2.)

```
/*
 * keyboard.c - read commands
 *
 *
 * Entry points:
 *
 *     k_donext(cmd)
 *     char *cmd;
 *             Arrange that cmd will be done next.
 *
 *     k_finish()
 *             Close down the keyboard manager.
 *
 *     int k_getch()
 *             Return the next character of the current command.
```

```
*
*      k_init()
*           Initialize the keyboard manager.
*
*      char k_lastcmd()
*           Return the first letter in the last command.
*
*      k_newcmd()
*           Prepare for reading a new command.
*
*      k_redo()
*           Redo the last buffer-change command.
*
*
* External procedure calls:
*
*      int b_changed()              .. file Bman.c
*           Tell if the buffer was changed by the last command.
*
*      b_newcmd(bit)                .. file Bman.c
*      int bit;
*           Inform the buffer module that a new command is starting and tell
*           whether it is from the keyboard (bit = 1) or not (bit = 0).
*
*      s_keyboard(bit)              .. file Sman.c
*      int bit;
*           Inform the screen module whether the next input character is
*           from the keyboard (bit = 1) or not (bit = 0).
*
*      s_savemsg(msg, count)        .. file Sman.c
*      char *msg;
*      int count;
*           Format msg and save it for the next screen
*/
#include "s.h"
#define CMD_MAX 500              /* longest command that can be redone */

static char
     change[CMD_MAX+2],          /* most recent buffer-change command */
     cmd_last,                   /* first letter in the last command */
     command[CMD_MAX+2],         /* accumulates the current command */
     *cmd_ptr = command,         /* next location in command */
     pushed[CMD_MAX],            /* pushed-back command */
     *push_ptr = pushed;         /* next location in pushed */

/* k_donext - push a command back on the input stream */
k_donext(cmd)
char *cmd;
{
     int cmd_size;
     char *s;

     cmd_size = strlen(cmd);
     if (push_ptr - pushed + cmd_size > CMD_MAX) {
          s_savemsg("Pushed commands are too long.", 0);
          UNKNOWN;
     } else if (cmd_size > 0) {
          /* copy cmd to pushed[] in reverse order */
          for (s = cmd + cmd_size - 1; s >= cmd; --s)
               *push_ptr++ = *s;
          s_keyboard(0);
     }
}
```

k_donext

```
/* k_finish - close down the keyboard manager */                              k_finish
k_finish()
{
    k_flip();
}

/* k_getch - get a character of the command */                                k_getch
int k_getch()
{
    int ch;

    /* get pushed character (preferably) or read keyboard */
    /* use logical AND operation with octal 0177 to strip the parity bit */
    ch = (push_ptr > pushed) ? *(--push_ptr) : getchar() & 0177;
    /* remember character if there is room */
    if (cmd_ptr <= command + CMD_MAX)
        *cmd_ptr++ = ch;
    s_keyboard(push_ptr == pushed);
    return(ch);
}

/* k_init - initialize the keyboard manager */                                k_init
k_init()
{
    k_flip();
}

/* k_lastcmd - get first letter of the last command */                        k_lastcmd
char k_lastcmd()
{
    return(cmd_last);
}

/* k_newcmd - start a new command */                                          k_newcmd
k_newcmd()
{
    char *s;

    *cmd_ptr = '\0';
    /* remember first letter of the old command */
    for (s = command; *s != '\0' && !isalpha(*s); ++s)
        ;
    cmd_last = *s;
    /* if the old command changed the buffer, remember it */
    if (b_changed())
        strcpy(change, command);
    cmd_ptr = command;                     /* prepare to collect the new command */
    b_newcmd(push_ptr == pushed);          /* mark buffer "unchanged" */
}

/* k_redo - redo the last buffer-change command */                            k_redo
k_redo()
{
    if (strlen(change) > CMD_MAX) {
        s_savemsg("Cannot redo commands longer than %d characters.",
            CMD_MAX);
        change[0] = '\0';
    }
    if (change[0] == '\0')
        UNKNOWN;
    else
        k_donext(change);
}
```

```
/*
 * k_flip - toggle keyboard input to and from noecho-raw mode   (UNIX)
 * Normally:
 *    1. typed characters are echoed back to the terminal and
 *    2. input characters are buffered until a complete line
 *       has been received.
 * Flipping to noecho-raw mode suspends all such input processing.
 */

#include <sgtty.h>
static k_flip()
{                                                                              k_flip
    struct sgttyb ttyb;

    ioctl(0, TIOCGETP, &ttyb);
    ttyb.sg_flags ^= ECHO | RAW;
    ioctl(0, TIOCSETP, &ttyb);
}
```

5.5 THE BUFFER MODULE

The buffer module handles the editor's copy of the file being edited; it consists of

> *Bman.c* buffer manager
> *buffer.c* data structure for the buffer

Beside providing the command processor with access functions that delete, insert, or replace text lines, the buffer manager's main duties are:

1. Keep track of the cursor location.
2. Supply a unique identification number for every text string added to the buffer.
3. Keep track of the mark for the *m* and ' commands.
4. Implement the *undo* command.
5. Maintain several bits telling if the buffer was modified recently.

The Cursor Location.   Monitoring the cursor is trivial. The cursor location is set by some procedures in the command processor and read by others; the buffer module need only remember it. The relevant code in *Bman.c* is self-explanatory:

```
static int
    b_count = 0,          /* number of lines in the buffer */
    ...
    cur_line, cur_pos,    /* cursor location */
    ...
```

```
/* b_getcur - get the cursor location */
b_getcur(line_ptr, pos_ptr)
int *line_ptr, *pos_ptr;
{
     *line_ptr = cur_line;
     *pos_ptr = cur_pos;
}
     ...
/* b_setcur - set buffer's record of the cursor location */
b_setcur(line, pos)
int line, pos;
{
     if (line < 1 || line > b_count)
          s_errmsg("b_setcur(): improper line %d", line);
     else if (pos < -1)
          /* address() uses pos == -1 to signal a line address */
          s_errmsg("b_setcur(): improper position %d", pos);
     else {
          cur_line = line;
          cur_pos = pos;
     }
}
```

Error checks like those in *b__setcur()* appear throughout *Bman.c*. They guard against internal errors in *s*, rather than improper user commands. These tests caught several errors as *s* was written; the checks were left there in case you make errors while modifying *s*.

ID's.   With each call to *b__insert()* or *b__replace()*, the new text string is assigned a unique identification (ID) number. In this implementation, *buffer.c* assigns ID's in the order 1, 2, . . . , but the only requirement is that each call generates a different number. The ID stays attached to the string even if the line number of the string changes because earlier lines are inserted or deleted.

ID's simplify the screen module's job of economically refreshing the screen. Suppose the screen is being updated after a buffer change and the screen module wants to display buffer line 20 in row 1. The ID of line 20 is retrieved from the buffer module by a call to *b__lineid(20)*, then compared to the ID's of displayed lines. (The screen module remembers ID's of the current screen contents.) If the ID of line 20 equals the ID of a displayed line, there is no need for a character-by-character check to see if they are identical; the screen module can delete rows (if necessary) to bring line 20 to the top of the screen. (If you have done Programming Assignment 2 of Section 3.3, it may be instructive to observe the similarities between a line ID and a file signature.)

The Mark.   As a side benefit, ID's provide a clean implementation of the mark.

```
static int
    ...
    mark_id, mark_pos,        /* ID of marked line; position of mark in line */
    ...

/* b_getmark - get the mark's location */
b_getmark(line_ptr, pos_ptr)
int *line_ptr, *pos_ptr;
{
    int line;

    for (line = 1; line <= b_count; ++line)
        if (b_lineid(line) == mark_id) {
            *line_ptr = line;
            *pos_ptr = mark_pos;
            return;
        }
    *line_ptr = *pos_ptr = 0;
}
    ...
/* b_setmark - set buffer's mark to the cursor location */
b_setmark()
{
    mark_id = b_lineid(cur_line);
    mark_pos = cur_pos;
}
```

The buffer manager remembers the ID of the marked line and the position of the mark within the line. The mark remains associated with the line unless the marked line is deleted or replaced; other lines can come and go. To locate the marked line, *b_getmark()* searches through the buffer for a line possessing the remembered ID.

Undo.   The implementation of *undo* is probably the most interesting part of the buffer module. The buffer manager records calls to *b_delete()*, *b_insert()*, and *b_replace()* with *modification records*:

```
/* definition of a modification record */
struct mod_rec {
    int type;                 /* DELETE, INSERT or REPLACE */
    int line;                 /* line number in the buffer */
    char *del_text;           /* deleted text (NULL for INSERT) */
    struct mod_rec *next;     /* link to next modification record */
};

static struct mod_rec
    *curr_recs,               /* mod recs for current user command */
    *prev_recs;               /* mod recs for previous user change */
```

Undo() traces the list of modification records for the previous buffer-change command and undoes their effects on the buffer. In pseudocode, the algorithm is

```
/* undo—undo the last user command that changed the buffer */
undo()
{
```

```
/*
 * Undo() marches down the list of modification records generated by
 * the last user change (the list starts with the most recent change).
 * A delete is undone by an insert, and vice versa. A replace is
 * undone by another replace.
 */

struct mod__rec *m;

for (m = prev__recs; m != NULL; m = m->next)
    switch (m->type) {
        case DELETE:
            b__insert(m->line, m->del__text);
            break;
        case INSERT:
            b__delete(m->line, m->line);
            break;
        case REPLACE:
            b__replace(m->line, m->del__text);
            break;
    }
}
```

The easiest way to see how *undo* works is to study an example. Suppose the cursor is located on line 2 of the file

```
line1
line2
line3
line4
line5
```

and the command is:

```
3ccnew1<return>new2<esc>
```

After *3cc* is typed, the procedure *operator()* of *operator.c* (Section 5.2) calls *b_delete(2, 3)* and *b_replace(2, '''')* to replace lines 2-4 by a blank line. This creates three modification records:

Type	Line	Del__text
DELETE	2	''line2''
DELETE	2	''line3''
REPLACE	2	''line4''

To save time and memory, the procedure *add__rec()* in *Bman.c* collapses a sequence of consecutive *REPLACE* records affecting a single line into one modification record. Intuitively, if line *k* is replaced, then immediately replaced again, the two *replace* operations could have been accomplished by a single *replace*. Thus, it is unnecessary to add modification records for the four calls to *b__replace()* resulting from the keystrokes

```
new1
```

When *<return>* is typed, *in__chars()* of *operator.c* calls *b__insert(3, ''''*) to insert a blank line. This adds a modification record:

Type	Line	Del__text
DELETE	2	''line2''
DELETE	2	''line3''
REPLACE	2	''line4''
INSERT	3	NULL

As the final characters

```
new2<esc>
```

are typed, *REPLACE* records are again collapsed. (An *insert* followed immediately by a replacement of the line is equivalent to a single *insert*.) The above four modification records accurately summarize the completed command.

The call to *k__newcmd()* at the top of the main loop in *s.c* in turn calls *b__newcmd()* with *keyboard = 1*. *B__newcmd()* transfers the above four modification records from the *curr__recs* list to the *prev__recs* list with

```
prev_recs = curr_recs;
```

If the next command is *u*, then *undo()* works through this list from bottom to top, generating the calls

```
b_delete(3, 3);
b_replace(2, "line4");
b_insert(2, "line3");
b_insert(2, "line2");
```

These calls change the modified text

```
line1
new1
new2
line5
```

back to

```
line1
line2
line3
line4
line5
```

Buffer-Modification Bits.   Whenever the buffer is modified, two global *static* bits are turned on by the statement

```
changed = modified = 1;
```

at the top of *add__rec()* in *Bman.c*. (To be precise, the "bits" are *int*s.) Roughly speaking, *changed* tells if the most recent command altered the buffer, and *modified* tells if the buffer has been altered during the edit session. However, a complete explanation involves differences between the meaning of *command* in the phrases *undoing the last buffer-change command* and *redoing the last buffer-change command*.

Consider the *star* command (Section 5.3), which is equivalent to a sequence of alternating *n* and *redo* commands. When the user follows a *star* with *u*, the editor should not undo just the last *redo* command pushed back on the input by *do__star()*. Rather, all of the *n* and *redo* commands generated internally by *s* must be undone. Let us distinguish a *user command* from a plain edit command, where a user command is characterized as coming from the keyboard. In general, *undo* undoes the last *user* command that changed the buffer. To do this, the buffer manager needs to be informed whether a command is being read from the keyboard or from the *pushed[]* array in *keyboard.c* (Section 5.4).

The situation is different with the *changed* bit that the buffer manager keeps for *redo*. Consider the problem of redoing a *redo* command. For example, suppose the user types

```
cweasy<esc>
```

then moves the cursor to another word, types '.', moves to a third word and types '.' again. When the second *redo* command is given, the command stored in the *change[]* array of *keyboard.c* should be the *cweasy<esc>* that was pushed back on the input by the first *redo* command, not the '.' itself. Thus, for purposes of *redo*, a "buffer-change command" means just a plain edit command, which need not be a user command.

The effects of these observations are apparent in the access function *b__newcmd()* of *Bman.c*.

```
/* b_newcmd - record the start of a command */
b_newcmd(keyboard)
int keyboard;
{
        changed = 0;    /* even if command was pushed back on input */

        if (!keyboard)
            return;

        /*
         * It is a user command.  If the last user command changed the buffer,
         * move its modification records to the prev_recs list.
         */
        if (curr_recs != NULL) {
            ...
```

The *changed* bit is always set to 0. It is reset to 1 by any buffer change. When next called, *k_newcmd()* uses *b_changed()* to test the bit and see if the last command should be saved for *k_redo()*. On the other hand, only if *keyboard* is non-zero will the current modification records be moved to the *prev_recs* list for *undo()*.

In summary, the buffer manager must answer the questions:

1. Was the buffer modified by the last edit command?
2. Was the buffer modified by the last user command?
3. Has the buffer been modified since it was last synchronized with the external file by an *edit* or *write* command?

Question 1 must be answered for proper implementation of *redo*; *b_changed()* supplies the answer. Question 2 affects the handling of *undo* by *Bman.c*; its answer is "Yes" if and only if *curr_recs* is non-*NULL*. Question 3 must be answered to prevent an accidental *q* command from disastrously ending a long edit session; *Bman.c* provides *b_unmod()* and *b_modified()* for that purpose.

Implementation of Buffer.c.   The essential implementation technique is illustrated by the code for insertion.

```
/* buffer.c - data structure for the buffer
   ...
 * Implementation:
 *
 *    Doubly-linked list with a pointer to a recently referenced line.
 */
   ...
struct b_line {
     char *b_text,            /* text of the line */
     int b_id,                /* ID of the line */
     struct b_line *next,     /* pointer to next line */
     struct b_line *prev;     /* pointer to previous line */
};
```

```
static struct b_line
        *ref_line;                  /* recently referenced line */

static int
        last_id = 0,                /* last ID assigned to a buffer line */
        ref_nbr;                    /* number of recently referenced line */
        ...
/* buf_insert - insert s as the k-th buffer line; tell if successful */
int buf_insert(k, s)
int k;
char *s;
{
        ... (declarations)

        p = (struct b_line *) malloc(sizeof(struct b_line));
        q = malloc((unsigned)strlen(s)+1);
        if (p == NULL || q == NULL)
            return(0);
        reference(k-1);
        p->b_text = strcpy(q, s);
        p->b_id = ++last_id;
            ... (node p is linked in after node ref_line)
        return(1);
}
        ...
/* reference - point ref_line to the n-th buffer line; update ref_nbr */
static reference(n)
int n;
{
        /* search forward from a recently referenced line ... */
        for ( ; ref_nbr < n; ++ref_nbr)
            ref_line = ref_line->next;
        /* ... or backward */
        for ( ; ref_nbr > n; --ref_nbr)
            ref_line = ref_line->prev;
}
```

Buf_insert() first checks that storage exists for (i) a structure that points to the line's text, contains the line's ID, and points to the adjacent buffer lines and for (ii) the text itself. If both allocations succeed, then *reference()* points *ref_line* to the $(k-1)^{st}$ buffer line. (Recent buffer references have probably been to nearby lines, so *reference()* need only search a short distance forward or backward in the buffer.) Finally, the structure giving the new line is linked into place.

EXERCISES

1. Show how to implement the mark so that *b_getmark()* returns the mark's location immediately, without searching through the buffer. Do you prefer this implementation to the one using ID's? Explain. Show how both implementations can be generalized to provide more than one mark. For example, there could be 26 marks named *a*, *b*, ... , *z*, and *mx* and *'x* could place and address mark *x*. Which implementation do you prefer for multiple marks?

2. Discuss the details of implementing the *undo* command using just (i) the last user change command, (ii) the cursor location, (iii) the location of the cursor at the start of the last user change command, and (iv) the contents of the yank buffer. Include the *read*, *write*, and *star* commands in your discussion.

3. Suppose the buffer initially contains, say, 10 lines and consider the sequence of calls:

```
buf_delete(9, 10);
x = buf_insert(9, "new10");
x = buf_insert(9, "new9");
```

Trace the evolution of the pointer *ref_line* and the integer *ref_nbr* of *buffer.c*.

PROGRAMMING ASSIGNMENTS

1. Measure the editor's performance. If calls to *malloc()* and *free()* are degrading performance, then keep a pool of *mod_rec* structures in *Bman.c* and a pool of *b_line* structures in *buffer.c*. Storage for the text of lines can also be kept in pools if the structures that point to the storage tell the allocated length. (Programming Assignment 2 of Section 5.2. can be extended in the same way.) The efficiency of *buffer.c* might also be increased by using a more sophisticated search strategy in *reference()*. For example, moving from the last line of the buffer to the first line currently involves a lengthy search.

2. Implement the buffer with a temporary file so that huge files can be edited. For satisfactory performance, arrange that there is no traffic with the temporary file while a line is being typed; if each keystroke while inserting text provokes a disk access, then the editor may be intolerably slow. The buffer manager can keep the current line in an array until attention turns to another line.

```
/*
 * Bman.c - buffer manager
 *
 *
 * Entry points:
 *
 *     int b_changed()
 *          Tell if the buffer has been modified since the last call to
 *          b_newcmd().
 *
 *     b_delete(from, to)
 *     int from, to;
 *          Manage deletion of a range of buffer lines.
 *
 *     b_free()
 *          Free the temporary buffer storage.
 *
 *     b_getcur(line_ptr, pos_ptr)
 *     int *line_ptr, *pos_ptr;
 *          Return the line and position of the cursor.
 *
 *     b_getmark(line_ptr, pos_ptr)
 *     int *line_ptr, *pos_ptr;
 *          Return the line and position of the mark.
 *
```

```
*     b_gets(k, s)
*     int k;
*     char *s;
*          Manage copying of the k-th buffer line to s.
*
*     b_init()
*          Initialize the buffer module.
*
*     b_insert(k, s)
*     int k;
*     char *s;
*          Manage insertion of s as the k-th buffer line; tell if
*          successful.
*
*     int b_lineid(k)
*     int k;
*          Return the ID of the k-th buffer line.
*
*     int b_modified()
*          Tell if the buffer has been modified since the last call to
*          b_unmod().
*
*     b_newcmd(keyboard)
*     int keyboard;
*          Record the start of a new edit command.  The argument tells
*          whether the command will be read from the keyboard.
*
*     b_replace(k, s)
*     int k;
*     char *s;
*          Manage replacement of the k-th buffer line with s.
*
*     b_setcur(line, pos)
*     int line, pos;
*          Set the cursor location.
*
*     b_setline(line)
*     int line;
*          Set the cursor to line's first nonwhite character.
*
*     b_setmark()
*          Set the mark to the cursor location.
*
*     int b_size()
*          Return the number of lines currently in the buffer.
*
*     b_unmod()
*          Record that the buffer contents match the external file.
*
*     undo()
*          Undo the most recent user command that changed the buffer.
*
*
* External procedure calls:
*
*     buf_delete(from, to)          .. file buffer.c
*     int from, to;
*          Delete a range of buffer lines.
*
*     buf_free()                    .. file buffer.c
*          Free the temporary buffer storage.
```

```
 *
 *      buf_gets(k, s)                    .. file buffer.c
 *      int k;
 *      char *s;
 *          Copy the k-th buffer line to s.
 *
 *      int buf_id(k)                     .. file buffer.c
 *      int k;
 *          Return the ID of the k-the buffer line.
 *
 *      buf_init()                        .. file buffer.c
 *          Initialize the buffer.
 *
 *      int buf_insert(k, s)              .. file buffer.c
 *      int k;
 *      char *s;
 *          Insert s as the k-th buffer line; tell if successful.
 *
 *      int buf_replace(k, s)             .. file buffer.c
 *      int k;
 *      char *s;
 *          Replace the k-th buffer line by s; tell if successful.
 *
 *      s_errmsg(msg, val)                .. file Sman.c
 *      char *msg;
 *      int val;
 *          Format and print msg; wait for a key to be pressed.
 *
 *      s_savemsg(msg, val)               .. file Sman.c
 *      char *msg;
 *      int val;
 *          Format msg and save it for the next screen refreshing.
 */

#include "s.h"

/* buffer operations */
#define DELETE      1
#define INSERT      2
#define REPLACE     3

static int
    b_count = 0,            /* number of lines in the buffer */
    changed,                /* did last command change the buffer? */
    cur_line, cur_pos,      /* cursor location */
    line_prev, pos_prev,    /* origin of previous user change */
    line_start, pos_start,  /* origin of this user command */
    mark_id, mark_pos,      /* ID of marked line; position of mark in line */
    modified;               /* does buffer differ from external file? */

/* definition of a modification record */
struct mod_rec {
    int type;               /* DELETE, INSERT or REPLACE */
    int line;               /* line number in the buffer */
    char *del_text;         /* deleted text (NULL for INSERT) */
    struct mod_rec *next;   /* link to next modification record */
};

static struct mod_rec
    *curr_recs,             /* mod recs for current user command */
    *prev_recs;             /* mod recs for previous user change */
```

```
/* b_changed - tell if last command changed the buffer */
int b_changed()                                                      b_changed
{
    return(changed);
}

/* b_delete - manage deletion of buffer lines */
b_delete(from, to)                                                    b_delete
int from, to;
{
    int count, line;
    char text[MAXTEXT-1];

    if ((count = to - from + 1) < 0)
        s_errmsg("b_delete(): cannot delete %d lines", count);
    else if (from < 1 || to > b_count)
        s_errmsg("b_delete(): improper line number %d",
            (from < 1) ? from : to );
    else {
        for (line = from; line <= to; ++line) {
            buf_gets(line, text);
            add_rec(DELETE, from, text);
        }
        buf_delete(from, to);
        b_count -= count;
    }
}

/* b_free - manage freeing of temporary buffer storage */
b_free()                                                              b_free
{
    buf_free();
}

/* b_getcur - get the cursor location */
b_getcur(line_ptr, pos_ptr)                                          b_getcur
int *line_ptr, *pos_ptr;
{
    *line_ptr = cur_line;
    *pos_ptr = cur_pos;
}

/* b_getmark - get the mark's location */
b_getmark(line_ptr, pos_ptr)                                        b_getmark
int *line_ptr, *pos_ptr;
{
    int line;

    for (line = 1; line <= b_count; ++line)
        if (b_lineid(line) == mark_id) {
            *line_ptr = line;
            *pos_ptr = mark_pos;
            return;
        }
    *line_ptr = *pos_ptr = 0;
}

/* b_gets - manage retrieval of a buffer line */
b_gets(k, s)                                                          b_gets
int k;
```

```
char *s;
{
    char *strcpy();

    if (k < 1 || k > b_count) {
        s_errmsg("b_gets(): improper line number %d", k);
        strcpy(s, "");
    } else
        buf_gets(k, s);
}

/* b_init - manage buffer initialization */
b_init()                                                                      b_init
{
    buf_init();
}

/* b_insert - manage insertion of s as k-th buffer line; tell if successful */
int b_insert(k, s)                                                            b_insert
int k;
char *s;
{
    if (k < 1 || k > b_count + 1)
        s_errmsg("b_insert(): improper line number %d", k);
    else if (buf_insert(k, s)) {
        add_rec(INSERT, k, (char *)NULL);
        ++b_count;
        return(1);
    }
    return(0);
}

/* b_lineid - return ID of buffer line k */
int b_lineid(k)                                                               b_lineid
int k;
{
    if (k < 1 || k > b_count) {
        s_errmsg("b_lineid(): improper line number %d", k);
        return(0);
    }
    return(buf_id(k));
}

/* b_modified - tell if buffer differs from external file */
int b_modified()                                                             b_modified
{
    return(modified);
}

/* b_newcmd - record the start of a command */
b_newcmd(keyboard)                                                           b_newcmd
int keyboard;
{
    changed = 0;          /* even if command was pushed back on input */

    if (!keyboard)
        return;

    /*
     * It is a user command.  If the last user command changed the buffer,
```

```
    * move its modification records to the prev_recs list.
    */
    if (curr_recs != NULL) {
        free_recs(prev_recs);
        prev_recs = curr_recs;
        curr_recs = NULL;

        /* remember where the user change started */
        line_prev = line_start;
        pos_prev = pos_start;
    }

    /* remember where the current user command started */
    line_start = cur_line;
    pos_start = cur_pos;
}

/* b_replace - manage replacement of a buffer line */
b_replace(k, s)                                                                   b_replace
int k;
char *s;
{
    char text[MAXTEXT-1];

    buf_gets(k, text);
    if (k < 1 || k > b_count)
        s_errmsg("b_replace(): improper line number %d", k);
    else if (buf_replace(k, s))
        add_rec(REPLACE, k, text);
}

/* b_setcur - set buffer's record of the cursor location */
b_setcur(line, pos)                                                               b_setcur
int line, pos;
{
    if (line < 1 || line > b_count)
        s_errmsg("b_setcur(): improper line %d", line);
    else if (pos < -1)
        /* address() uses pos == -1 to signal a line address */
        s_errmsg("b_setcur(): improper position %d", pos);
    else {
        cur_line = line;
        cur_pos = pos;
    }
}

/* b_setline - set cursor to first nonwhite character of line */
b_setline(line)                                                                   b_setline
int line;
{
    int pos;
    char text[MAXTEXT-1];

    b_gets(line, text);
    for (pos = 0; isspace(text[pos]); ++pos)
        ;
    if (text[pos] == '\0')
        pos = max(pos-1, 0);
    b_setcur(line, pos);
}
```

```
/* b_setmark - set buffer's mark to the cursor location */
b_setmark()                                                                    b__setmark
{
    mark_id = b_lineid(cur_line);
    mark_pos = cur_pos;
}


/* b_size - return the number of lines currently in the buffer */
int b_size()                                                                   b__size
{
    return(b_count);
}


/* b_unmod - record that the buffer matches the external file */
b_unmod()                                                                      b__unmod
{
    modified = 0;
}


/* undo - undo the last user command that changed the buffer */
undo()                                                                         undo
{
    struct mod_rec *m;

    if (curr_recs != NULL) {
        /* happens if star operation tries to redo an undo */
        s_savemsg("Improper undo operation.");
        return;
    }

    /*
     * Undo() marches down the list of modification records generated by
     * the last user change (the list starts with the most recent change).
     * A delete is undone by an insert, and vice versa.  A replace is
     * undone by another replace.
     */

    for (m = prev_recs; m != NULL; m = m->next)
        switch (m->type) {
            case DELETE:
                b_insert(m->line, m->del_text);
                break;
            case INSERT:
                b_delete(m->line, m->line);
                break;
            case REPLACE:
                b_replace(m->line, m->del_text);
                break;
            default:
                s_errmsg("Undo(): cannot happen", 0);
                break;
        }

    /* change starting location so this undo command can be undone */
    line_start = cur_line;
    pos_start = cur_pos;
    if (b_size() > 0)
        b_setcur(line_prev, pos_prev);
    else {
        s_savemsg("No lines in buffer.", 0);
```

```
        b_insert(1, "");
        b_setcur(1, 0);
    }
}


/* add_rec - add to the list of current modification records */
static add_rec(type, line, del_text)                                          add_rec
int type, line;
char *del_text;
{
    struct mod_rec *new;
    static int nospace = 0;        /* are we out of memory? */
    char *malloc(), *p, *strcpy();

    changed = modified =  1;

    /* look for the possibility of collapsing modification records */
    if (curr_recs != NULL && curr_recs->line == line
       && type == REPLACE && curr_recs->type != DELETE)
        return;

    /* do nothing if space has been exhausted */
    if (nospace)
            return;

    new = (struct mod_rec *) malloc(sizeof(struct mod_rec));
    if (new == NULL || del_text != NULL &&
       (p = malloc((unsigned)strlen(del_text)+1)) == NULL) {
        nospace = 1;
        free_recs(curr_recs);
        curr_recs = NULL;
        s_errmsg("Ran out of memory!", 0);
        return;
    }
    new->type = type;
    new->line = line;
    new->del_text = (del_text != NULL) ? strcpy(p, del_text) : NULL;
    new->next = curr_recs;
    curr_recs = new;
}


/* free_recs - free storage for modification records */
static free_recs(m)                                                           free_recs
struct mod_rec *m;
{
    struct mod_rec *a;

    for ( ; m != NULL; m = a) {
        a = m->next;
        if (m->del_text != NULL)
            free(m->del_text);
        free((char *)m);
    }
}


/*
* buffer.c - data structure for the buffer
*
*
* Only procedures in Bman.c should access buffer.c.  Entry points:
```

```
*
*     buf_delete(from, to)
*     int from, to;
*         Delete a range of buffer lines.
*
*     buf_free()
*         Free temporary buffer storage.
*
*     buf_gets(k, s)
*     int k;
*     char *s;
*         Copy the k-th buffer line to s.
*
*     int buf_id(k)
*     int k;
*         Return the ID of the k-th buffer line.
*
*     buf_init()
*         Initialize the buffer.
*
*     int buf_insert(k, s)
*     int k;
*     char *s;
*         Insert s as the k-th buffer line; tell if successful.
*
*     int buf_replace(k, s)
*     int k;
*     char *s;
*         Replace the k-th buffer line by s; tell if successful.
*
*
* Implementation:
*
*     Doubly-linked list with a pointer to a recently referenced line.
*/

#include "s.h"

struct b_line {
    char *b_text;           /* text of the line */
    int b_id;               /* ID of the line */
    struct b_line *next;    /* pointer to next line */
    struct b_line *prev;    /* pointer to previous line */
};

static struct b_line
    line0,                  /* points to first and last buffer lines */
    *ref_line;              /* recently referenced line */

static int
    last_id = 0,            /* last ID assigned to a buffer line */
    ref_nbr;                /* number of recently referenced line */

/* buf_delete - delete buffer lines */
buf_delete(from, to)                                                    buf_delete
int from, to;
{
    struct b_line *b;
    int count = to - from + 1;
```

```
        reference(from);
        while (count-- > 0) {
            b = ref_line->next;
            b->prev = ref_line->prev;
            b->prev->next = b;
            free(ref_line->b_text);
            free((char *)ref_line);
            ref_line = b;
        }
}

/* buf_free - free temporary buffer storage */
buf_free()                                                              buf_free
{
/*
* This implementation does nothing.  Implementations using a temporary file
* can unlink it here.
*/
}

/* buf_gets - get a line from the buffer */
buf_gets(k, s)                                                          buf_gets
int k;
char *s;
{
    char *strcpy();

    reference(k);
    strcpy(s, ref_line->b_text);
}

/* buf_id - return the ID of a line  */
int buf_id(k)                                                          buf_id
int k;
{
    reference(k);
    return(ref_line->b_id);
}

/* buf_init - initialize the buffer */
buf_init()                                                             buf_init
{
    line0.b_text = NULL;
    line0.b_id = 0;
    ref_line = line0.next = line0.prev = &line0;
    ref_nbr = 0;
}

/* buf_insert - insert s as the k-th buffer line; tell if successful */
int buf_insert(k, s)                                                   buf_insert
int k;
char *s;
{
    struct b_line *p;
    char *malloc(), *q, *strcpy();

    p = (struct b_line *) malloc(sizeof(struct b_line));
    q = malloc((unsigned)strlen(s)+1);
    if (p == NULL || q == NULL)
        return(0);
```

```
    reference(k-1);
    p->b_text = strcpy(q, s);
    p->b_id = ++last_id;
    /* link node p in after node ref_line */
    p->next = ref_line->next;
    p->prev = ref_line;
    ref_line->next->prev = p;
    ref_line->next = p;
    return(1);
}

/* buf_replace - replace a buffer line; tell if successful */
int buf_replace(k, s)                                                          buf_replace
int k;
char *s;
{
    char *malloc(), *p, *strcpy();

    if ((p = malloc((unsigned)strlen(s)+1)) != NULL) {
        reference(k);
        free(ref_line->b_text);
        ref_line->b_text = strcpy(p, s);
        ref_line->b_id = ++last_id;
        return(1);
    }
    return(0);
}

/* reference - point ref_line to the n-th buffer line; update ref_nbr */
static reference(n)                                                            reference
int n;
{
    /* search forward from a recently referenced line ... */
    for ( ; ref_nbr < n; ++ref_nbr)
        ref_line = ref_line->next;
    /* ... or backward */
    for ( ; ref_nbr > n; --ref_nbr)
        ref_line = ref_line->prev;
}
```

5.6 THE SCREEN MANAGER

The screen module keeps the screen's image of the buffer up to date. The module consists of

> *Sman.c*   screen manager
>
> *screen.c* terminal-specific procedures

This section describes the *screen manager*, which applies a screen-update algorithm based on an idealized computer terminal. The next section covers low-level specifics of real terminals and presents *screen.c*.

The main entry point to the screen manager is *s_refresh()*, which is called by several procedures in the command processor. The most notable calls occur (i) just before an edit command is read (the top of the *for* loop of *main()* in *s.c* of

Section 5.3), and (ii) just after a character is typed in "insert mode" (the bottom of the *while* loop of *in__chars()* in *operator.c* of Section 5.2).

In outline, the screen manager maintains a record of the screen's appearance. When *s__refresh()* is called to update the display, the screen manager gets the cursor location and up-to-date text from the buffer module, compares screen rows with buffer lines, and produces an economical sequence of screen update commands that moves the cursor, inserts characters, deletes a screen row, etc. The changes are applied systematically from the top of the screen to the bottom, and left to right in a row. Once the changes are completed, the cursor is moved to the current location.

A complete description of the screen-update algorithm requires discussion of:

1. The algorithm's input.
2. Cases where *s__refresh()* should postpone screen updating.
3. Selection of the line to be displayed at the top of the screen.
4. The method of using entire rows that are already displayed.
5. The method of using portions of rows that are already displayed.

After covering these topics, this section briefly compares *s*'s screen-update algorithm with several alternative approaches.

Input for the Screen-Update Algorithm.   The algorithm has two primary sources of information. One is the buffer, which determines the desired screen contents. The screen manager accesses this information using four functions:

b__getcur()	return the location of the cursor
b__gets()	return a buffer line
b__lineid()	return the ID of a buffer line
b__size()	return the number of lines in the buffer

The algorithm's other main source of information is the screen manager's record of the current screen contents:

```
static int
    first_line = 0,         /* line number of first screen row */
    id[MAXROWS+1],          /* ID of line at row i (subscript 0 unused) */
    keyboard,               /* is command coming from keyboard? */
    last_row,               /* last row displaying buffer contents */
    ncols,                  /* number of columns on the screen */
    nrows;                  /* number of rows on the screen */

static char
    msg_save[MAXCOLS+1],    /* message saved for next screen refreshing */
    *text[MAXROWS+1];       /* text of line at row i (subscript 0 unused) */
```

Text[i] gives an exact copy of screen row i; tab characters are expanded to the appropriate number of <*space*> characters.

To facilitate the task of comparing buffer lines with screen rows, the buffer module generates a unique identification (ID) number for each *insert* or *replace* operation and assigns the number to the new text string. Although the line number of the string changes if earlier buffer lines are inserted or deleted, its ID is unaffected unless the line itself is deleted or replaced. Whenever the screen manager displays a new line, it associates the line's ID with the screen row. To check whether a buffer line matches a screen row, the screen manager simply compares the two ID's. An existing screen row with ID matching a desired line is moved to its new position by inserting and deleting earlier rows.

Postponing the Screen Update.   The screen manager's *keyboard* bit (actually an *int*) is "on" when the next input character will come directly from the keyboard; it is "off" when the edit command was pushed back on the input (see Section 5.4). When *keyboard* is on, the display must be accurate so the user can determine what to type. However, when *keyboard* is off, displaying is suspended and *s_refresh()* returns without doing any work:

```
/* s_refresh - refresh the screen */
s_refresh()
{
    if (keyboard) {
        last_row = nrows - s_ismsg();
        if (first_line == 0)        /* initial refreshing */
            repaint();
        else
            changes();              /* economical refreshing */
    }
}
```

The screen update is postponed so that buffer modifications can be accumulated before they are displayed. Consider the command:

```
    2ccHere are two<return>replacement lines.<esc>
```

1. After

```
                        2cc
```

is typed, the two screen rows beginning with the current row are replaced by a single blank row. Later rows are shifted up, and a new row is written to the bottom of the screen.

2. After

```
            Here are two<return>
```

is typed, the block of rows that was previously shifted up is shifted back down to its original position, and the newly added row disappears off the bottom of the screen.

On the other hand, if the *change* command is repeated by a *redo* command, there is no need to display the intermediate buffer states. Instead, the screen manager overwrites the two changed rows without moving later rows.

Positioning the Window.   The first step in screen refreshing is picking *first__line*, the number of the line to be displayed at the top of the screen. As long as the current line appears somewhere on the screen, *first__line* can be chosen to maximize the visual appeal of the screen changes. As characters are typed in insert mode, the screen update algorithm is applied for every keystroke, and recomputation of *first__line* is inadvisable because of both the execution delay and the undesirable appearance of changing the displayed segment of the buffer. On the other hand, a fairly careful recomputation of *first__line* is quite acceptable if the screen will be substantially changed.

The function *changes()* in *Sman.c* picks *first__line* as follows:

```
/* determine the first buffer line that will be on the screen */
if (cur_line >= s_firstline() && cur_line <= s_lastline() + 1)
        /* the old first line will probably display the current line */
        new_first = first_line;
/* else compute the first line that optimally reuses existing rows */
else if ((new_first = good_first()) == 0) {
        /* there is no good choice; repaint the screen */
        repaint();
        return;
}
```

Changes() first considers using the old value of *first__line*. This choice is adopted if it will make the current line visible. *S__firstline()* and *s__lastline()* return the line numbers of the first and last visible lines. The condition $cur\_line \leq s\_lastline() + 1$ covers the case that the last screen row displays a message that will be replaced by the current line when the screen is updated. If the current line falls a short distance below the screen, then the procedure *bottom()* will rectify the problem, as described later.

If the old value of *first__line* cannot be used, then *good__first()* is called to determine a new value. *Good__first()* picks *first__line* to maximize the number of existing screen rows that can be reused when refreshing the screen. If the best achievable overlap does not provide a worthwhile savings, then *changes()* calls *repaint()* to redraw the screen from scratch.

In essence, *good__first()* tries all values of *first__line* that display the current line. For each candidate, it computes how many lines in the screen-sized section of the buffer beginning at *first__line* are currently visible. (All such lines can be reused to produce the desired screen; see Exercise 2.) For example, suppose that the current line is line 40, that the screen holds 24 rows, and that the bottom row must be reserved for a message that is waiting to be displayed.

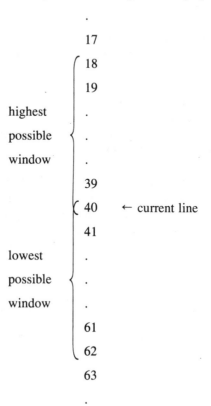

(For now, assume that each buffer line fits in a single screen row; the problem of folded lines is addressed below.) The smallest possible value of *first__line* is 18, which would display the current line just above the message. The largest possible value of *first__line* is 40. Suppose there are 10 buffer lines in the highest possible window whose ID matches that of a screen row. That is, the overlap between the current screen and the desired screen is ten rows if *first__line* is 18. If instead *first__line* is set to 19, then the overlap must be nine, ten, or eleven rows, and the correct value can be computed from the overlap for *first__line* = 18 by

> **if** the ID of line 18 equals that of a screen row
>   −−overlap
> **if** the ID of line 41 equals that of a screen row
>   ++overlap

Thus, once the overlap has been determined for one value of *first__line*, the others are easy.

In pseudocode, the algorithm used by *good__first()* is:

```
/* good__first—return a good first line for window; 0 = no good choice */
int good__first()
{
    /* start with the highest window containing the current line */
    first = max (current line − number of rows on screen + 1, 1)
    last = min (first + number of rows on screen − 1, buffer size)
    overlap = number of lines between first and last that are currently displayed
    (where "currently displayed" means its ID matches that of a displayed line)

    /* try other possible windows */
    max__overlap = overlap
    best__first = first
    while + +first ≤ current line {        /* next window */
        if buffer line number first− 1 is currently displayed
            − −overlap
        if buffer line number + +last is currently displayed
            + +overlap
        if overlap ≥ max__overlap {
            max__overlap = overlap
            best__first = first
        }
    }
    if max__overlap is sufficiently large
        return best__first
    else
        return 0
}
```

The choice between ≥ and > in the test

```
                    if overlap ≥ max__overlap
```

has interesting consequences; see Exercise 1.

The computation of *overlap* is imperfect because *Sman.c* folds long lines onto several screen rows, causing some windows to hold fewer lines. Thus, setting *first_line* = *good_first()* may not actually display the current line. The problem is corrected by the procedure *bottom()* in *Sman.c*, which adds lines to the bottom of the screen until the current line appears.

Deleting, Inserting, Keeping, and Replacing Screen Rows.   Once *first_line* is chosen, the screen manager can determine the ID's of lines that should appear on the screen by calling *b_lineid(first_line)*, *b_lineid(first_line+1)*, ... The function *changes()* in *Sman.c* loops over buffer lines *first_line*, *first_line+1*, . . . , displaying each line in the proper row. Denote:

line   buffer line being displayed

row   screen row where *line* will begin

visible   next buffer line with ID matching an existing screen row

useful_row row where line *visible* begins

Given

Current ID's		Desired ID's	
row 1	428	428	line *first_line*
	.	.	
	.	.	
	481	481	
row →	432	526	← *line*
useful_row →	491	521	
	.	491	← *visible*
	.	.	

changes() of *Sman.c* would:

1. replace the text at *row* by the buffer line having ID 526 (the line labeled *line*),

2. increment *line* and *row*, and

3. insert the buffer line having ID 521 (the one labeled *line*) at *row*.

Step 3 moves the row having ID 491 down to its desired position.

   In general, if *useful_row* is defined (that is, unless existing rows *row*, *row+1*, . . . , *nrows* must all be replaced), then *row* ≤ *useful_row* and *line* ≤ *visible*. One possibility is that *row* < *useful_row* and *line* = *visible*, as in

Current ID's		Desired ID's	
	.	.	
	481	481	
row →	432	526	← *line* = *visible*
	.	.	
useful_row →	526	.	
	.	.	

Then rows *row*, *row+1*, . . . , *useful_row−1* should be deleted. A second case is *row* < *useful_row* and *line* < *visible*, as in

Current ID's	Desired ID's
.	.
481	481
$row \rightarrow$ 432	521 $\leftarrow$ *line*
$useful\_row \rightarrow$ 526	526 $\leftarrow$ *visible*
.	.

In that case, *row* should be replaced by *line*. A third case is *row* = *useful_row* and *line* < *visible*, as in

Current ID's	Desired ID's
.	.
481	481
$row = useful\_row \rightarrow$ 432	521 $\leftarrow$ *line*
.	432 $\leftarrow$ *visible*
.	.

Then, *line* should be inserted at *row*. The remaining possibility is that *row* = *useful_row* and *line* = *visible*, which requires no work. In summary, *line* is displayed at *row* by

```
if row < useful_row and line == visible
    delete row through useful_row−1 from the screen
else if row < useful_row
    replace row by line
else if line < visible
    insert line at row
/* else line is already displayed at row */
```

Direct application of this rule for *row* = 1, 2, . . . has visually unpleasant consequences. Consider refreshing the screen when row 1 holds line 40 and the command is *control-U* (move the window up twelve lines).

Current lines	Desired lines
$row = useful\_row \rightarrow$ 40	28 $\leftarrow$ *line*
41	29
.	.
.	40 $\leftarrow$ *visible*
.	41
.	.

The rule would insert line 28 at row 1. The screen then holds lines 28, 40, 41, 42, ... The rule continues by inserting line 29 at row 2, line 30 at row 3, and so on. A more attractive approach is to insert line 39 at row 1, insert line 38 at row 1, insert line 37 at row 1, and so on. In that way, the screen always displays a block of consecutive buffer lines.

The rule's results are also unattractive for the command *control-D* (move the window down twelve lines). For example, suppose row 1 holds line 28:

Current lines	Desired lines
row → 28	40 ← *line = visible*
29	41
.	.
.	.
useful_row → 40	.
41	.
.	.

Lines 28–39 would be deleted from the top of the screen, creating 12 blank lines at the bottom, which would then be filled in. Identical conditions result when a block of lines at the top of the screen is the lower portion of a block being deleted from the buffer. In both cases, it is preferable to *scroll*, meaning to add the appropriate lines to the bottom of the screen and shift up the preceding rows; the screen is always full of a block of consecutive buffer lines. Scrolling is done only if the lines at the bottom of the screen can be used without alteration; the complete screen update is accomplished by moving the cursor to the last screen row, depositing the additional lines, then moving the cursor to the current location.

The basic rule does not cover the case when *useful_row* is undefined (no row at or below *row* can be reused). Rather than moving unusable rows up or down by *delete* or *insert* operations, it looks better to simply replace them.

The following screen-update algorithm incorporates modifications that improve the appearance of *control-U*, *control-D*, and several other operations.

```
determine first_line
last_line = last line that might possibly be displayed
for (row = 1, line = first_line;
        row ≤ last_row and line ≤ last_line;
        row = row after the current line, ++line) {

    /* determine the next buffer line that is already visible */
    useful_row = next reusable row
    visible = line appearing at useful_row
    (useful_row = 0 and visible = last_line + 1 if no such row exists)
```

```
    if row < useful__row and line == visible {
        if row == 1 and scrolling completes the update process {
            scroll the screen
            break
        }
        delete row through useful__row − 1
    } else if row < useful__row
        or useful__row == 0          /* no more useful rows */
        replace row by line
    else if line < visible
        /* insert in reverse order so scrolling up looks OK */
        insert lines visible − 1, visible − 2, . . . , line at row
    /* else line is already displayed at row */
}
if a message is waiting to be displayed
    display the message
if the last buffer line is displayed above some unused rows
    set each unused row to '' ~ ''
```

This algorithm is implemented by *changes()* of *Sman.c*. *Changes()* also handles lines that fit only partially on the screen. Whereas screen row 1 always contains the 0th segment of a line, a long line can begin too near the last row for all of its segments to be visible. Deletion of earlier rows pulls such a broken line up the screen, and *changes()* must add the segments that move into view.

Changes() calls other procedures in *Sman.c* that handle details of scrolling the screen, deleting rows, etc. These procedures (1) call still lower level procedures in *screen.c* that alter the screen and (2) simultaneously modify the screen manager's record of the screen contents. Consider *delete()*:

```
/* delete - delete rows from the screen */
static delete(from, to)
int from, to;
{
    int k, nbr_rows = to - from + 1;

    /* don't let message move up */
    if (id[nrows] == MESSAGE) {
        id[nrows] = CLEAR;
        strcpy(text[nrows], "");
        scr_move(nrows, 1);
        scr_delr();
    }

    /* remember the rows that are shifted up */
    for (k = from; k <= nrows - nbr_rows; ++k) {
```

```
            id[k] = id[k+nbr_rows];
            strcpy(text[k], text[k+nbr_rows]);
      }
      /* remember the bottom rows that are cleared */
      for (k = nrows - nbr_rows + 1; k <= nrows; ++k) {
            id[k] = CLEAR;
            strcpy(text[k], "");
      }
      /* delete rows from the screen */
      scr_move(from, 1);
      while (nbr_rows-- > 0)
            scr_delr();
}
```

Delete() calls *scr_move()* to position the cursor on a row, then calls *scr_delr()* to delete the row. (These two lower level screen functions, and eight others, are implemented by *screen.c*; see the next section.) In parallel, *delete()* modifies the arrays *id[]* and *text[]*. Each of the pointers *text[1], . . . , text[nrows]* is initialized by *s_init()* of *Sman.c* to point to a space capable of holding a string of length *ncols*, so *strcpy(text[k], . . .)* can be used to save the text of row *k*. A few bogus ID's like *MESSAGE* and *CLEAR* (identified by being negative numbers) indicate screen rows that are not displaying buffer lines.

Deleting, Inserting, Keeping, and Overwriting Characters.   To re-place a line, *changes()* calls *replace()*, which in turn calls *repl_text()*. (This two-step approach allows *repl_text()* to be applied to the message row.) *Repl_text()* displays the desired line using portions of the current displayed line. The following screen operations are assumed available:

scr_clr()

        Clear the remainder of the row, i.e., delete characters under and to the right of the cursor.

scr_delc(i)
int i;

        Delete *i* characters, starting at the cursor location. Later characters in the row are shifted left.

scr_instr(s)
char *s;

        Insert the string *s*. Characters under and to the right of the cursor are shifted right.

scr_move(row, col)
int row, col;

        Move the cursor to the given row and column of the screen.

scr__puts(s)
char *s;

> Overwrite with the string *s*. The cursor is positioned just after the printed string.

Of all the possible combinations of these screen operations, *repl__text()* considers only a *move cursor*, followed by an *overwrite*, followed by one of *clear row*, *delete characters*, or *insert string*. This implies that the desired line borrows only a prefix and possibly a suffix from the current displayed text. *Repl__text()* evaluates two general strategies for converting the current text to the desired text, then employs the method that appears more economical. For both methods, *repl__text()* starts by finding the longest common prefix of the old and new lines and calling *scr__move()* to move the cursor to the first differing character. The strategies are first described assuming that every buffer line fits on a screen row, then line folding is accommodated.

Following *move cursor*, the first approach uses *scr__puts()* to overwrite existing characters with the rest of the desired text and calls *scr__clr()* to clear any characters that remain from the old row. Any given text line can be converted to any other line by this method.

The second replacement strategy, which also works for any old and new lines, determines the longest common suffix, leaving mismatching internal substrings, as in

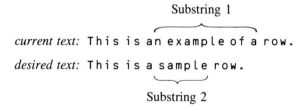

To start converting current text to desired text, characters from Substring 2 are written over Substring 1 until either Substring 1 has been completely replaced or Substring 2 has been completely copied. If Substring 1 is longer than Substring 2 (equivalently, if the current text is longer than the desired text), then the conversion is finished by deleting the remainder of Substring 1. If Substring 2 is longer, then the remainder of Substring 2 is inserted. If the substrings have the same length, the overwrite step completes the conversion.

In the above example the overwrite step would produce:

        This is a samplele of a row.

Then

                le of a

would be deleted by calling *scr__delc(7)*.

In this example, the call *scr__delc(7)* is probably more costly than adding the five characters

```
<space>row.
```

to the overwrite step, producing

```
This is a sample row._a row.
```

and clearing the remainder of the row. Suppose that *scr__delc(i)* sends *i* individual *delete character* instructions to the screen and that the terminal's *delete character* and *clear row* commands are each three bytes long. Then, the calls

```
scr_puts(" sample");
scr_delc(7);
```

would send $7 + 3 \times 7 = 28$ bytes to the screen, while

```
scr_puts(" sample row.");
scr_clr();
```

would send only $12 + 3 = 15$. In general, *repl__text()* uses the rule of thumb that deleting or inserting a character costs three times as much as overwriting one; accordingly, it selects the overwrite-clear approach.

Repl__text() implements the algorithm

> **if** Substring 1 is longer than Substring 2
>   prepare for possible overwrite-delete
> **else**
>   prepare for possible overwrite-insert
> **if** overwrite-clear costs less than overwrite-delete or overwrite-insert
>   prepare instead for overwrite-clear
> move the cursor to the first improper character
> overwrite the appropriate characters (if any)
> perform the proper operation: clear row, delete, or insert (if any)

If buffer lines were never longer than a screen row, then the following implementation of *repl__text()* would suffice:

```
#define D_OR_I_COST  3    /* delete/insert cost per character */

/* repl_text - economically replace the text of a short line */
static repl_text(row, line_id, new_text)
int row, line_id;
char *new_text;
{
    int d_count, do_clear, i_count, o_count, scr_instr(), scr_puts(), tail_len;
    char *p1, *p2, *s1, *s2;
```

```
/* point p1 and p2 to first differing characters */
for (p1 = text[row], p2 = new_text;
     *p1 != '\0' && *p1 == *p2; ++p1, ++p2)
     ;
id[row] = line_id;   /* update before possible return */
if (*p1 == '\0' && *p2 == '\0')              /* identical lines */
    return;

/* point s1 and s2 to the starts of longest common suffix */
tail_len = strlen(p2);   /* length of remainder of new line */
for (s1 = p1 + strlen(p1), s2 = p2 + tail_len;
     s1 > p1 && s2 > p2 && s1[-1] == s2[-1]; --s1, --s2)
     ;
strcpy(text[row], new_text);   /* old text no longer needed */

/* compare overwrite-clear cost against overwrite-(delete/insert) */
d_count = s1 - p1 - (s2 - p2);   /* counts deleted chars (< 0 for insert) */
o_count = min(s1 - p1, s2 - p2);   /* counts overwritten chars */
do_clear = (tail_len < o_count + D_OR_I_COST*abs(d_count));
if (do_clear)
    o_count = tail_len;   /* overwrite with entire tail */

/* move cursor to first improper character */
scr_move(row, p2 - new_text + 1);

/* overwrite if appropriate */
if (o_count > 0)
    chop_arg(scr_puts, p2, o_count);

/* clear row if appropriate */
if (do_clear) {
    if (d_count > 0)   /* old text is longer than new text */
        scr_clr();
/* else delete text if appropriate */
} else if (d_count > 0)
    scr_delc(d_count);
/* else insert text if appropriate */
else if ((i_count = -d_count) > 0)
    chop_arg(scr_instr, p2 + o_count, i_count);
/* else d_count = 0; do nothing */
}
```

If the old text is longer than the new, then *repl_text()* computes

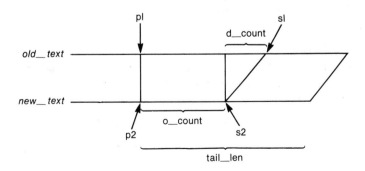

The first replacement strategy simply overwrites *tail__len* characters then clears the remainder of the row. Its cost, in terms of the number of bytes sent to the screen, is taken as *tail__len*, which ignores the less significant cost of the *clear row* command. (Care is needed in modifying the formula to account for the potential *clear row* command; see Exercise 5.) The overwrite-delete cost is computed as *o__count* $+ 3 \times$ *d__count*.

The function *chop__arg()* is used by *repl__text()* to apply a given function to a truncated character string. Thus, the call to

```
chop_arg(scr_puts, p2, o_count);
```

overwrites with the *o__count* characters that *p2* points to. The implementation in *Sman.c* is

```
/* chop_arg - chop a function's argument to a maximum length */
static chop_arg(fcn, arg, maxlen)
int (*fcn)(), maxlen;
char *arg;
{
    char save;

    save = arg[maxlen];
    arg[maxlen] = '\0';
    fcn(arg);
    arg[maxlen] = save;
}
```

The implementation of *repl__text()* in *Sman.c* is more complicated because long lines are divided into row-sized segments. Segments are numbered from 0 and columns are numbered from 1, so a pointer to the character at column *col* of segment *seg* of a line beginning at *row* is given by

```
/* text at a given segment and column */
#define TEXT text[row+seg] + col - 1;
```

If the *o__count* characters being overwritten extend past the current segment, then the extra characters are normally printed starting at column 1 of the next segment. For example, suppose *redo* repeats the command *cwconvert<esc>* in the two-segment line

```
row:       ... should repl
```
```
row+1: ace the word.
```

The calls

```
scr_puts("conv");
scr_move(row + 1, 1);
scr_puts("ert");
```

produce

row: `...should conv`

row+1: `ert_the word.`

The overwrite operation may be continued to a later segment by other means when *repl__segs*, the number of segments to be replaced, does not include all the line's segments. This happens if the new line has more segments than the old one or segments fall below the last screen row. (It is essential that *scr__move()* not attempt to move the cursor to the row below the bottom of the screen; chaos would result on many terminals.) For example, suppose the *J* (join) command is used when

line at row: `This is the start of a two-line sentence that`

next buffer line: `is just a little too long to fit in a row.`

Since a one-segment line is being replaced by a two-segment line, *repl__segs* = 1. With 80-character screen rows, *repl__text()* performs a *move cursor* and calls:

```
scr_puts(" is just a little too long to fit i");
```

Then the test

```
if (++seg < repl_segs)
```

fails, which terminates the overwrite step of *repl__text()*. The additional segment of the new line is handled by cases. If the segment does not fall below the bottom of the screen, then *repl__text()* determines whether the segment should (i) overwrite the next row or (ii) be inserted. In this case, the ID of the next row is not the ID of a current buffer line, so the next row is deemed useless; *repl__text()* calls *displ__text()* to overwrite the next row with the remaining segment, producing

row: `This is the start of a two-line sentence that_is just a little too long to fit i`

row+1: `n a row.`

On the other hand, if the next segment falls below the last screen row, then *repl__text()* simply returns. (The procedure *bottom()* of *Sman.c* displays the other segment if *line* is the current line.)

This approach to overwriting characters in multisegment lines is implemented in *repl__text()* with the code

```
for ( ; o_count > 0 && seg < repl_segs; o_count -= count)
    /* if overwrite operation reaches the segment's end ... */
    if ((count = ncols - col + 1) <= o_count) {
        /* overwrite with remainder of desired row */
        scr_puts(TEXT);
        /* move to start of next segment */
        if (++seg < repl_segs)
            scr_move(row + seg, col = 1);
    } else {
        /* overwrite internal substring */
        chop_arg(scr_puts, TEXT, count = o_count);
        col += count;
    }
```

Overwriting continues to exhaustion of either (1) the characters to be overwritten or (2) the segments to be treated. In the first case, the *for* loop terminates because *o_count* reaches 0, leaving *seg* and *col* at the first location after the last over-written character. This is the location affected by a subsequent *clear row*, *delete characters*, or *insert characters* command. In the second case, the loop terminates with *seg* = *repl_segs* and no subsequent screen commands are generated by *repl_text()*. For example, the code for *clear row* changes from

```
if (do_clear) {
    if (d_count > 0)      /* old text is longer than new text */
        scr_clr();
}
```

(when lines are not folded) to

```
        if (do_clear) {
            if (d_count > 0 && seg < repl_segs)
                /* old text is longer than new text */
                scr_clr();
        }
```

When a substring is deleted from a segment other than the line's last one, the terminal will not automatically transfer characters to the end of the segment from the start of the next segment. The editor must explicitly append characters to the end of the current segment and delete them from the start of the following segment. This creates a "ripple effect"; all subsequent visible segments of the line must be modified.

For example, suppose a *dw* command is given for the three-segment line

> *row*:   ... the r̲igh
>
> *row+1*: t end of ... this
>
> *row+2*: <*space*>very long ...

The calls

```
scr_delc(4);
scr_puts("end ");
scr_move(row + 1, 1);
scr_delc(6);
scr_move(row + 1, ncols - 5);
scr_puts(" very ");
scr_move(row + 2, 1);
scr_delc(6);
```

produce:

> *row*:   . . . t h e   e n d < *space* >
>
> *row+1*:   o f . . . t h i s   v e r y < *space* >
>
> *row+2*:   l o n g . . .

Note that the first call to *scr__delc()* is unnecessary because the deleted text reaches to the end of segment 0. See Exercise 7.

Using the approach illustrated by the above example, *repl__text()* deletes text from potentially multisegment lines with

```
while (seg < repl_segs) {
    /* don't delete beyond the segment's end */
    count = min(d_count, ncols - col + 1);
    scr_delc(count);
    /* if there are later segments in the old text ... */
    if (seg < old_segs - 1) {
        /* append characters from the next segment */
        scr_move(row + seg, col = ncol - count + 1);
        scr_puts(TEXT);
    }
    if (++seg < repl_segs)
        scr_move(row + seg, col = 1);
}
```

When a substring is inserted, any characters pushed off the end of the row must be inserted at the front of the next segment. If the inserted substring reaches to the end of the current segment, it suffices to overwrite with the substring instead of inserting it.

For example, suppose "right< *space* >" is inserted in the three-segment line

> *row*:   . . . t h e   e̲n d < *space* >
>
> *row+1*:   o f . . . t h i s   v e r y < *space* >
>
> *row+2*:   l o n g . . .

Not all $i\_count = 6$ characters can be inserted in the current row; only ''righ'' will fit. Since these four characters go at the end of the segment, overwriting with them is equivalent to inserting them. Accordingly, *Sman.c* uses a call to

```
scr_puts("righ");
```

to produce

  row: . . . the righ

  row+1: of . . . this very *<space>*

  row+2: long . . .

(The cursor's position depends on factors discussed in the next section.) The calls

```
scr_move(row + 1, 1);
scr_instr("t end ");
scr_move(row + 2, 1);
scr_instr(" very ");
```

then display the modified line

  row: . . . the righ

  row+1: t end of . . . this

  row+2: *<space>*very long . . .

This approach to inserting text in potentially multisegment lines is implemented in *repl_text()* by

```
while (seg < repl_segs) {
    /* if inserted text reaches the segment's end ... */
    if (i_count > ncols - col)
        scr_puts(TEXT);    /* just overwrite with it */
    else
        chop_arg(scr_instr, TEXT, i_count);
    if (++seg < repl_segs)
        scr_move(row + seg, col = 1);
}
```

Program Simplicity vs. Optimal Display Refreshing. The screen manager balances clean code against smooth screen updates. Program development saw *Sman.c* grow until screen updates became visually pleasant. For instance, line-folding was added to the already obscure code after weeks of trying to accept an editor that let long lines fall off the screen. Though the following examples show that the screen manager is not perfect, unpleasant displays are infrequent.

Line ID's illustrate the balance between simplicity and effectiveness. Their use greatly simplifies the task of matching a buffer line with a screen row; the matching row is the one (if any) with the same ID. The difficulties that plague computation of maximal traces (Exercise 6 of Section 3.2) never arise. However, the reliance on ID's occasionally causes suboptimal updating. Suppose the command

```
ccsome text<return>another line<esc>
```

is typed, the cursor is moved to a line that coincidently holds the text ''another line'', and a *redo* command is given. The editor replaces ''another line'' with ''some text'', and then inserts ''another line'' instead of merely inserting ''some text''.

Further display anomalies arise from the simple ''one-pass'' update strategy. Given a *control-D* command, the editor starts scrolling the screen without checking out the possibility that the twelve lines below the screen won't all fit on the screen. Thus, it is possible for a single refresh step to write text on the bottom of the screen and immediately push it off the top.

Conversely, the editor may push text off the screen then immediately write it back. Consider the command sequence

```
/the<return>
cwsome<esc>
*
```

Suppose the *star* command first encounters *the* as a word in a line that fills one screen row. The substitution increases the line's length by one and necessitates inserting a second row for that line. The bottom row is pushed off the screen. Suppose *the* next occurs in *their* within a line that exceeds a row by one character. The substitution produces a one-row line. If the screen holds a third occurrence of *the* like the second, then a side effect of the three substitutions is to replace the bottom row by a blank row, and the row's original contents must be redrawn. (The third substitution is needed to pull the blank row above the message

```
3 changes
```

that *s* writes.)

Program Simplicity vs. Efficiency.   Again, a pragmatic approach was adopted; *s* was built and used, then augmented until it was adequate. In the case of efficiency, this meant increasing the cooperation between the buffer and screen modules using ID's. The amount of cooperation could be further increased to make updates faster, but that would involve a cost in code complexity. See Programming Assignment 3.

Other Display Algorithms.   The use of ID's to simplify screen updating was suggested in the paper "The design of the PEN video editor display module" by David Barach, David Taenzer and Robert Wells (*Proceedings of the ACM Symposium on Text Manipulation*, 1981, pp. 130–136). My first implementation of *Sman.c* instead utilized the modification records needed for *undo*. This approach has advantages. First, no space is needed to save ID's in the buffer module. Moreover, most screen updating is very fast. For example, when text is being inserted, the screen manager sees immediately that only one modification record needs to be displayed; it need not check if the other screen rows are up to date. (Comparable efficiency can be obtained with *Sman.c*; see Programming Assignment 3.) However, the idea of making the modification records available to the screen manager is inferior to using ID's. (See Exercise 10.) A third display algorithm uses general string-comparison techniques, like the one discussed in Section 3.2, to determine a minimal set of *insert* and *delete* operations for converting the current screen to the desired one. This approach is discussed by James Gosling in "A redisplay algorithm" (pp. 123–129 of the proceedings mentioned above). Its results are not entirely satisfactory; see Exercise 9. However, it is possible to modify the algorithm of Section 3.2 to find an "optimal" set of row-update commands; see "Row replacement algorithms for screen editors" by Eugene W. Myers and Webb Miller.

EXERCISES

1. It is possible for several values of *first_line* to maximize the overlap with current screen contents. For each of the following scenarios, describe how *s_refresh()* would update the screen (i) if *good_first()* picked the smallest optimal *first_line* and (ii) if it picked the largest.

   • The screen holds lines 100–111, each folded onto two screen rows. The command is *113g*.

   • The current line is line 100, which appears near the middle of the screen. The command is *d50–*.

   • The current line is line 1 of a long file. The command sequence is

     g
     H
     –

   Does *good_first()* select the smallest or the largest optimal *first_line*? Which choice maximizes the likelihood that the current line will be displayed without additional scrolling? Explain. Which choice is preferable?

2. Show that if *m* and *n* are ID's of both buffer lines and screen rows, then they appear in the same order in the buffer as on the screen. How is this fact used implicitly in *changes()*? Why does this fact imply that the value *overlap* computed by *good_first()* gives the number of screen rows that can be reused?

3. Just after lines are inserted by the screen-update algorithm, the variables *row* and *line*

can be raised to avoid unnecessary passes through the main *for* loop. Give the appropriate pseudocode.

4. Show how to make *delete()* more efficient.

5. Suppose a character is appended to the end of *current text* to give *new text*. What are the values of *d_count*, *o_count* and *tail_len* in *repl_text()*? Which of the procedures *scr_clr()*, *scr_delc()*, *scr_instr()*, and *scr_puts()* are called? What are the arguments in the calls?

6. (a) The editor's line replacement policy uses the operations (1) clear the remainder of the row, (2) delete *i* characters, (3) insert a string of characters, and (4) overwrite with a string of characters. After moving the cursor, the algorithm performs one of the operator pairs

> overwrite and clear
> overwrite and delete
> overwrite and insert

These are just three of the sixteen possible ways of picking a pair of the four operations. Are there cases where one of the thirteen other pairs would update the line more efficiently? Explain.

   (b) Exhibit a case where using more than two operations, possibly including additional *move cursor* instructions, would produce dramatically more efficient line updating.

7. Suppose that a substring being deleted by *repl_text()* falls at the end of a segment. The call to *scr_delc()* is unnecessary if the characters are going to be overwritten by characters from the start of the following segment. Show how to make this improvement to *repl_text()*. Are the execution-time savings worth the cost in code complexity?

8. Whenever the code in *repl_text()* for overwriting a substring reaches the end of a segment, it moves the cursor to the start of the next segment (assuming there is a later visible segment). Under what conditions is this call to *scr_move()* unnecessary? Show how to make this improvement to *repl_text()*. Are the execution-time savings worth the cost in code complexity?

9. Compare the operation of changing *acaacaacaac* to *aabaabaabab* by (1) inserting and deleting the fewest possible characters with (2) simply overwriting the entire line.

10. Discuss the details of implementing *s_refresh()* using only *b_getcur()*, *b_gets()*, *b_size()*, and the new access function

```
int b_getmod(type_ptr, line_ptr, del_text)
int *type_ptr, *line_ptr;
char *del_text;
    /* Return the next undisplayed buffer modification record.  The function's
    value is 0 if and only if all modification records have been displayed. */
```

In particular, how can you curtail the conditions under which lines will be written to the screen, then removed later in the same refresh step (or removed, then rewritten)?

11. Devise a substantially more efficient algorithm for *good_first()*. (*Hint:* The intersection between two lists of *n* numbers can be computed in time $O(n \log n)$ by sorting the lists.)

PROGRAMMING ASSIGNMENTS

1. Implement a command that completely rewrites the screen. Such a command is useful when unwanted characters (e.g., a message from another user) appear on the screen during an edit session. (*Hint:* Why won't it work to add

```
case ctrl(l):
        k_donext("g'");    /* g<backquote> */
        break;
```

to *simp__cmd()* of *commands.c* of Section 5.3?)

2. Describe the screen's appearance when *s* deletes the first character from a line that begins with many blanks. Revise *Sman.c* to improve the appearance of this operation.

3. Use *s* when your system is heavily loaded. If response is annoyingly slow in "insert mode," then determine if the problem lies in the screen-update algorithm (including calls to *b__lineid()*). If so, arrange that as text is inserted, the screen manager makes just a call or two to the buffer manager for each keystroke. For example, you might add an access function *b__onerepl()* that tells if the only buffer change since the previous call to *b__onerepl()* replaced a line; it can return the line number, ID, etc. through its arguments.

```
/*
 * Sman.c - screen manager
 *
 *
 * Entry points:
 *
 *    s_errmsg(msg, val)
 *    char *msg;
 *    int val;
 *        Format and print msg; wait for a key to be pressed.
 *
 *    s_finish()
 *        Adjust the screen at the end of an edit session.
 *
 *    int s_firstline()
 *        Return the number of the first line on the screen.
 *
 *    char *s_getmsg(msg)
 *    char *msg;
 *        Print msg on the last row; return the user's reply.
 *
 *    s_init()
 *        Initialize the screen module.
 *
 *    int s_ismsg()
 *        Tell whether a message is pending.
 *
 *    s_keyboard(bit)
 *    int bit;
 *        Record if input is from the keyboard.
 *
 *    int s_lastline()
 *        Return the number of the last line on the screen.
```

```
*
*     s_putmsg(msg)
*     char *msg;
*          Print msg on the last row.
*
*     s_refresh()
*          Bring the screen up to date after a buffer change.
*
*     s_savemsg(msg, val)
*     char *msg;
*     int val;
*          Format msg and save it for the next screen refreshing.
*
*
* External procedure calls:
*
*     b_getcur(line_ptr, pos_ptr)        .. file Bman.c
*     int *line_ptr, *pos_ptr;
*          Return the line and position of the cursor.
*
*     b_gets(k, s)                       .. file Bman.c
*     int k;
*     char s[];
*          Copy the k-th buffer line to s.
*
*     int b_lineid(k)                    .. file Bman.c
*     int k;
*          Return the ID of the k-th buffer line.
*
*     int b_size()                       .. file Bman.c
*          Return the number of lines in the buffer.
*
*     int k_getch()                      .. file keyboard.c
*          Return the next character of the current command.
*
*     scr_clr()                          .. file screen.c
*          Clear the remainder of the row, i.e., delete the characters
*          under, and to the right of, the cursor.  Characters to the
*          left and in other rows remain.
*
*     scr_cls()                          .. file screen.c
*          Remove all characters from the screen.
*
*     scr_delc(i)                        .. file screen.c
*     int i;
*          Delete i characters.  All characters that follow on the same
*          row are shifted left i positions and i blank characters are
*          placed at the right end of the row.
*
*     scr_delr()                         .. file screen.c
*          Delete the row under the cursor.  Later rows on the screen are
*          shifted up, and a blank row is placed at the bottom of the
*          screen.
*
*     scr_inr()                          .. file screen.c
*          Insert a blank row at the cursor location.  Rows at and below
*          the current row are shifted down and the last row is lost.
*
*     scr_instr(s)                       .. file screen.c
*     char *s;
*          Insert the string s.  Characters under, and to the right of, the
```

```
*           cursor are shifted right.  Characters shifted beyond the right
*           margin of the screen are lost.  No assumption is made about
*           what happens if the line contains tabs or newline characters
*           or if the cursor reaches the right margin of the screen.
*
*      scr_move(row, col)                  .. file screen.c
*      int row, col;
*           Move the cursor to the given row and column of the screen.  The
*           upper left corner of the screen is considered row 1, column 1.
*
*      scr_puts(s)                         .. file screen.c
*      char *s;
*           Print the line s.  No assumption is made about what happens
*           if the line contains tabs or newline characters or if the cursor
*           reaches the right margin of the screen.
*
*      scr_scrl()                          .. file screen.c
*           Scroll screen rows up and place a blank row on the bottom.
*           The top screen row is lost.
*
*      scr_shape(nrow_ptr, ncol_ptr)       .. file screen.c
*      int *nrow_ptr, *col_ptr;
*           Return the number of rows and columns on the screen.
*/

#include "s.h"

#define CLEAR             -1        /* "ID" for cleared row */
#define D_OR_I_COST        3        /* delete/insert cost per character */
#define MESSAGE           -2        /* "ID" for message row */
#define MAXCOLS           80        /* maximum possible screen width */
                                    /* size of buffers for expanded text */
#define MAXEXPAND         MAXTEXT+100
#define MAXROWS           24        /* maximum possible screen height */
                                    /* text at given segment and column */
#define TEXT              text[row+seg] + col - 1
#define TILDE             -3        /* "ID" for "~" row */
#define USEFUL             8        /* repaint screen if fewer rows can be reused */

static int
    first_line = 0,                 /* line number of first screen row */
    id[MAXROWS+1],                  /* ID of line at row i (subscript 0 unused) */
    keyboard,                       /* is command coming from keyboard? */
    last_row,                       /* last row displaying buffer contents */
    ncols,                          /* number of columns on the screen */
    nrows;                          /* number of rows on the screen */

static char
    msg_save[MAXCOLS+1],            /* message saved for next screen refreshing */
    *text[MAXROWS+1];               /* text of line at row i (subscript 0 unused) */

/* s_errmsg - format and print msg; wait for the user to read it */
s_errmsg(msg, val)                                                      s__errmsg
char *msg;
int val;
{
    char message[MAXCOLS+1];

    sprintf(message, msg, val);
    s_putmsg(message);
    getchar();
}
```

```
/* s_finish - terminate the edit session */
s_finish()                                                                    s_finish
{
    scr_scrl();
    scr_move(nrows, 1);
}

/* s_firstline - return the number of the first line on the screen */
int s_firstline()                                                             s_firstline
{
    return(first_line);
}

/* s_getmsg - write a message; return the reply */
char *s_getmsg(msg)                                                           s_getmsg
char *msg;
{
    static char last_text[MAXCOLS+1];
    char expanded[MAXCOLS+2], *reply, *s;

    strcpy(last_text, msg);
    if (keyboard)
        s_putmsg(last_text);
    s = reply = last_text + strlen(last_text);
    for ( ; s - last_text < MAXCOLS && (*s = k_getch()) != CR; ++s) {
        if (*s == '\b')
            if (s == reply) {
                s[1] = '\0';    /* return the '\b' */
                return(reply);
            } else
                s -= 2;
        else if (!isprint(*s) && *s != '\t') {
            UNKNOWN;
            --s;
            continue;
        }
        if (keyboard) {
            s[1] = '\0';
            if (expand(expanded, last_text, sizeof(expanded)) > 1)
                /* exceeds one row; don't display */
                return(reply);
            repl_text(nrows, MESSAGE, 1, 0, expanded);
        }
    }
    *s = '\0';      /* trim off the final CR */
    return(reply);
}

/* s_init - initialize for an edit session */
s_init()                                                                      s_init
{
    int row;
    char *ckalloc();

    /* save constants giving terminal characteristics */
    scr_shape(&nrows, &ncols);
    if (ncols > MAXCOLS)
        s_errmsg("The screen has too many columns.", 0);
    else if (nrows > MAXROWS)
        s_errmsg("The screen has too many rows.", 0);
```

```
        else /* allocate storage for remembering screen contents */
            for (row = 1; row <= nrows; ++row) {
                text[row] = ckalloc((unsigned)(ncols+1));
                strcpy(text[row], "");
            }
}

/* s_ismsg - tell if a message is waiting to be displayed */
int s_ismsg()                                                                s__ismsg
{
    return(msg_save[0] != '\0');
}

/* s_keyboard - record if command is from the keyboard */
s_keyboard(bit)
int bit;                                                                     s__keyboard
{
    keyboard = bit;
}

/* s_lastline - return the number of the last line on the screen */
int s_lastline()                                                            s__lastline
{
    int last_line = first_line, row;

    for (row = 2; row <= nrows; ++row)
        if (id[row] > 0 && id[row] != id[row-1])
            ++last_line;
    return(last_line);
}

/* s_putmsg - print a message on the last screen row */
s_putmsg(msg)
char *msg;                                                                   s__putmsg
{
    scr_move(nrows, 1);
    if (id[nrows] != CLEAR)
        scr_clr();
    id[nrows] = MESSAGE;
    expand(text[nrows], msg, ncols+1);
    scr_puts(text[nrows]);
}

/* s_refresh - refresh the screen */
s_refresh()                                                                  s__refresh
{
    if (keyboard) {
        last_row = nrows - s_ismsg();
        if (first_line == 0)          /* initial refreshing */
            repaint();
        else
            changes();                /* economical refreshing */
    }
}

/* s_savemsg - save msg for the next screen refreshing */
s_savemsg(msg, val)
char *msg;                                                                    s__savemsg
int val;
{
    sprintf(msg_save, msg, val);
}
```

```
/* ---------- static procedures for refreshing the screen ---------- */

/* after_line - return the first screen row of the next buffer line */
static int after_line(row)                                                      after_line
int row;
{
     while (row < nrows && id[row+1] == id[row])
          ++row;
     return(row+1);
}


/* bottom - make current location visible; handle TILDE lines and messages */
static bottom()                                                                     bottom
{
     int cur_col, cur_id, cur_line, cur_pos, cur_row, cur_seg, idr, junk,
          last_seg, n, r, tilde_row;
     char cur_text[MAXTEXT-1];

     /* guarantee that current line is completely visible */
     b_getcur(&cur_line, &cur_pos);
     b_gets(cur_line, cur_text);
     pos_to_seg(cur_text, strlen(cur_text)-1, &last_seg, &junk);
     cur_id = b_lineid(cur_line);
     n = 0;
     while ((cur_row = row_of_id(cur_id, 1)) == 0
       || cur_row + last_seg > last_row)
          if (++n < 20)
               scroll(1, s_lastline());
          else {
               s_savemsg("Screen repainted because of display error.", 0);
               repaint();
               return;
          }

     /* fill in TILDE rows below last line of buffer */
     /* (first condition avoids long buffer search) */
     if (b_size() < first_line + nrows &&
        (r = row_of_id(b_lineid(b_size()), cur_row)) > 0)
          for (tilde_row = after_line(r); tilde_row <= last_row; ++tilde_row)
               if ((idr = id[tilde_row]) != TILDE) {
                    scr_move(tilde_row, 1);
                    if (idr != CLEAR)
                         scr_clr();
                    scr_puts("~");
                    id[tilde_row] = TILDE;
                    strcpy(text[tilde_row], "~");
               }

     /* if a message is waiting, print it */
     if (s_ismsg()) {
          s_putmsg(msg_save);
          strcpy(msg_save, "");
     }

     /* move the cursor into position */
     pos_to_seg(cur_text, cur_pos, &cur_seg, &cur_col);
     if (cur_row + cur_seg <= nrows)
          scr_move(cur_row + cur_seg, cur_col);
}

/* can_scroll - try to scroll the window down; tell if successful */
static int can_scroll(new_row1, new_first)                                       can_scroll
```

```
int   new_row1,        /* row to be moved to the top of the screen */
      new_first;       /* number of the line currently at new_row1 */
{
      int count, line, row;

      /* don't scroll if the bottom part of the screen requires updating */
      for (row = new_row1, line = new_first; ++row <= nrows && id[row] > 0; )
            if (id[row] != id[row-1])
                  if (++line > b_size() || id[row] != b_lineid(line))
                        return(0);

      /* count lines to be removed from the top of the screen */
      for (count = row = 1; row < new_row1 - 1; ++row)
            if (id[row+1] != id[row])
                  ++count;

      scroll(count, line);
      return(1);
}


/* changes - economically update the screen */
static changes()                                                    changes
{
      int   line,        /* buffer line being displayed */
            row,         /* row where line will begin */
            visible,     /* next buffer line already on the screen */
            useful_row,  /* row where the visible line begins */
      cur_line, cur_pos, n, new_first, last_line, partial;

      b_getcur(&cur_line, &cur_pos);

      /* determine the first buffer line that will be on the screen */
      if (cur_line >= s_firstline() && cur_line <= s_lastline() + 1)
            /* the old first line will probably display the current line */
            new_first = first_line;
      /* else compute the first line that optimally reuses existing rows */
      else if ((new_first = good_first()) == 0) {
            /* there is no good choice; repaint the screen */
            repaint();
            return;
      }

      /* determine the last displayed line, assuming one row per line */
      last_line = min(new_first + nrows - 1, b_size());

      /* record ID of line that may have segments falling below the screen */
      if ((partial = id[nrows]) <= 0)
            partial = id[nrows-1];

      for (row = 1, line = new_first;
            row <= nrows && (row <= last_row || line == cur_line) && line <= last_line;
            row = after_line(row), ++line) {

            /* determine the next buffer line that is already visible */
            for (visible = line; visible <= last_line; ++visible)
                  if ((useful_row = row_of_id(b_lineid(visible), row)) > 0)
                        break;

            if (row < useful_row && line == visible) {
                  /* if screen update can be performed by scrolling .. */
```

```
                    if (row == 1 && can_scroll(useful_row, new_first))
                        break;
                    delete(row, useful_row - 1);
            } else if (row < useful_row
                || useful_row == 0    /* no more useful rows */
                || id[row] == partial)    /* may need additional segments */
                replace(row, line, useful_row);
            else if (line < visible)
                /* insert in reverse order so scrolling up looks OK */
                for (n = visible - 1; n >= line; --n)
                    insert(row, n);
            /* else line is already displayed at row */
        }

    first_line = new_first;
    bottom();      /* handle TILDE rows, message, etc */
}


/* chop_arg - chop a function's argument to a maximum length */
static chop_arg(fcn, arg, maxlen)                                            chop_arg
int (*fcn)(), maxlen;
char *arg;
{
    char save;

    save = arg[maxlen];
    arg[maxlen] = '\0';
    fcn(arg);
    arg[maxlen] = save;
}


/* chop_cpy - copy at most maxlen characters from s to t; add '\0' */
static chop_cpy(s, t, maxlen)                                                chop_cpy
char *s, *t;
{
    while (maxlen-- > 0 && (*s++ = *t++) != '\0')
            ;
    *s = '\0';
}


/* delete - delete rows from the screen */
static delete(from, to)                                                      delete
int from, to;
{
    int k, nbr_rows = to - from + 1;

    /* don't let message move up */
    if (id[nrows] == MESSAGE) {
        id[nrows] = CLEAR;
        strcpy(text[nrows], "");
        scr_move(nrows, 1);
        scr_delr();
    }

    /* remember the rows that are shifted up */
    for (k = from; k <= nrows - nbr_rows; ++k) {
        id[k] = id[k+nbr_rows];
        strcpy(text[k], text[k+nbr_rows]);
    }
    /* remember the bottom rows that are cleared */
```

```
        for (k = nrows - nbr_rows + 1; k <= nrows; ++k) {
            id[k] = CLEAR;
            strcpy(text[k], "");
        }
        /* delete rows from the screen */
        scr_move(from, 1);
        while (nbr_rows-- > 0)
            scr_delr();
}

/* display - display a line */
static display(row, line)                                                   display
int row, line;
{
        int nsegs;
        char buf[MAXTEXT-1], expanded[MAXEXPAND];

        b_gets(line, buf);
        nsegs = expand(expanded, buf, sizeof(expanded));
        displ_text(row, b_lineid(line), nsegs, expanded);
}

/* displ_text - print the text of a line */
static displ_text(row, line_id, nsegs, s)                                   displ_text
int row, line_id, nsegs;
char *s;
{
        int do_clear;

        for ( ; nsegs-- > 0 && row <= last_row; ++row, s += ncols) {
            scr_move(row, 1);
            do_clear = (id[row] != CLEAR && strlen(text[row]) > strlen(s));
            id[row] = line_id;
            chop_cpy(text[row], s, ncols);
            scr_puts(text[row]);
            if (do_clear)
                scr_clr();
        }
}

/* expand - expand t to s; return the number of segments */
static int expand(s, t, maxchars)                                           expand
char *s, *t;
int maxchars;
{
        char *start = s;

        for ( ; s - start < maxchars - 1 && *t != '\0' ; ++s, ++t)
            if ((*s = *t) == '\t') {
                *s = ' ';      /* overwrite the tab */
                while (s - start < maxchars - 2
                  && (s - start + 1)%TAB_WIDTH != 0)
                    *++s = ' ';
            }
        *s = '\0';
        return(1 + (s - start - 1)/ncols);
}

/* good_first - return a good first line for window; 0 = no good choice */
static int good_first()                                                     good_first
{
        int best_first, cur_line, cur_pos, first, last, line, max_overlap, overlap;
```

```
    /*
     * find the window containing the current line and as many of the
     * currently visible lines as possible
     */

    b_getcur(&cur_line, &cur_pos);

    /* start with the highest window that (probably) contains cur_line */
    first = max(cur_line - nrows + 1 + s_ismsg(), 1);

    /* determine the last possible line in the highest window */
    last = min(first + nrows - 1 - s_ismsg(), b_size());

    /* compute overlap between current screen and highest window */
    overlap = 0;
    for (line = first ; line <= last; ++line)
        if (row_of_id(b_lineid(line), 1) > 0)
            ++overlap;

    /* try other possible windows */
    max_overlap = overlap;
    best_first = first;
    while (++first <= cur_line) {    /* next window */
        if (row_of_id(b_lineid(first-1), 1) > 0)
            --overlap;
        if (++last <= b_size() && row_of_id(b_lineid(last), 1) > 0)
            ++overlap;
        /* in case of a tie, pick the lower window */
        if (overlap >= max_overlap) {
            max_overlap = overlap;
            best_first = first;
        }
    }
    return((max_overlap >= USEFUL) ? best_first : 0);
}

/* insert - insert a line */
static insert(row, line)                                                        insert
int row, line;
{
    int nsegs;
    char buf[MAXTEXT-1], expanded[MAXEXPAND];

    b_gets(line, buf);
    nsegs = expand(expanded, buf, sizeof(expanded));
    ins_text(row, b_lineid(line), nsegs, expanded);
}

/* ins_text - insert the text of a line */
static ins_text(row, lineid, nsegs, t)                                          ins_text
int row, lineid, nsegs;
char *t;
{
    int r;

    nsegs = min(nsegs, nrows - row + 1);
    /* remember the rows that are shifted down */
    for (r = nrows; r >= row + nsegs; --r) {
        id[r] = id[r-nsegs];
        strcpy(text[r], text[r-nsegs]);
    }
```

```
        /* insert blank rows on the screen */
        scr_move(row, 1);
        for (r = 1; r <= nsegs; ++r)
            scr_inr();
        displ_text(row, lineid, nsegs, t);
}

/* pos_to_seg - convert a line position to a screen segment and column */
static pos_to_seg(t, pos, seg_ptr, col_ptr)                                pos_to_seg
char *t;
int pos, *seg_ptr, *col_ptr;
{
        int c, p;

        for (c = 1, p = 0; p < pos && t[p] != '\0'; ++c, ++p)
            /* keep column c corresponding to position p */
            if (t[p] == '\t')
                while (c%TAB_WIDTH != 0)
                    ++c;

        *seg_ptr = (c - 1)/ncols;
        *col_ptr = 1 + (c-1) % ncols;
}

/* repaint - completely repaint the screen */
static repaint()                                                           repaint
{
        int cur_line, cur_pos, line, row;
        /* clear the screen */
        scr_cls();
        for (row = 1; row <= nrows; ++row) {
            id[row] = CLEAR;
            strcpy(text[row], "");
        }

        b_getcur(&cur_line, &cur_pos);
        for (row = 1, line = first_line = max (cur_line - 8, 1);
            row <= last_row && line <= b_size();
            row = after_line(row), ++line)
                display(row, line);
        bottom();
}

/* replace - replace a line */
static replace(row, line, useful_row)                                      replace
int row, line, useful_row;
{
        int nsegs;
        char buf[MAXTEXT-1], expanded[MAXEXPAND];

        b_gets(line, buf);
        nsegs = expand(expanded, buf, sizeof(expanded));
        repl_text(row, b_lineid(line), nsegs, useful_row, expanded);
}

/* repl_text - economically replace the text of a line */
static repl_text(row, line_id, new_segs, useful_row, new_text)             repl_text
int  row,           /* row containing 0-th segment of the line */
     line_id,       /* ID of the new line */
     new_segs,      /* number of segments in the new line */
     useful_row;    /* next row that should not be overwritten */
```

```
char *new_text;        /* text of the new line */
{
    int  add_segs,       /* number of segments to be added */
         col,            /* column of current interest */
         count,          /* character count for current segment */
         d_count,        /* number of characters to be deleted */
         do_clear,       /* is overwrite/clear strategy used? */
         i,              /* generic loop index */
         i_count,        /* number of characters to be inserted */
         o_count,        /* number of characters to be overwritten */
         old_segs,       /* number of segments in the old line */
         repl_segs,      /* number of segments to be replaced */
         scr_instr(),    /* argument to chop_arg() */
         scr_puts(),     /* argument to chop_arg() */
         seg,            /* segment of current interest */
         tail_len;       /* length of new text after mismatch */
    char old_text[MAXEXPAND],  /* current displayed line */
         *p1,            /* first mismatching character in old text */
         *p2,            /* first mismatching character in new text */
         *s1,            /* start of matching suffix in old text */
         *s2,            /* start of matching suffix in new text */
         *t;             /* generic character pointer */

    /* build the old line from screen segments */
    strcpy(old_text, text[row]);
    for (i = row + 1; i <= nrows && id[i] == id[row] && id[i] > 0; ++i)
        strcat(old_text, text[i]);
    old_segs = i - row;
    /* don't consider segments below the screen */
    new_segs = min(new_segs, nrows - row + 1);
    /* don't replace segments that should be inserted or deleted */
    repl_segs = min(old_segs, new_segs);

    /* update id[] and text[] */
    for (seg = 0, t = new_text; seg < repl_segs; ++seg, t += ncols) {
        chop_cpy(text[row+seg], t, ncols);
        id[row+seg] = line_id;
    }

    /* point p1 and p2 to first differing characters */
    for (p1 = old_text, p2 = new_text;
        *p1 != '\0' && *p1 == *p2; ++p1, ++p2)
            ;
    if (*p1 == '\0' && *p2 == '\0')     /* identical lines */
        return;

    /* point s1 and s2 to the starts of longest common suffix */
    tail_len = strlen(p2);                /* length of remainder of new line */
    for (s1 = p1 + strlen(p1), s2 = p2 + tail_len;
        s1 > p1 && s2 > p2 && s1[-1] == s2[-1]; --s1, --s2)
            ;

    /* compare overwrite-clear cost against overwrite-(delete/insert) */
    d_count = s1 - p1 - (s2 - p2);      /* counts deleted chars (<0 for insert) */
    o_count = min(s1 - p1, s2 - p2);    /* counts overwritten chars */
    do_clear = (tail_len < o_count + D_OR_I_COST*abs(d_count));
    if (do_clear)
        o_count = tail_len;             /* overwrite with entire tail */

    /* move cursor to first improper character */
    seg = (p2 - new_text)/ncols;
```

```
        col = 1 + (p2 - new_text) % ncols;
        if (seg < repl_segs)
            scr_move(row + seg, col);

        /* overwrite if appropriate */
        for ( ; o_count > 0 && seg < repl_segs; o_count -= count)
            /* if overwrite operation reaches the segment's end ... */
            if ((count = ncols - col + 1) <= o_count) {
                /* overwrite with remainder of desired row */
                scr_puts(TEXT);
                /* move to start of next segment */
                if (++seg < repl_segs)
                    scr_move(row + seg, col = 1);
            } else {
                /* overwrite internal substring */
                chop_arg(scr_puts, TEXT, count = o_count);
                col += count;
            }

        /* clear remainder of row if appropriate */
        if (do_clear) {
            if (d_count > 0 && seg < repl_segs)
                /* old text is longer than new text */
                scr_clr();
        /* else delete text if appropriate */
        } else if (d_count > 0)
            while (seg < repl_segs) {
                /* don't delete past the segment's end */
                count = min(d_count, ncols - col + 1);
                scr_delc(count);
                /* if there are later segments in old text ... */
                if (seg < old_segs - 1) {
                    /* append characters from the next segment */
                    scr_move(row + seg, col = ncols - count + 1);
                    scr_puts(TEXT);
                }
                if (++seg < repl_segs)
                    scr_move(row + seg, col = 1);
            }
        /* else insert text if appropriate */
        else if ((i_count = -d_count) > 0)
            while (seg < repl_segs) {
                /* if inserted text reaches the segment's end ... */
                if (i_count > ncols - col)
                    scr_puts(TEXT);     /* just overwrite with it */
                else
                    chop_arg(scr_instr, TEXT, i_count);
                if (++seg < repl_segs)
                    scr_move(row + seg, col = 1);
            }
        /* else d_count = 0; do nothing */

        /* overwrite or insert any additional segments */
        if ((add_segs = new_segs - old_segs) > 0) {
            t = new_text + old_segs*ncols;   /* points to remaining text */
            if (useful_row == 0 || row + new_segs <= useful_row)
                displ_text(row+old_segs, line_id, add_segs, t);
            else
                ins_text(row+old_segs, line_id, add_segs, t);
        }
    }
```

```
/* row_of_id - return the screen row having a given id */
static int row_of_id(i, row)
int   i,             /* ID being sought */
      row;           /* first row to be searched */
{
      for ( ; row <= nrows; ++row)
          if (id[row] == i)
              return(row);
      return(0);
}


/* scroll - scroll the window down */
static scroll(k, line)
int   k,             /* number of lines to be pushed off the top of the screen */
      line;          /* last visible line */
{
      int      desired,     /* desired top line */
               i,           /* generic loop index */
               nsegs,       /* number of segments in last visible line */
               row,         /* row holding last visible segment */
               seg;         /* number of last visible segment */
      char     *s,          /* points to last visible segment */
               buf[MAXTEXT-1], expanded[MAXEXPAND];

      /* determine desired first line; initialize nsegs, row, seg and s */
      desired = first_line + k;
      b_gets(line, buf);
      nsegs = expand(expanded, buf, sizeof(expanded));
      for (row = nrows; row > 1 && id[row] < 0; --row)
          ;
      for (i = row; i > 1 && id[i-1] == id[row]; --i)
          ;
      seg = row - i;
      s = expanded + seg*ncols;

      /* keep adding segments or TILDE rows to produce desired first line */
      while (first_line != desired) {
          /* get next values of nsegs, seg and s */
          if (line <= b_size() && ++seg < nsegs)
              s += ncols;
          else if (++line <= b_size()) {
              b_gets(line, buf);
              nsegs = expand(expanded, buf, sizeof(expanded));
              seg = 0;
              s = expanded;
          }
          /* get next value of row; make a space for the next segment */
          if (row < nrows)
              ++row;
          else {
              scr_scrl();
              if (id[1] != id[2] && id[2] > 0)
                  ++first_line;
              for (i = 0; i < nrows; ++i) {
                  id[i] = id[i+1];
                  text[i] = text[i+1];
              }
              id[nrows] = CLEAR;
              text[nrows] = text[0];
              strcpy(text[nrows], "");
              /* don't write segment then cover by a message */
```

row_of_id

scroll

```
            if (first_line == desired && s_ismsg())
                break;
    }
    /* write the segment or "~" */
    if (line <= b_size()) {
        scr_move(row, 1);
        if (id[row] != CLEAR)
            scr_clr();
        id[row] = b_lineid(line);
        chop_cpy(text[row], s, ncols);
        scr_puts(text[row]);
    } else if (id[row] != TILDE) {
        scr_move(row, 1);
        if (id[row] != CLEAR);
            scr_clr();
        id[row] = TILDE;
        strcpy(text[row], "~");
        scr_puts("~");
    }
  }
}
```

5.7 THE SCREEN

The file *screen.c* provides the ten low level, screen-handling procedures needed by *Sman.c*:

scr_clr()

> Clear the remainder of the row, i.e., delete the characters under and to the right of the cursor.

scr_cls()

> Clear all characters from the screen.

scr_delc(i)
int i;

> Delete *i* characters. Characters that follow on the same row are shifted left *i* positions, and *i* blank characters are placed at the right end of the row.

scr_delr()

> Delete the row under the cursor. Later screen rows are shifted up, and a blank row is placed at the bottom of the screen.

scr_inr()

> Insert a blank row at the cursor location. Rows at and below the current row are shifted down, and the last row is lost.

scr_instr(s)
char *s;

> Insert the string *s*. Characters under and to the right of the cur-

sor are shifted right. Characters shifted beyond the right margin
of the screen are lost. The calling procedure must not allow *s*
to contain tab or newline characters and must reset the cursor
after a character is inserted at the right margin of the screen.
No attempt should be made to insert a character at the extreme
lower right corner of the screen.

scr__move(row, col)
int row, col;

> Move the cursor to the given row and column of the screen.
> The upper left corner of the screen is considered row 1, column
> 1.

scr__puts(s)
char *s;

> Print the string *s*, overwriting existing characters. The calling
> procedure must not allow *s* to contain tab or newline characters
> and must reset the cursor after a character is printed at the right
> margin of the screen. A character may be printed at the extreme
> lower right corner of the screen.

scr__scrl()

> Scroll the screen rows up and place a blank row on the bottom.
> The top screen row vanishes.

scr__shape(nrow__ptr, ncol__ptr)
int *nrow__ptr, *col__ptr;

> Return the number of rows and columns on the screen.

Screen handling is the least portable part of *s*. *Sman.c* limits its demands on
screen.c to simplify the job of accommodating a new terminal. For example, tab
characters are never printed or inserted because terminals would respond differently. Instead, *Sman.c* translates each tab character into an appropriate number of
<*space*> characters, guaranteeing that its interpretation of tabs is reflected on the
screen. Moreover, *Sman.c* breaks long buffer lines into several screen rows without any assistance (or hindrance) from the terminal. Problems associated with
printing a character at the extreme lower right corner of the screen are limited to
scr__puts(). (The problem is described below, under "autowrap.")

Capabilities of "Intelligent" Terminals.   A screen editor sends special
character sequences to the terminal to accomplish such tasks as deleting a character
or moving the cursor. The appropriate sequences vary widely. The following table
gives some of the sequences for two models. Consult a manual to get the sequences
for your terminal.

Instruction	ANSI Standard	IBM 3101
clear to end of row	$<esc>$[K	$<esc>$I
clear entire screen	$<esc>$[2J	$<esc>$L
delete char	$<esc>$[P	$<esc>$Q
delete row	$<esc>$[M	$<esc>$O
enter insert mode	$<esc>$[4h	—
insert char	—	$<esc>$P$<char>$
leave insert mode	$<esc>$[4l	—
insert row	$<esc>$[L	$<esc>$N

Note that a string of characters is inserted on some screens by (i) sending a byte sequence to put the terminal in "insert mode," (ii) sending the desired characters, then (iii) sending a byte sequence to exit from insert mode. On other terminals, each character in the sequence is preceded by a few bytes that say, in effect, "insert the following character."

The cursor can be positioned at a given row and column of an ANSI-standard terminal with

```
printf("\033[%d;%dH", row, col);
```

(The octal constant 33 is the ASCII code for $<esc>$.) The command for the 3101 is

```
printf("\033Y%c%c", row + 31, col + 31)
```

To experiment with escape sequences, put the terminal "off line," type the sequence, and see what happens. For example, do the four keystrokes $<esc>$[2J clear the screen?

Autowrap. The most difficult problems faced in implementing *screen.c* arose because my terminal (a Zenith Z29) automatically resets the cursor to the start of the next row whenever a character is written or inserted at the right margin of the screen. In particular, if the cursor is positioned in the extreme lower right corner of the screen, then emitting a character scrolls the screen. That is, a blank row is added to the bottom of the screen, earlier rows move up, and the top row vanishes.

The approach taken by *screen.c* works in practice, but is ugly and imperfect. To place a character at the lower right corner, *screen.c* writes it one position to the left, then backs up and inserts the appropriate character before it. Thus, if the last few characters of the bottom row are

```
. . . 123
```

then . . . *13* is printed and *2* is inserted in front of the *3*. These measures are limited to *scr__puts()* because *scr__instr()* will never try to insert a character in the troublesome corner. *Sman.c* makes the entire current line visible, so insertions at the right margin always come above another visible segment of the same line. (An insertion in the corner with a *star* command is not displayed because the number of changes is reported on the last screen row.) However, it seemed too complicated to make the strategy work when insertions have shifted down a row of length one less than the screen width; *screen.c* lapses into a warning message in that improbable circumstance.

Minor Considerations

- *Output Processing by the Terminal Driver.* A '\n' transmitted by a program will ordinarily be converted to the character pair <*return*> <*line feed*> before being transmitted to the terminal. However, in raw mode this processing may be turned off; in the computing environment used, a transmitted '\n' (ASCII code 10) moves the cursor down one row, but not back to the start of the row. *Screen.c* economizes cursor motion to the start of a nearby row by printing a <*return*> and the appropriate number of <*line feed*> characters.

- *Pad Characters.* If the Z29 terminal is sent certain escape sequences too quickly, it displays printable characters from the sequences instead of performing screen operations. The solution was to follow the sequences by an appropriate number of '\0' characters. Experiments determined adequate amounts of padding. (The Z29 supports "handshaking" by transmitting *XOFF* whenever the contents of its 32-character buffer reaches 22 characters. However, this feature cannot be used in raw mode. See Section 5.4, especially Exercise 3.)

PROGRAMMING ASSIGNMENTS

1. If using standard I/O makes *s* too slow on your system, replace it with system-dependent I/O. Consider both (1) I/O between the file and the buffer and (2) I/O between the terminal and *s*.

```
/*
 * screen.c - terminal-specific procedures
 *
 *
 * Only procedures in Sman.c should access screen.c.  Entry points:
 *
 *     scr_clr()
 *         Clear the remainder of the row, i.e., delete the characters
 *         under, and to the right of, the cursor.
 *
 *     scr_cls()
 *         Clear all characters from the screen.
```

```
 *
 *      scr_delc(i)
 *      int i;
 *          Delete i characters.  Characters that follow on the same row are
 *          shifted left i positions and i blank characters are placed at
 *          the right end of the row.
 *
 *      scr_delr()
 *          Delete the row under the cursor.  Later screen rows are shifted
 *          up and a blank row is placed at the bottom of the screen.
 *
 *      scr_inr()
 *          Insert a blank row at the cursor location.  Rows at and below
 *          the current row are shifted down and the last row is lost.
 *
 *      scr_instr(s)
 *      char *s;
 *          Insert the string s.  Characters under, and to the right of, the
 *          cursor are shifted right.  Characters shifted beyond the right
 *          margin of the screen are lost.  The calling procedure must not
 *          allow s to contain tab or newline characters and is responsible
 *          for resetting the cursor after a character is inserted at the
 *          right margin of the screen.  No attempt should be made to insert
 *          a character at the extreme lower right corner of the screen.
 *
 *      scr_move(row, col)
 *      int row, col;
 *          Move the cursor to the given row and column of the screen.  The
 *          upper left corner of the screen is considered row 1, column 1.
 *
 *      scr_puts(s)
 *      char *s;
 *          Print the string s, overwriting existing characters.  The
 *          calling procedure must not allow s to contain tab or newline
 *          characters and is responsible for resetting the cursor after a
 *          character is printed at the right margin of the screen. A
 *          character may be printed at the extreme lower right corner of
 *          the screen.
 *
 *      scr_scrl()
 *          Scroll screen rows up and place a blank row on the bottom.
 *          The top screen row is lost.
 *
 *      scr_shape(nrow_ptr, ncol_ptr)
 *      int *nrow_ptr, *col_ptr;
 *          Return the number of rows and columns on the screen.
 */

#include "s.h"

/* screen control commands for ANSI terminals */
#define AUTOWRAP          1
#define CLEAR_ROW         "K"
#define CLEAR_SCREEN      "2J"
#define DELETE_CHAR       "P"
#define DELETE_ROW        "M"
#define INSERT_BEGIN      "4h"
#define INSERT_END        "4l"
#define INSERT_ROW        "L"
#define LONG_COUNT        10
```

```
#define MOVE(row,col)       printf("\033[%d;%dH",row,col)                    MOVE
#define NCOL                80        /* columns per screen row */
#define NROW                24        /* rows per screen */
#define PAD_CHAR            '\0'
#define SCREEN(x)           printf("\033[%s",x)                              SCREEN
#define SHORT_COUNT         4

static int cur_row = 0, cur_col;           /* cursor location */
static char save = '\0';            /* character in location (NROW, NCOL-1) */

/* scr_clr - clear the current row */
scr_clr()                                                                   scr_clr
{
    SCREEN(CLEAR_ROW);
    wait(LONG_COUNT);
}

/* scr_cls - clear the screen */
scr_cls()                                                                   scr_cls
{
    SCREEN(CLEAR_SCREEN);
    wait(LONG_COUNT);
}

/* scr_delc - delete characters */
scr_delc(i)                                                                 scr_delc
int i;
{
    while (i-- > 0) {
        SCREEN(DELETE_CHAR);
        wait(SHORT_COUNT);
    }
    if (cur_row == NROW)
        save = '\0';
}

/* scr_delr - delete the current row */
scr_delr()                                                                  scr_delr
{
    SCREEN(DELETE_ROW);
}

/* scr_inr - insert a row */
scr_inr()                                                                   scr_inr
{
    SCREEN(INSERT_ROW);
    save = '\0';
}

/* scr_instr - insert a string */
scr_instr(s)                                                                scr_instr
char *s;
{
    int s_len = strlen(s);

    if (cur_col + s_len > NCOL + 1) {
        errmsg("scr_instr(): line extends past column %d", NCOL);
        s_len = NCOL + 1 - cur_col;
        s[s_len] = '\0';
    }
```

```
        cur_col += s_len;
        if (cur_row == NROW && cur_col == NCOL + 1) {
            errmsg("scr_instr(): cannot insert in lower, right corner", 0);
            return;
        }
        SCREEN(INSERT_BEGIN);
        while (*s != '\0') {
            putchar(*s++);
            wait(SHORT_COUNT);
        }
        SCREEN(INSERT_END);
        if (AUTOWRAP && cur_col == NCOL + 1) {
            cur_col = 1;
            ++cur_row;
        }
}


/* scr_move - move the cursor */
scr_move(row, col)                                                                  scr__move
int row, col;
{
        if (row < 1 || row > NROW)
            s_errmsg("scr_move(): illegal row %d", row);
        else if (col < 1 || col > NCOL)
            s_errmsg("scr_move(): illegal col %d", col);
        else if (col == 1 && cur_row > 0
            && cur_row <= row && row <= cur_row + 5) {
            putchar('\r');         /* move to the start of the current row ... */
            for ( ; cur_row < row; ++cur_row)
                putchar('\n');       /* ... and down to the desired row */
            cur_col = col;
        } else if (col != cur_col || row != cur_row ) {
            MOVE(row, col);
            wait(LONG_COUNT);
            cur_row = row;
            cur_col = col;
        }
}


/* scr_puts - overwrite characters on the screen */
scr_puts(s)                                                                         scr__puts
char *s;
{
        static int bad_bytes = 0;
        int s_len = strlen(s);
        char buf[NCOL+1], *t;

        for (t = s; *t != '\0'; ++t)
            if (!isprint(*t)) {
                if (++bad_bytes < 5)
                    errmsg("scr_puts(): replacing byte with value %d by '#'",
                        (int)*t);
                *t = '#';
            }
        if (cur_col + s_len > NCOL + 1) {
            errmsg("scr_puts(): line extends past column %d", NCOL);
            s_len = NCOL + 1 - cur_col;
            s[s_len] = '\0';
        }
        cur_col += s_len;
```

```
        if (cur_row == NROW && cur_col == NCOL)
            save = s[s_len-1];
        else if (cur_row == NROW && cur_col == NCOL + 1 && s_len > 1)
            save = s[s_len-2];
        if (AUTOWRAP && cur_row == NROW && cur_col == NCOL + 1) {
            if (save == '\0') {
                scr_move(NROW, 1);
                scr_puts("Improbable display error; refresh this line.");
                scr_clr();
                return;
            }
            if (s_len > 1) {
                strcpy(buf, s);
                buf[s_len-2] = buf[s_len-1];
                buf[s_len-1] = '\0';
                fputs(buf, stdout);
            } else {
                scr_move(NROW, NCOL-1);
                putchar(*s);
            }
            cur_col = NCOL;
            scr_move(NROW, NCOL-1);
            SCREEN(INSERT_BEGIN);
            putchar(save);
            SCREEN(INSERT_END);
            cur_col = NCOL;
        } else {
            fputs(s, stdout);
            if (AUTOWRAP && cur_col == NCOL + 1) {
                cur_col = 1;
                ++cur_row;
            }
        }
    }
}

/* scr_scrl - scroll screen rows up */
scr_scrl()                                                                       scr_scrl
{
    scr_move(NROW, 1);
    putchar('\n');
}

/* scr_shape - return the number of rows and columns on the screen */
scr_shape(nrow_ptr, ncol_ptr)                                                    scr_shape
int *nrow_ptr, *ncol_ptr;
{
    *nrow_ptr = NROW;
    *ncol_ptr = NCOL;
}

/* errmsg - print an error message and return cursor to current location */
static errmsg(msg, val)                                                          errmsg
char *msg;
int val;
{
    int col = cur_col, row = cur_row;

    s_errmsg(msg, val);
    scr_move(row, col);
}
```

```
/* wait - pause, allowing the screen to catch up */
static wait(count)                                                wait
int count;
{
    while (count-- > 0)
        putchar(PAD_CHAR);
}
```

5.8 ADDITIONAL PROGRAMMING ASSIGNMENTS

Increase Efficiency.   Use *s* to see if it runs fast enough to suit you. If necessary, speed it up. Potential performance bottlenecks include:

1. *Malloc()* and *free()*; see Programming Assignment 1 of Section 5.5.
2. Screen updates in insert mode; see Programming Assignment 3 of Section 5.6.
3. Standard I/O; see Programming Assignment 1 of Section 5.7.

Squeeze the Editor onto a Small Computer.   The editor was implemented for a virtual-memory machine; the file buffer, yank buffer, and lists of modification records are assumed to all fit in memory. However, use of abstract data types should simplify the task of reimplementing them using temporary files. See Programming Assignment 2 of Section 5.5.

Greater Terminal Independence.   How can a screen editor be written so it can be moved among various terminals without being recompiled? The list of differences between ANSI-standard terminals and the IBM 3101 given in Section 5.7 illustrates the main problems. Not only do terminals differ in their capabilities, but a given capability is sometimes provided in incompatible ways. Imagine the scope of the problem facing the writer of a screen editor who hopes to support dozens, or even hundreds, of terminal models.

The UNIX operating system uses an approach developed by Bill Joy, then a student at University of California, Berkeley. The basic idea is to store a data base of terminal capabilities (hence the name *termcap*). A screen editor, or other program, can read the data base to get information about a particular terminal.

The UNIX termcap data base is just an ordinary file with entries like the following, which gives the capabilities and command sequences for a hypothetical terminal, the *foo100*. (The syntax has been changed in trivial ways.)

```
foo100
    li#24
    co#80
    autowrap
    clr = <esc>[K
    cls = <esc>[2J
```

```
.
.
move = "\033[%d;%dH"
.
.
```

The first three entries tell that a screen has 24 lines and 80 columns and automatically wraps long lines onto several screen rows. Next come the *clear row* and *clear screen* sequences, and the *move* entry gives a format control string for a *printf()* statement to position the cursor.

The real complexity of this project comes from terminals that do not adequately support the facilities provided by *screen.c*. For example, it is difficult to deal with terminals that cannot insert and delete individual characters.

If you have UNIX documents, read about termcap and "curses" for further ideas.

Handle Special Keys.   *S* uses only keys that can be found on any keyboard. Adding less common keys, such as those labeled with arrows, requires learning what byte sequences these keys transmit. Instead of extracting this information from a manual, it may prove easier and more reliable to run the program:

```
#include <stdio.h>
main()
{
      int c1, c2, c3, c4;

      k_flip();
      c1 = getchar() & 0177;
      c2 = getchar() & 0177;
      c3 = getchar() & 0177;
      c4 = getchar() & 0177;
      k_flip();
      printf("ascii values: %d %d %d %d\n", c1, c2, c3, c4);
}
```

(*K_flip()* is discussed in Section 5.4.)

When the program is executed, press the key in question, then hit the <*space*> bar until output appears. The typed spaces will appear as the ASCII code 32; the other printed values are the characters sent by the key. For example, on some terminals the key labeled → sends the three-character sequence <*esc*>*[D*. With the above program, the → key and <*space*> bar produce

```
ascii values: 27 91 68 32
```

(A table of ASCII codes shows that 27, 91, and 68 are the codes for <*esc*>, *[*, and *D*.)

Conversely, problems may arise if the user accidently hits a special key that is unknown to *s*. For example, the key labeled → often sends the three-byte sequence *<esc>[D*. Currently, *s* responds with two "beeps" (in response to the illegal commands *<esc>* and *[*), then deletes the rest of the line (in response to the *D* command). How can *s* be modified to recover more gracefully from a mistyped special key? The UNIX *vi* editor waits a second after receiving an *<esc>* character. If the *<esc>* and the other characters typed in that period do not constitute the byte sequence sent by a special key, then *vi* figures that the user actually pressed the *<esc>* key. However, this solution cannot be implemented in a portable way.

Extend Existing Capabilities.   You might provide several file buffers. This would simplify such jobs as building a file by cutting and pasting pieces of other files. Similarly, multiple yank buffers and marks are useful, as is the ability to undo or redo change commands that were issued before the most recent one. *Undo* might restore more of the editing environment, such as marks, the remembered search string, contents of the yank buffer, etc. A very useful project is to give the editor several screen "windows" so that several edit buffers can be viewed simultaneously. However, independence of the screen manager in *s* makes this modification difficult.

The '/' string-search command can be extended in several useful ways. One possibility is to use more flexible patterns, such as the regular expressions of Chapter 4. Another possibility is "incremental" search: as each character of the search string is typed, the editor finds and displays the next occurrence of what has been typed so far. This lets you type the fewest characters that identify the desired position in the file.

Abbreviations and Macros.   One or two typed characters might be interpreted as a longer sequence. For example, you might want *control-C* expanded to

```
a/*<space><space>*/<esc><backspace><backspace>i
```

This produces the three characters on either end of a C comment and leaves you ready to type in the rest. Similar macros can be entered while editing, or read from a file when the editor is invoked. The function *k_donext()* in *keyboard.c* is quite useful for this project.

Support for Editing Programs.   A simple but useful facility is automatic indentation. In its basic form, pressing the *<return>* key moves to the next line and automatically inserts the same number of *<tab>* characters as appeared on the previous line. (Either there must be a way to turn off this feature, or another key, such as the *<line feed>* key, can be used.) At the cost of language dependence, you might try something fancier; for example, if the preceding line ends with {, an additional <*tab*> could be inserted.

A way of addressing the matching delimiter is useful. If the cursor is positioned on (or {, then a certain key might move the cursor to the matching) or }, and vice versa. When) or } is entered in insert mode, the cursor might momentarily move to the matching (or {.

A harder project is to smooth the interaction between the editor and the C compiler. The compiler's syntax error messages might be redirected to a file, and the editor modified to read the file a line at a time. Each diagnostic message might be kept on the screen until the problem is located and fixed. The editor might even inspect the messages, fetch the proper file, and move to the offending line. (Recording ID's of lines that provoke error messages helps when line numbers change as errors are fixed.) Such a capability might also be used with tools other than compilers, such as the *find* program of Section 1.1.

If you have UNIX documents, read about "ctags" for further ideas.

Support for Editing Documents.   The editor might automatically start a new line if a <*space*> is inserted near the right margin of the screen. That way, text can be entered without thinking about when the <*return*> key should be pressed.

A *fill* operator could be used to make a range of lines have approximately the same length. If characters to the left of the cursor position are ignored in this process, then the capability would be quite useful for C program comments. For example, suppose the cursor is positioned at *Set* in

```
*     loc_string(ch)
*     char ch;
*         Set cursor to the next instance
*         of a user-supplied string.
*         If ch = '\', then the search is backward in the file.
```

A *fill* command that addresses the last line might produce

```
*     loc_string(ch)
*     char ch;
*         Set cursor to the next instance of a user-supplied string. If
*         ch = '\', then the search is backward in the file.
```

Commands to locate and correct misspelled words are quite useful. A command analogous to the '/' string-searching command might address the next potentially misspelled word. If a program to locate misspelled words is already available, it may be quite easy for the editor to run the program and cycle through the output, making each potentially misspelled word the string for the '/' command.

However, this approach is limited, since misspelled words embedded in longer words are often uninteresting. Moreover, a multicommand correction like

$$<space><space>rx$$

which replaces the third letter with x, cannot be repeated with a *redo* command.

A much more ambitious project is to build a spelling checker/corrector into the editor. For an introduction to the problem read

- "Programming pearls: a spelling checker" by Jon Bentley (*Communications of ACM*, May 1985, pp. 456–462)
- "Computer programs for detecting and correcting spelling errors" by James L. Peterson (*Communications of ACM*, Dec. 1980, pp. 676–687)

Since building a spelling checker into the editor requires the editor to "know" roughly 25,000 words, the size of a small dictionary, the memory requirements are formidable. Ideas for storing a dictionary can be found in:

- "Hash-bucket search: a fast technique for searching an English spelling dictionary" by Douglas Comer and Vincent Shen (*Software—Practice and Experience*, July 1982, pp. 669–682)
- "Reducing dictionary size by using a hashing technique" by D. J. Dodds (*Communications of ACM*, June 1982, pp. 368–370)
- "Experience with a space efficient way to store a dictionary" by Robert Nix (*Communication of ACM*, May 1981, pp. 297–298)

The last two papers describe data structures that occasionally report that a word is in the dictionary when, in fact, it is not there.

For example, the approach advocated by Nix works as follows. Suppose the dictionary contains 25,000 words, averaging eight characters apiece. Just storing the characters requires 200,000 bytes, and the additional pointers, etc., required for efficient lookup add to the total. Instead, Nix uses an array T of 500,000 *bits*. Ten independent hash functions $h_0, h_1, \ldots, h_9$ are picked, each mapping words into the range 0 to 499,999. The ith bit of T is initialized to 1 if and only if one of the hash functions maps one of the dictionary words to i. At most 250,000 bits can equal 1, so the probability is at most 0.5 that a random bit is 1.

Searching the dictionary for a word x involves testing the 10 bits $T[h_0(x)]$, $T[h_1(x)], \ldots, T[h_9(x)]$. If any of these is 0, then x is definitely not in the dictionary. If all 10 bits equal 1, then x is considered legitimate. The chance of being mistaken is just the probability of 10 randomly-chosen bits being 1, which is less than $(0.5)^{10}$, roughly 1 in 1000. In other words, this way of storing the dictionary will cause the spelling checker to accept an incorrectly spelled word about 0.1 percent of the time. (It is probably more common for a misspelled word to be accepted because it produces the name of, e.g., an old Russian coin.) The main attraction of this approach is that it requires far less space than explicitly storing the dictionary's words; in one real-world use it needed only one fifth the array storage. However, the process of searching the dictionary for a word is liable to be slower than if the explicit dictionary is stored as a monster hash table; one study observed a factor of 2.3 for the time difference.

The following function implements 10 hash functions.

```
/*
* hash - compute hash function i for the word w
*
* The j-th character of w is multiplied by the (7j)-th power of 2 and
* the resulting products are added.  All arithmetic is modulo a prime p[i].
*/
long hash(i, w)
int i;
char *w;
{
    long hval, power;
    char *wp;

    /* p holds the 10 largest primes less than 500,000 */
    static long p[] = { 499979, 499973, 499969, 499957,
        499943, 499927, 499903, 499897, 499883, 499879};

    hval = 0;
    power = 1;
    for (wp = w; *wp != '\0'; wp++) {
        power = (power << 7) % p[i];
        hval += (*wp)*power;
    }
    return(hval % p[i]);
}
```

Efficiency might be gained by precomputing the successive values of *power*.

When the editor thinks a word is misspelled, it might remember if the user determined that the word was correct or what the word was changed to. In addition, the editor might ''suggest'' a proper spelling, i.e., it might try deleting, inserting, and changing single letters, and search its dictionary for each such mutant.

Increased Safety.   The user will be very unhappy if the file buffer's contents are accidently lost. Currently, *s* guards against such disasters as accidently quitting without saving a modified buffer, and buffer changes can be undone. A simple way to provide additional insurance is to automatically store the contents of the buffer in a known place after a certain number of editor commands. (This may be unnecessary if the buffer is implemented with a temporary file.) Such ''checkpoints'' are extremely welcome after a system crash.

Efficiency at Low Transmission Rates.   At speeds of 120 characters per second (1200 baud) or less, the editor is annoyingly slow. A smaller window (less than 24 lines) may help, and many cursor-motion optimizations are possible. For example, many terminals have short commands to move the cursor up, down, left, or right, and an autowrap capability is sometimes useful.

Another approach is to give screen updating lower priority than buffer changing. For example, suppose you edit a new file and type *107g* when the editor has painted only a few lines on the screen. (You might be responding to a compiler diagnostic message about line 107 of a file.) The screen manager might notice that a new command has been typed, stop what it is doing, and let the command processor go to work. Implementing this capability requires some (nonportable) way of polling to see if a character has been typed, but the editor's autonomous screen manager helps make it easy. Read about nonblocking I/O in Chapter 4 of *Advanced UNIX Programming* by Marc J. Rochkind (Prentice-Hall, 1985).

Expand the Range of Uses.   The editor can be adapted to provide a standard user interface for other utility programs, such as the computer mail system. An editor command could mail lines from the buffer to another user, just as the lines can be written to a file. More generally, an editor could be the primary interface to the operating system; it could record past commands and allow the user to form new commands by editing old ones.

The paper ''A generalized text editor'' by Christopher W. Fraser (*Communications of ACM*, March 1980, pp. 154–158) explores this theme with several interesting examples, including the following. UNIX provides ad hoc commands to

- change the access rights for a file or directory,
- change the ownership of a file or directory,
- remove a file,
- remove a directory, or
- rename a file or directory.

These commands can be eliminated if directories can be ''edited.'' When applied to a directory, *s* might list the directory's files and subdirectories and indicate ownership and permissions, as in

```
fastfind        webb    -rwxr-x

fastfind.c      webb    -rw-r--

lib.o           webb    -rw-r--

match           webb    drwxr-x
```

The first character in the third column tells if the directory entry is itself a directory. The next three characters give the read, write, and execute permissions for the owner, while the last three give those permissions for all other users. For example, *fastfind* is a nondirectory file that can be read or executed by anyone, but only the owner, *webb*, can modify it.

Each of the five file or directory operations mentioned above could be performed by editing this listing of the directory. Thus, the ownership of *fastfind* could be given to *root* by moving the cursor to the second word of the first row and typing

```
cwroot<esc>
```

However, it may be difficult to implement this capability so that (i) the editor complains immediately about an improper change (such as trying to convert an ordinary file to a directory) and (ii) the *undo* command works for any change.

APPENDIX

A

REQUIRED FUNCTIONS
AND MACROS

The programs in this book assume the availability of certain primitive functions and macros that are typically supplied by standard run-time libraries and header files. These primitives fall into four categories:

1. The standard I/O library.
2. Standard string functions.
3. Character-classification macros.
4. System-specific functions.

For each function or macro, the types of the arguments and value (if any) are specified below and the behavior is described.

Only the capabilities needed by programs listed in Chapters 1–5 are given. In particular, most implementations of the functions in categories 1 and 2 return values, though the programs often ignore those values. The UNIX *lint* program will consequently warn of improper use. (Many C compilers provide a *void* type that can be used to explicitly discard unused function values.)

For functions in categories 2–4, suggestions are provided to help you construct appropriate facilities if you do not already have them.

A.1 STANDARD I/O LIBRARY

Any source file that uses this library of functions should have the line

```
#include <stdio.h>
```

near the beginning.

int EOF;

> *EOF* is a predefined constant that differs from every legitimate
> character. It is returned by *getc()* and *getchar()* if no character
> was read.

fclose(fp)
FILE *fp;

> Buffers for the specified file are emptied and the file is closed.
> The connection between *fp* and the file is broken.

fflush(fp)
FILE *fp;

> Buffered data destined for the specified file is written to the file.
> The file remains open.

char *fgets(s, maxchars, fp)
char *s;
int maxchars;
FILE *fp;

> At most *maxchars* $-$ 1 characters, or up to and including the
> first newline character (whichever comes first), are read from
> the specified file to *s*, and the string is terminated with a null
> character. (Note: *gets(s)* differs from *fgets(s, n, stdin)* in that
> *gets()* removes the newline character.) If one or more charac-
> ters are successfully read, then *s* is returned; *NULL* is returned
> at the end of file or upon a read error.

/* *FILE is a data type* */

> An object of type *FILE* is a structure holding information about
> a file or an I/O device. A *FILE* pointer is returned by *fopen()*
> and used to identify the file in subsequent I/O requests.

FILE *fopen(filename, mode)
char *filename, *mode;

> The specified file is opened and a value is returned to identify
> the file in subsequent input and output operations. *NULL* is
> returned if the file cannot be opened. *Mode* specifies the in-
> tended use of the file. The modes used in this book are:
> ''r''   Open an existing file for reading.
> ''w''   Create for writing. (If the file already exists, then its
>   contents are discarded.)
> ''r+''   Open an existing file for reading and writing, beginning
>   with the first character of the file. This mode does not
>   exist on all systems. Its only use in this book is in
>   *tweak()*. (See Section 1.1.)

fprintf(fp, format [,arg] . . .)
FILE *fp;
char *format;

Output is formatted and sent to the specified file. The *format* and the optional arguments are the same as for *printf()*.

fputs(s, fp)
char *s;
FILE *fp;

The string *s* is copied to the specified file. (Note: *fputs(s, stdout)* differs from *puts(s)* in that *puts()* appends a newline character to *s*.)

int getc(fp)
FILE *fp;

The next character is returned from the specified file. *EOF* is returned at the end of file or upon a read error.

int getchar()

The next character is returned from standard input. *EOF* is returned at the end of file or upon a read error. *Getchar()* is equivalent to *getc(stdin)*.

char *gets(s)
char *s;

A string of characters from standard input is read into *s*. Standard input is read up to and including the next newline character. The newline character is not placed in *s*, but is replaced by the null character. (Note: *gets(s)* differs from *fgets(s,n,stdin)* in that *fgets()* keeps the newline character.) If characters are successfully read, then *s* is returned; *NULL* is returned at the end of file or upon a read error.

FILE *NULL;
char *NULL;

Every pointer type has a special value, denoted *NULL*, that "points to nothing." *Fopen()* returns *NULL* if the file cannot be opened. *Gets()* and *fgets()* return *NULL* if no character was read.

printf(format [,arg] . . .)
char *format;

Format is printed on standard output, but with *conversion specifications* replaced by the corresponding converted *args*. The programs in this book use the following conversion specifications:

%s   A character string.
%c   A character.
%d   An integer.
%ld A long integer.

%7ld A long integer preceded by enough blanks to fill out at least seven characters.

putc(c, fp)
char c;
FILE *fp;

> The character *c* is written to the specified file. Since *putc* is usually implemented as a macro, evaluation of the expression *c* should not have any side effects because the evaluation may be done more than once. For example,

$$putc(*s++, fp)$$

> is dangerous.

putchar(c)
char c;

> The character *c* is written to standard output. *Putchar(c)* is equivalent to *putc(c, stdout)*.

puts(s)
char *s;

> The specified string is written to standard output and a newline character is appended. (Note: *fputs(s, stdout)* differs from *puts(s)* in that it does not append a newline.)

rewind(fp)
FILE *fp;

> The specified file is adjusted so that the next input or output operation occurs at the beginning of the file.

sprintf(s, format [,arg] . . .)
char *s, *format;

> Output is formatted and placed in the character array pointed to by *s*. *Format* and the optional arguments are the same as for *printf()*.

FILE *stderr;

> When a C program begins execution, *stderr* is open for writing. In an interactive environment, *stderr* will usually be associated with the user's terminal.

FILE *stdin;

> When a C program begins execution, *stdin* is open for reading. In an interactive environment, *stdin* will usually be associated with the user's keyboard.

FILE *stdout;

> When a C program begins execution, *stdout* is open for writing.

In an interactive environment, *stdout* will usually be associated with the user's terminal.

A.2 STANDARD STRING FUNCTIONS

char *index(s, c)
char *s, c;

> The string *s* is searched for the first occurrence of *c*. If *c* is found, then a pointer to its first occurrence is returned. *NULL* is returned if *c* is not found.

strcat(s, t)
char *s, *t;

> A copy of the string *t* is appended to the end of the string *s*. The null character at the end of *s* is replaced by the characters from *t* and a terminating null character. *Strcat()* does not check for overflow in the new string. If the two original strings overlap in memory, then the results are unpredictable.

int strcmp(s, t)
char *s, *t;

> 0 is returned if and only if the contents of the two strings are identical.

char *strcpy(s, t)
char *s, *t;

> The contents of the string *s* are replaced by the contents of the string *t*, terminating with a null character, and a pointer to the first character of *s* is returned. *Strcpy()* does not check for overflow in the new string. If the two original strings overlap in memory, then the results are unpredictable.

int strlen(s)
char *s;

> The number of characters in the string *s*, not counting the terminating null character, is returned.

If these string functions are not available, then the implementations listed at the end of this appendix can be used.

A.3 CHARACTER-CLASSIFICATION MACROS

Any source file that uses these macros should have the line

```
#include <ctype.h>
```

near the beginning.

```
int isalnum(c)
char c;
```
> A nonzero value is returned if and only if c is a digit ('0'–'9'), a lower case letter ('a'–'z') or an upper case letter ('A'–'Z').

```
int isalpha(c)
char c;
```
> A nonzero value is returned if and only if c is a lower case letter or an upper case letter.

```
int isdigit(c)
char c;
```
> A nonzero value is returned if and only if c is a digit.

```
int islower(c)
char c;
```
> A nonzero value is returned if and only if c is a lower case letter.

```
int isprint(c)
char c;
```
> A nonzero value is returned if c is alphanumeric, a punctuation character, or a blank; 0 is returned if c is a control character (including '\n' and '\t').

```
int isspace(c)
char c;
```
> A nonzero value is returned if c is a ' ', '\t', or '\n'. For printing characters, e.g., letters, digits, and punctuation marks, zero is returned.

```
int isupper(c)
char c;
```
> A nonzero value is returned if and only if c is an upper case letter.

With the ASCII character representation and controlled use of the macros, a file containing the following definitions could be substituted for *ctype.h*:

```
#define islower(c)     ('a' <= c && c <= 'z')
#define isupper(c)     ('A' <= c && c <= 'Z')
#define isalpha(c)     (islower(c) || isupper(c))
#define isdigit(c)     ('0' <= c && c <= '9')
#define isalnum(c)     (isalpha(c) || isdigit(c))
#define isprint(c)     (32 <= c && c <= 126)
#define isspace(c)     (c == ' ' || c == '\t' || c == '\n')
```

Controlled use is required because the dummy argument c appears more than once on the right side of each definition, so that the actual argument should be an expression without side effects. Thus, character constants and variables are safe, but uses such as

```
while (isalpha(*s++))
```

may not work as expected.

These shortcomings can be avoided by implementing the capabilities as functions. Alternatively, it is an interesting exercise to implement them as macros in such a way that the dummy argument appears just once on the right side of each *#define* line.

A.4 SYSTEM-SPECIFIC FUNCTIONS

Three system-specific functions, *exit()*, *free()*, and *malloc()*, are used throughout the book. Others are introduced in Chapters 2 and 5.

> exit(status)
> int status;
>
> > *Exit()* immediately terminates execution of the program. The program's files are closed, and *status* is made available to the parent process. *Status* is not meaningful on all systems.
>
> free(p)
> char *p;
>
> > The space pointed to by *p* is freed. It is absolutely essential that *p* point to a block of space that was previously allocated by *malloc()*. The cost of not having *free()* available is that programs may run out of space sooner.
>
> char *malloc(amount)
> unsigned amount;
>
> > *Malloc()* returns the pointer to a block large enough to hold an object whose size, as measured by the *sizeof* operator, is *amount*. NULL is returned if *malloc()* fails. If *malloc()* is used to allocate storage for objects other than character arrays, then the returned valued should be cast to a pointer of the appropriate type; otherwise, the program may not be portable.
>
> > The following rudimentary storage allocator could be used to achieve some of the desired functionality.

```
#include <stdio.h>

#define MAX_ALLOC 1000        /* whatever amount you can spare */

static char buf[MAX_ALLOC];   /* memory be to parceled out */
static char *b = buf;         /* next free location in buf */

char *malloc(amount)
unsigned amount;
{
```

```
    if (b + amount >= &buf[MAX_ALLOC])
        return(NULL);
    b += amount;
    return(b - amount);
}
```

A.5 AN IMPLEMENTATION OF THE STANDARD STRING FUNCTIONS

```
#include <stdio.h>

/* index - return the location of a character in a string */
/* In some C implementations this function is called strchr. */
char *index(s, c)                                                          index
char *s, c;
{
    while (*s != '\0' && *s != c)
        ++s;
    return( (*s == c) ? s : NULL );
}

/* strcat - append a copy of t to the end of s */
strcat(s,t)                                                                strcat
char *s, *t;
{
    /* move to the end of s */
    while (*s != '\0')
        ++s;
    /* copy t */
    while ((*s++ = *t++) != '\0')
        ;
}

/* strcmp - dictionary order of two strings */
int strcmp(s,t)                                                            strcmp
char *s, *t;
{
    for ( ; *s == *t; ++s, ++t)
        if (*s == '\0')
            return(0);
    return(*s - *t);
}

/* strcpy - copy t to s; return s */
char *strcpy(s,t)                                                          strcpy
char *s, *t;
{
    char *start = s;

    while ((*s++ = *t++) != '\0')
        ;
    return(start);
}

/* strlen - return the length of s */
int strlen(s)                                                              strlen
char *s;
{
    char *start = s;

    while (*s != '\0')
        ++s;
    return(s - start);
}
```

BIBLIOGRAPHY

AHO, ALFRED V. and MARGARET J. CORASICK, "Efficient string matching: an aid to bibliographic search," *Comm. Assoc. Comput. Mach.*, **18**(6), June 1975, pp. 333-340.

AHO, ALFRED V., DANIEL S. HERSHBERG and J. D. ULLMAN, "Bounds on the complexity of the longest common subsequence problem," *Journal Assoc. Comput. Mach.*, **23**(1), Jan. 1976, pp. 1-12.

AHO, ALFRED V., RAVI SETHI and J. D. ULLMAN, *Compilers: Principles, Techniques and Tools*, Reading, MA: Addison-Wesley, 1986.

BARACH, DAVID, DAVID TAENZER and ROBERT WELLS, "The design of the PEN video editor display module," *Proceedings of the Assoc. Comput. Mach. Symposium on Text Manipulation, SIGPLAN Notices*, **16**(6), June 1981, pp. 130-136.

BENTLEY, JON, *Writing Efficient Programs*, Englewood Cliffs, NJ: Prentice-Hall, 1982.

————, "Programming pearls: a spelling checker," *Comm. Assoc. Comput. Mach.*, **28**(5), May 1985, pp. 456-462.

BOYER, ROBERT S. and J. STROTHER MOORE, "A fast string searching algorithm," *Comm. Assoc. Comput. Mach.*, **20**(10), Oct. 1977, pp. 762-772.

COMER, DOUGLAS and VINCENT SHEN, "Hash-bucket search: a fast technique for searching an English spelling dictionary," *Software—Practice and Experience*, **12**(7), July 1982, pp. 669-682.

DODDS, D. J., "Reducing dictionary size by using a hashing technique," *Comm. Assoc. Comput. Mach.*, **25**(6), June 1982, pp. 368-370

FELDMAN, STUART I., "Make − a program for maintaining computer programs," *Software—Practice and Experience*, **9**(4), April 1979, pp. 255-265.

FRASER, CHRISTOPHER W., "A compact, portable CRT-based text editor," *Software—Practice and Experience*, **9**(2), Feb. 1979, pp. 121-125.

————, "A generalized text editor," *Comm. Assoc. Comput. Mach.*, **23**(3), March 1980, pp. 154-158.

————, "Maintaining program variants by merging editor scripts," *Software—Practice and Experience*, **10**(10), Oct. 1980, 817-821.

GAREY, MICHAEL R. and DAVID S. JOHNSON, *Computers and Intractability: A Guide to the Theory of NP-Complete Problems*, San Francisco, CA: W. H. Freeman, 1979.

GOSLING, JAMES, "A redisplay algorithm," *Proceedings of the Assoc. Comput. Mach. Symposium on Text Manipulation, SIGPLAN Notices*, **16**(6), June 1981, pp. 123-129.

HARBISON, SAMUEL P. and GUY L. STEEL, JR., *A C Reference Manual*, Englewood Cliffs, NJ: Prentice-Hall, 1984.

HUNT, JAMES. W. and THOMAS G. SZYMANSKI, "A fast algorithm for computing longest common subsequences," *Comm. Assoc. Comput. Mach.*, **20**(5), May 1977, pp. 350-353.

KERNIGHAN, BRIAN W. and P. J. PLAUGER, *Software Tools*, Reading, MA: Addison-Wesley, 1976.

KERNIGHAN, BRIAN W. and DENNIS M. RITCHIE, *The C Programming Language*, Englewood Cliffs, NJ: Prentice-Hall, 1978.

KERNIGHAN, BRIAN W. and JOHN MASHEY, "The UNIX programming environment," *IEEE Computer*, April 1981, pp. 12-24.

KERNIGHAN, BRIAN W. and ROB PIKE, *The UNIX Programming Environment*, Englewood Cliffs, NJ: Prentice-Hall, 1984.

KNUTH, DONALD E., JAMES H. MORRIS and VAUGHAN R. PRATT, "Fast pattern matching in strings," *SIAM J. Computing*, **6**(2), June 1977, pp. 323-350.

MILLER, WEBB and EUGENE W. MYERS, "A file comparison program," *Software—Practice and Experience*, **15**(11), Nov. 1985, pp. 1025-40.

———, "Side-effects in automatic file updating," *Software—Practice and Experience*, **16**(9), Sept. 1986, pp. 809–820.

MYERS, EUGENE W., "An O(ND) difference algorithm and its variants," *Algorithmica*, **1**, 1986, pp. 251–266.

MYERS, EUGENE W. and WEBB MILLER, "Row replacement algorithms for screen editors," TR 86-19, Department of Computer Science, The University of Arizona, Tucson, Arizona 85721.

NIX, ROBERT, "Experience with a space efficient way to store a dictionary," *Comm. Assoc. Comput. Mach.*, **24**(5), May 1981, pp. 297-298.

PETERSON, JAMES L., "Computer programs for detecting and correcting spelling errors," *Comm. Assoc. Comput. Mach.*, **23**(12), Dec. 1980, pp. 676-687.

ROCHKIND, MARC J., "The source code control system," *IEEE Transactions on Software Engineering*, **1**(4), Dec. 1975, pp. 364-370.

———, *Advanced UNIX Programming*, Englewood Cliffs, NJ: Prentice-Hall, 1985.

TICHY, WALTER F., "The string-to-string correction problem with block moves," *Assoc. Comput. Mach. Transactions on Computer Systems*, **2**(4), Nov. 1984, pp. 309-321.

———, "RCS—a system for version control," *Software—Practice and Experience*, **15**(7), July 1985, pp. 637-654.

WALDEN, KIM, "Automatic generation of Make dependencies," *Software—Practice and Experience*, **14**(6), June 1984, pp. 575-585.

ZELKOWITH, MARVIN, ALAN SHAW and JOHN GANNON, *Principles of Software Engineering and Design*, Englewood Cliffs, NJ: Prentice-Hall, 1979.

INDEX